Free Market Democracy and the Chilean and Mexican Countryside

This book examines the relationship between free markets and democracy. It demonstrates how the implementation of even very painful free market economic reforms in Chile and Mexico have helped to consolidate democratic politics without engendering a backlash against either reform or democratization. This national-level compatibility between free markets and democracy, however, is founded on their rural incompatibility. In the countryside, free market reforms socially isolate peasants to such a degree that they become unable to organize independently and thus are vulnerable to the pressures of local economic elites. This helps to create an electoral coalition behind free market reforms that is critically based in some of the market's biggest victims: the peasantry. The book concludes that the contemporary prevalence of comparatively stable free market democracy in Latin America hinges critically on its defects in the countryside; conservative, free market elites may consent to open politics only if they have a rural electoral redoubt.

Marcus J. Kurtz is an Assistant Professor of Political Science at Ohio State University after having taught at both the University of Miami and the University of Michigan. He has published articles in the areas of political science, sociology, and Latin American studies in such journals as *Comparative Politics*, *Comparative Political Studies*, *Politics & Society*, *Theory and Society*, *Comparative Studies in Society and History*, and *The Journal of Latin American Studies*. He is also on the editorial board of *Latin American Politics* and *Society* and is a member of the American Political Science Association, the Latin American Studies Association, and the Midwest Political Science Association.

Free Market Democracy and the Chilean and Mexican Countryside

MARCUS J. KURTZ

Ohio State University

CAMBRIDGE
UNIVERSITY PRESS

JL
2681
.K87
2004

CAMBRIDGE UNIVERSITY PRESS
Cambridge, New York, Melbourne, Madrid, Cape Town, Singapore, São Paulo

Cambridge University Press
The Edinburgh Building, Cambridge CB2 2RU, UK

Published in the United States of America by Cambridge University Press, New York

www.cambridge.org
Information on this title: www.cambridge.org/9780521827379

© Marcus J. Kurtz 2004

First published 2004
This digitally printed first paperback version 2006

A catalogue record for this publication is available from the British Library

Library of Congress Cataloguing in Publication data

Kurtz, Marcus J.
Free market democracy and the Chilean and Mexican countryside / Marcus J. Kurtz.
    p.   cm.
Includes bibliographical references and index.
ISBN 0-521-82737-X
1. Democracy – Chile.   2. Democracy – Mexico.   3. Free enterprise – Chile.
4. Free enterprise – Mexico.   5. Rural population – Chile.   6. Rural population –
Mexico.   7. Political participation – Chile.   8. Political participation – Mexico.
I. Title.
JL2681.K87   2004
320.972–dc22   2003065316

ISBN-13 978-0-521-82737-9 hardback
ISBN-10 0-521-82737-X hardback

ISBN-13 978-0-521-53474-1 paperback
ISBN-10 0-521-53474-7 paperback

70844642

Contents

Acknowledgments

I must begin these acknowledgments with the start of this project. It was in Ruth Berins Collier's graduate course on Latin American politics that I first became acquainted with the at-times utopian and at-times tragic reality that has been post-war Chilean politics. Little did I know that the interest sparked at that moment would evolve into an obsession that consumed nearly a decade of my life. It is for this spark – and many other things – that I owe Ruth an enormous debt of gratitude. Once launched, this project took many turns, and it was David Collier who persistently and insistently kept my work from straying down dead ends and false paths, and at least on one occasion, kept me from dropping out of the discipline of political science. David and Ruth were the co-chairs of the dissertation in which the central ideas for this book were conceived, and without their support, insight, and guidance it is obvious to me that neither would have been completed, much less have merited reading. I know that it is customary to thank one's advisors, but I want to make clear I mean far more than that: David and Ruth are ongoing sources of advice, inspiration, and most importantly constructive criticism. It has been a rare privilege to have worked so closely with both of them over the years, and I am grateful that they have tolerated my anxieties and bouts of ill-humor with their customary aplomb.

No book is written in isolation, and mine is certainly no exception. At different points over the years an enormous number of scholars, friends, and listeners unable to escape the room have cheerfully read, heard, and/or commented on different aspects of this work.

Particular thanks go to Felipe Agüero, Andrew Barnes, Juliet Gainsborough, Larry King, Tom Koelble, Steve Levitsky, James Mahoney, Carol Medlin, Eric Oliver, Pierre Ostiguy, Rudy Sil, Jeff Sluyter, Bill Smith, Rich Snyder, Dave Stuligross, Arun Swamy, Elaine Thomas, and Michael Watts. Two reviewers for Cambridge University Press provided very helpful comments and critcisms. Many of my colleagues at Ohio State have been important sources of advice and encouragement, including Tim Frye, Anthony Mughan, Kira Sanbonmatsu, Allan Silverman, Alex Thompson, Alan Wiseman, and Kuba Zielinski. Special thanks also go to Peter Houtzager, who forced much greater precision in my thinking over the course of our multiyear collaboration. Ken Greene has been a steadfast colleague, engaging critic, and friend. Similarly, I must thank Aaron Schneider for being willing to discuss the manuscript only during marathon training runs; both the book and my health are better for it.

The initial work on this project was made possible by the National Science Foundation, and was facilitated by my affiliation with the Grupo de Investigaciones Agrarias (GIA) in Santiago, Chile. I sincerely thank Estanislao Gacitúa and the other researchers at GIA for providing tremendous assistance as well as making me feel at home during a difficult time. My heartfelt thanks also go to Chileans and Mexicans too numerous to mention – from peasants to bureaucrats – that made my research possible, and saved me from (some of) my gringo naïveté. Additional research was supported by the University of Miami through both the Jame MacLamore Summer grant and several research support awards.

Preliminary versions of some of the ideas in this book appeared in "Free Markets and Democratic Consolidation in Chile: The National Politics of Rural Transformation" *Politics & Society* vol. 27: 2 (June 1999), as well as in "The Institutional Roots of Popular Mobilization: State Transformation and Rural Politics in Brazil and Chile" (with Peter Houtzager) *Comparative Studies in Society and History* vol. 42: 2 (April 2000).

Several colleagues and friends here deserve very special mention. Elizabeth Armstrong many years ago convinced me that my future lay in the social sciences. Teresa Wright reminded me that there is more to life than the social sciences, and talked me through more tough times than I can count. Ken Shadlen has by this time read and commented on the entire manuscript many times over, and I can only hope that I have been half as helpful to him over the years as he has been to me. I have been lucky to have had such a friend, critic, and colleague, literally since we met on our first day in graduate school in the Fall of 1988. Andrew Schrank probably more than anyone has helped to shape my intellectual development. We have been close friends since our undergraduate days at the University of Michigan, and I am hard-pressed to think of anything I have written that has not benefited from his advice. My debt to him for his intellectual support, solidarity, and friendship is beyond repayment.

Sarah Brooks has managed the unenviable task of being simultaneously my partner and my colleague. I doubt very much that I could have accomplished what I have without her, and I know that I am a far better and happier person for having the opportunity to share my life with her. I only hope that the burden has not been too great, and that I can repay the favor. Finally, I must thank my parents Margot and J Kurtz. Despite the fact that the academy is the family business, they never wanted me to go to graduate school. Of course, like so many rebellious children, I ignored their advice. But their love, constant support, and the examples they set carried me through the periods of both light and dark. I will be lucky indeed to accomplish a fraction of what they have as people, parents, and scholars. It is to them that this book is dedicated.

M. J. K.
Columbus, Ohio

PART I

THE FRAMEWORK AND
THEORETICAL ARGUMENT

I

Posing the Right Questions

This book begins with an odd contrast: while the recent emergence of many "free market democracies" in Latin America and much of the rest of the underdeveloped world is not in doubt, this outcome stands in marked conflict with almost two decades of scholarship that suggested that the process of free market *democratization* should at best be difficult and conflictual and at worst be impossible. However stable an equilibrium liberal capitalist democracy might be in both political and economic terms, the costs of transition, particularly among the historically statist and inward-oriented late developers, ought be very high. Economically, the abandonment of import substitution policies induces unemployment, uncertainty, mass bankruptcies, and increases in inequality and poverty. Politically, processes of economic reform typically entail attacks on a broad swath of powerful vested interests, including protected industrialists, organized labor, peasants, and even the state bureaucracy. Yet despite these challenges – huge economic costs and politically powerful opponents – free market democracy has sometimes emerged in the unlikeliest of settings, often with a minimum of instability and upheaval.

Chile, long one of the most statist political economies and stable democracies on the South American continent, had by 1970 elected a Marxist president and launched a peaceful transition to socialism. Three years later the military seized power in the context of hyper-mobilization and paralyzed politics (Valenzuela 1978), eventually setting the stage for radical economic transformation. In an uneven and

3

piecemeal fashion, the subsequent military government of General Augusto Pinochet (1973–89) imposed a wide-ranging and coherent neoliberal developmental model (Silva 1996; Kurtz 1999a). This free market transformation inserted Chile into the international economy and eventually, after two severe economic crises, produced high rates of growth. But it also dramatically widened income inequality, more than doubled the rate of poverty, and reduced large segments of the labor force to informality (Vergara 1994). From 1983–6, in the midst of a severe economic downturn, protests rocked the country and threatened the very survival of the authoritarian regime – though they were harshly repressed and in the end unable to force a transition. Instead, defeat in a plebiscite in 1988 over the continuation of General Pinochet's military government ushered in a democratic transition. What emerged was a rapidly consolidated free market democracy. Political freedom and op-position victory did not, however, bring a rollback of neoliberal reforms or a return to the polarized redistributive politics of the early 1970s. Instead, three successive elected governments dominated by Christian Democratic and Socialist opponents of military rule have, if anything, extended the free market development model. Nor has democratization been accompanied by the political turmoil and/or blocked reform ef-forts that have characterized posttransition Argentina, Peru, Ecuador, and of late, Venezuela.

This has led some to argue that what is needed is a firm hand in the implementation of market-oriented economic reforms until such time as their economic merits can be demonstrated, *after which* de-mocratization can be accomplished in a comparatively unproblematic fashion.[1] While such an explanation is consistent with the sequence of

---

[1] It is precisely this concern for the short-run problems involved in imposing neoliberal reforms on an economically prostrate and potentially unwilling population that has led some analysts to counsel political centralization, bureaucratic insulation, and decree powers in order to consolidate reform rapidly before politics are loosened (Lipton and Sachs 1990; Williamson 1994). Remmer (1990), however, points out that democra-cies may be no less able than authoritarian regimes to respond to economic crisis and initiate painful reforms. This suggests implicitly that even authoritarian regimes can face serious barriers to policy reform. Others, equally expecting popular resistance to reform, have proposed gradualist approaches that might allow for the construction of viable reform-oriented political coalitions. Geopolitical differences may matter as well. In the postsocialist context, marketization and democratization may be mutually

reform and political opening that took place in Chile, it cannot be sustained on other grounds – a clear majority of the population at the time of democratization continued to suffer materially from neoliberalism. Moreover, some of the most reliable supporters of conservative, free market political parties came from those peasant population segments *most* adversely affected by economic opening. Whatever the causes of support for neoliberal parties, for this segment it is not economic self-interest.

A comparative perspective casts further doubt on sequencing explanations. First, free market reforms do not always produce sustained growth over the medium to long term (e.g., Argentina and Mexico). Second, they are often implemented coterminously with or subsequent to democratization itself (e.g., at roughly the same time in Mexico, and after democratization in Brazil). In Mexico, the dual process of economic and political liberalization culminated in the consolidation of open economic policies with the North American Free Trade Agreement (NAFTA) of 1993 and the establishment of national-level democracy with the first opposition legislative victory in 1997 and a presidential victory in 2000. Both marketization and democratization occurred alongside each other without sustained or widespread political upheaval, serious efforts to turn back reform, or the interruption of secular progress toward greater political and market openness. This was despite the two catastrophic economic downturns in the 1980s and 1990s.

So how is stable free market democracy brought about? The empirical task this book sets itself is to provide a socially grounded political account of the construction of free market democracy in both countries. It is an account that will avoid the tautological assertion that the institutional foundations of the market economy are intrinsic to the definition of democracy, as well as the claim made on the political right that free market reforms are *in themselves* inherently democratizing – there

reinforcing for unique political reasons (Bunce 2000, 719), though some disagree (Kurtz and Barnes 2002). Bienen and Herbst (1996) have argued that efforts at joint liberalization and democratization in Africa face additional, and daunting, challenges. A few have suggested either that market reforms need not produce severe costs, or, at a minimum, that they are far lower than the price of inaction (Rodrik 1996, 29), and thus may not be so politically difficult to implement after all.

are far too many free market authoritarianisms for this to be the case. Equally, however, it rejects the assumption prevalent on the left that market economics and meaningful democracy are incompatible. Rather, this book focuses the discussion on when, why, and how free market economics and democratic politics come together in a stable political equilibrium.

Before the question can be adequately answered, however, it must be correctly posed. This chapter will be focused around two questions that frame the theoretical emphasis presented in Chapter 2 and the empirical analysis that comprises the remainder of the book. First, what is it about the process of economic liberalization that poses challenges for democracy's establishment, and how have these barriers been overcome? Second, moving beyond the question of consolidation, we must ask what is the relationship between consolidated free market democracy and the prospects for the *deepening* of democratic social relations? This is an issue that is a matter of ongoing debate among the "first wave" democratizers and it represents a set of new challenges in the underdeveloped world. Finally, I consider the relationship between these two processes, arguing that efforts to extend and deepen democracy introduce trade-offs with its consolidation. It is this, usually unacknowledged and unhappy dilemma that stands at the center of the relationship between markets and democracy.

OVERCOMING THE ANTINOMIES OF FREE MARKET REFORM AND DEMOCRATIZATION

The point here is to understand how states overcome the challenges that face them in attempting to render free markets and democratic politics compatible in the underdeveloped world. Not all scholars, however, accept that the twin phenomena are anything but mutually reinforcing. Prominent proponents of economic liberalism have long held that it is essential to human freedom (Hayek 1944; Friedman 1962), while arguing that statism (and particularly state socialism) are inherently corrosive of democracy (Friedrich and Brzezinski 1956; Fainsod 1957). More recently scholars have promoted a more nuanced argument that rejects a deterministic linkage, but suggests that liberal economies foster the conditions that are propitious for the survival of democratic politics (Fukuyama 1989, 8). Others, like Huntington (1984, 24) suggest that key features of the market economy – private property rights and the dispersion of political power they are said to entail – are at least necessary conditions for the maintenance of democratic politics.

The vast majority of scholars, however, have argued that the dual transition (away from statism and authoritarianism) is inherently difficult in the short term. The crux of the problem is that the economic reforms essential to economic liberalization – *inter alia* privatization, deregulation, trade opening, fiscal austerity, and tax reform – produce harmful material consequences for the vast majority of citizens (Przeworski et al. 1995, 68). In the context of democratic politics, this provides fertile ground for the emergence of "nationalist" or "populist" politicians seeking office based on promises to reverse the reforms (Nelson 1989). Rodrick (1996, 10) has captured the crux of this problem: "Good economics does often turn out to be good politics, but only eventually.... Conversely, bad economics can be popular, if only temporarily."

From this perspective one would expect opposition to liberal economic reform from powerful vested industrial and commercial interests with a stake in continued statism (Krueger 1974). On the other hand, the beneficiaries of economic liberalization tend to be at their weakest politically at the time at which reforms are initiated. Indeed, many of the economic sectors that stand to benefit from reform may not even have a meaningful presence at the time of opening, and thus they cannot be its political author. The key to reconciling democracy and the market thus involves the construction of a political coalition capable of sustaining reforms in a politically open context. The paradox is that if voters, firms, unions, and peasants act on their interests defined in material terms, no such coalition can be assembled. Implicitly, either democracy will consume the market, or marketization must take place in the absence of democracy. Should politicians endeavor to launch economic liberalization, they would still face the orthodox paradox: entrenched bureaucrats unwilling to engage in the retrenchment of the state, but who would nonetheless be responsible for implementing liberalization (Kahler 1989, 55).

Understanding free market democracy, then, involves understanding how these twin paradoxes can be solved. Empirical reality – in stark contrast to theory – suggests that they can, even in unfavorable circumstances (Remmer 1990). In Chile, the very same polity that had in 1970 produced the world's first elected Marxist government had by 1989 generated a political system in which nearly all political actors supported open, market-based economic organization (Roberts 1995). In Argentina, a democratic government was able to push through and consolidate a package of economic liberalizations far more ambitious than those even a previous savage bureaucratic authoritarian government was unable to impose, and more extensive than those undertaken in the East Asian newly industrializing countries over the course of decades (Rodrik 1993, 356). In Mexico, a long-standing dominant party founded on revolutionary nationalist economic policies was able to open the economy, induce catastrophic declines in living standards for the broad majority of citizens, open up political competition to an unprecedented degree, remain in power throughout the transition, and eventually pass the presidency to an opposition party equally committed to free market policies.

Four perspectives dominate the efforts to explain this apparent paradox. The first emphasizes the sequencing of reforms, such that marketization precedes democratization and can become a fait accompli by the time political opening is achieved. A second perspective suggests that a sufficiently gradualist approach to economic liberalization – despite potential efficiency costs – can help to make reform politically palatable (and thus durable). A third suggests that the galvanizing force of economic crisis can make otherwise unpalatable reforms politically feasible. Finally, some have pointed to a new form of "populist" politics that combines free market economic positions with a charismatic and antioligarchic political style and/or targeted side payments (social welfare programs) that can be used to mitigate opposition to neoliberal reforms.

Arguments about sequencing have been most prominent in the literature on transitions in the formerly communist countries (Williamson 1994). And they mirror the conventional understanding of the Chilean case, a stylized scenario in which an ideologically committed military government imposed sudden and harsh neoliberal reforms on the economy, which after a severe downturn eventually produced a sustained high-growth outcome (Edwards and Edwards 1987). In addition to inducing adjustment and efficiency, the neoliberal reforms were also consciously designed to disarticulate remaining supporters of statism (Piñera 1991). By the time of democratic transition in 1988, the benefits of liberalization were said to have been manifest, leading to the commitment even of most of the opposition parties to the free market model (Puryear 1994, 112; Roberts 1995).

There are three principal problems with the sequencing argument, however. First, in most empirical cases the return to growth has either not materialized (as in much of the formerly communist world) or has not been sustained (e.g., Argentina, Brazil, Peru, and Mexico). Moreover, even in Chile where rapid growth was maintained, this did not imply material improvements for the vast majority of the population. Near the time of transition, free market policies had raised rates of poverty and indigence to nearly triple and quadruple their 1970 levels, with over 42 percent of the urban and over 53 percent of the rural population impoverished (León 1994, 11). While there is debate as to the merits of neoliberalism as a growth strategy, few argue that in the medium term it produces anything but regressive distributional outcomes that are hardly conducive to constructing a mass following. Thus the second problem is political – arguments about the long-term benefits of growth only make sense if politicians can construct coalitions based in the winners from neoliberalism. But in Chile the free market political forces on the right have as a large portion of their political base peasants who were among the greatest victims of the neoliberal transformation. This is despite the reduction in poverty achieved during the post-transition reformist administrations. That is, the neoliberals have constructed a viable political coalition, but it is not the one predicted by sequencing approaches. Finally, arguments about sequencing would expect that the more simultaneous the reforms the more severe the resistance (as losers from the reform process have greater ability to resist in more democratic settings). But in Mexico a much more contemporaneous process of political and economic reform – despite catastrophic economic results in the mid-1980s and again in the mid-1990s – produced far less open resistance than experienced in Chile during the 1980s in a decidedly more authoritarian setting.

Others scholars, also operating under the assumption that painful reforms will provoke serious societal resistance, have argued that politicians should take a gradualist and more democratic approach to economic reform. In the process, political coalitions supporting reform can be constructed (Bresser Pereira et al. 1994, 182). Nelson (1992, 259–60) contends that failure to do so may require either a reversion to authoritarian practices or the abandonment of reform, but she does suggest ways in which even fiscally constrained states might construct reform coalitions.[2] Buttressing this perspective are arguments by Rodrik that suggest that economic reforms are not as painful in the short run as commonly assumed (1996, 29), and Bunce's (2000, 719) observation that neoliberal reforms have the political side "benefit" of disarticulating reform opponents. Finally, and most compellingly, Schamis (1999) points out how the process of neoliberal reform can create rents for potential reform beneficiaries, and thereby help construct a viable proreform coalition.

While there is some merit in this second general perspective, it ignores several crucial points. Rodrik's claim that economic reform is not as painful as is usually argued makes sense only in comparison to a counterfactual – the potential consequences of failure to reform. But it is not likely that the vast majority of citizens will make that comparison in place of a judgment of relative change in material well-being since the onset of reform. By the latter yardstick, short-run costs have been enormous almost everywhere. Gradual approaches to economic reforms also raise the strong possibility that opposition majorities can be mobilized to slow, block, or roll back liberalization (e.g., crucial pension reforms in Brazil). Certainly liberalization's rents can create allies among powerful interests (e.g., privatized firms, the finance sector), but it is difficult to see how mass electoral support could thusly be generated. Indeed, these rents can sometimes cause the reform process to stall in unfavorable partial reform equilibria (Hellman 1998). And surprisingly frequently specific economic reforms are taken in a rapid way, while accompanying social welfare programs designed to mitigate dissent and build overall support for politicians implementing the model are typically inadequate to the task, if they are present at all.[3]

---

[2] A recent examination of the Argentine reform experience by Etchemendy (2001) suggests that a coalition for reform was established by transforming (but not eliminating) the rents provided key members of business and labor, as well as by the avoidance of wholesale liberalization in sectors dominated by the powerful traditional beneficiaries of import substitution.

[3] It is clear that in important instances politicians have used social development expenditures in an effort to build political support (Horcasitas and Weldon 1994 for Mexico; Schady 2000 on Peru). But whether they are adequate to the task of compensating for neoliberal reforms is an open question. Weyland (1998), argues that

A third prominent perspective suggests that economic crisis is a key ingredient to successful reform. Typically, such an approach argues that where hyperinflation is present, economic reform is made easier by the fact that the *status quo ante* is decidedly harmful to almost all social actors, making stabilization a win-win outcome. While this is undoubtedly true, it applies only narrowly. First, while all the Latin American cases suffered some degree of economic downturn after the debt crisis, only some reached hyperinflationary proportions (Brazil, Argentina, Peru, Bolivia, Nicaragua, and less clearly Chile). Second, while all political players in such contexts would benefit from stabilization, this is only a small component of the overall neoliberal reform package of structural adjustments that includes policies that are decidedly harmful to labor and capital alike. It is true that in the wake of inflationary imbalances one would expect monetary tightening and fiscal austerity, but why would one expect support for trade opening, privatization, deregulation, or labor "flexibilization"?

A refreshing move in the direction of more overtly political explanation can be found in the literature on neoliberal populism. Roberts (1996, 88), for example, explains reform outcomes in terms of leaders who reconcile harsh economic policies with mass followings by emphasizing personalist appeals, antioligarchical discourse, mobilization that bypasses existing institutions, and redistributive or clientelistic social spending. While welcome for its explicit focus on the process by which a neoliberal political coalition is constructed, this form of populism is comparatively unusual. Particularly because of its emphasis on bypassing existing forms of institutional intermediation, it seems likely to emerge only in settings in which traditional parties and social organizations are notably weak or absent (post-1990 Peru, possibly Brazil, but not Mexico, Argentina, or Chile). An alternative and extremely useful approach can be found in Gibson's (1997) analysis of market reform in Mexico and Argentina, that emphasizes the ability of

---

compensatory packages are simply too small to create a coalition in favor of the initiation of neoliberal reform, but might help consolidate support behind them once they are fully implemented. Instead, he contends that only where preceded by hyperinflationary crises did neoliberal reforms manage to receive substantial immediate approval. It is important to note that in some cases the funds for social development, for example in Peru, in large part came from former allocations to municipal and line ministry budgets, and thus do not reflect dramatic increases in new spending.

traditionally statist parties to impose economic reform without losing electoral viability – though in both cases losing elections – through the construction of a two-sector coalition that includes urban beneficiaries of economic reform and a crucial bastion of rural voters providing a mass electoral base for the reformist party.

The key insight here is that the social coalition that appears to support neoliberal reforms is both sectoral and extremely heterogeneous. It incorporates masses of peasants who are among the most materially disadvantaged by free market reforms alongside business and middle-sector elites who have benefited disproportionately from liberalization and the ensuing rise of wealth and income inequality. It is a "sandwich coalition"[4] that is *prima facie* implausible, yet empirically present in both Mexico and Chile. It is the task that this book sets for itself to answer three questions framed around the construction of just such a coalition: (1) Why are the victims of liberalization in a freely democratic setting among its chief electoral supporters? (2) How does economic liberalization drive this political reorientation of the rural sector, especially given that neoliberal policies are corrosive of traditional clientelistic patterns of control? (3) What are the longer term implications for democratic deepening of a marriage of economic liberalization and political democracy?

THE POLITICAL CONSTRUCTION OF A NEOLIBERAL COALITION IN CHILE AND MEXICO

We now turn briefly to Chile and Mexico. It is widely accepted that for democratic transitions to be stable, incumbent elites must believe that the opening of politics will not create political conditions that are threatening to their fundamental interests, and that a reversion to authoritarianism is on the whole undesirable or excessively costly (Linz and Stepan 1996, 6). But how do elites provide for the sort of democratic "outcome insurance" that keeps regime-threatening issues off the political agenda? Indeed, fears of such a return to redistributive politics led the Chilean military government, with the support of prominent private-sector allies, to savagely repress an enormous wave

---

[4] I thank Arun Swamy for this term.

of urban popular mobilization against continued military rule between 1983 and 1986. But then only a few years later a rapid and almost violence-free transition to democracy was launched in the wake of the 1988 plebiscite defeat of the military; and it was a transition that had the (grudging) support of some of the military's crucial upper class allies. Or, at least, they saw it as less costly than efforts to subvert the plebiscite results. What had happened to make democratization palatable to at least some economic elites and (barely) tolerable for soldiers?

By 1988 neither the military nor its civilian allies felt directly threatened by democratization – they were confident that freely elected leaders would not (or could not) alter property rights or other fundamental aspects of the free market development model, in decisive contrast to the 1970–3 period. But why? Part of the answer is to be found in the conventional wisdom and has to do with institutional features of the Chilean transition "pact."[5] Embedded in the military-drafted constitution of 1980 and the accessory organic constitutional laws enacted after the 1988 plebiscite were features that introduced appointed senators (some from the military itself) into the legislature, electoral rules that in practice favor the right, and requirements for supermajorities in both houses of congress to introduce changes to existing laws in important issue areas. Linked to this were protections for the autonomy of the military as an institution and the tenure of military-era judges. These institutional features helped to guarantee the broad outlines of the neoliberal model even in the face of opposition victory at the polls.

This explanation is part of a broader set of recent advances in our understanding of democratization that have emphasized institutional variables (Snyder and Mahoney 1999). But for progress to continue we must explicitly connect these insights to the social formations in which they are necessarily embedded. Institutional rules, then, provided a modicum of security for the privileged classes in Chilean society

---

[5] Strictly speaking, of course, the Chilean transition was not pacted but rather carried out under the terms of the military-imposed 1980 constitution. Nevertheless, in the final years of military rule fundamental changes were negotiated with respect to postmilitary political institutions as a condition for opposition participation under the basic terms of the 1980 constitution.

against distributive demands from below, but they operate only if con-servative forces *also* have a substantial electoral base – one the extends well beyond the privileged sectors. Thus, institutional safeguards are only half the story. Without mass support for the right, even a biased electoral law would produce an overwhelming opposition victory. And given the brutality of Chilean authoritarianism, an economic system that created record levels of poverty and inequality at the same time it produced record economic growth, and a recent experience of mas-sive democratic and distributive popular demands, it is surprising that Chilean elites were comparatively confident of just such a mass base.

How such an electoral base can be constructed in a free market con-text is the central issue for this book. My argument is that neoliberal reforms made possible the construction of an unusual social coalition for the neoliberal right in Chile: it is a "sandwich coalition" of tradi-tional well-off supporters in urban areas coupled with a mass rural base of some of neoliberalism's greatest victims. This has stabilized Chilean democracy, giving conservatives a veto role over key policies, and thus bringing elites into the democratic game. But how was such an improb-able bloc created? The answer to this question hinges on the dynamics of economic liberalization. As liberal forms of economic organization were introduced in the 1970s and 1980s in Chile – reversing course in what had been among the most statist economies on the continent – the political consequences of these reforms differed markedly in urban and rural settings. While marketization was consonant with compet-itive politics and the survival of, albeit diminished, associational life in urban centers (Oxhorn 1995), in the countryside it provoked social fragmentation, economic dependence, immiseration, and the near col-lapse of organization. Certainly, urban areas also suffered from social decapitalization and demobilization relative to their precoup experi-ences, but the point is that this result was so much more severe in rural areas as to constitute a qualitatively different phenomenon.

When market-induced rural atomization was coupled with a po-litical system in which the reformist center and left support almost identical agrarian policies as those of the neoliberal right, the conser-vative voice in the countryside has become a monologue. And because high levels of rural economic dependence and vulnerability to local elites was another consequence of the neoliberal reforms, it is unsur-prising that the countryside has become not only a repository for a large number of votes for conservatives, but also an area of decidedly underdeveloped democratic competition. This rural base, magnified by institutional biases, has made democratization safe for elites. The sectorally uneven social transformations induced by marketization are the crucial complement to conventional explanations of Chilean democratic consolidation – they give political meaning to the institutional variables usually highlighted.

Herein lies the paradox of free market democracy. The reconciliation of the inherently austere policies of free market reform with open politics is based not in a sequence of imposition but rather a *segmentation of social effect*. It is precisely the democracy-inhibiting character of specifically rural free market reforms that make national-level neoliberalism compatible with open politics. Neoliberal elites, whether on the Chilean right or within the Institutional Revolutionary Party (PRI) in Mexico, stabilize their power even in the course of severe economic contraction because of their hold in rural areas. In the absence of this sandwich coalition, however, free market reform or democracy might well fail either through the victory of illiberal politicians, or through the unwillingness of authoritarian elites (and their supporters) to open up politics in the first place.

If the conventional sequencing explanation fails to withstand scrutiny in Chile, it is decidedly less plausible for Mexico. There political and economic opening were much more simultaneous, and the latter has yet to produce a sustained return to growth, to say nothing of improvements in average living standards. Long an unusual case of "inclusionary" authoritarianism and statist economic development, Mexico took up the path toward market opening and democratization in the wake of the debt crisis of 1982. While newly elected President de la Madrid (1982–8) did put an end to the populist experiment that characterized the final years of López Portillo's (1976–82) presidency, his efforts at stabilization took on at first a decidedly heterodox complexion. In 1988, however, in the closest election in postrevolutionary Mexican history, Carlos Salinas eked out a fraud-marred victory. Not only was this a sign of the beginnings of meaningful political liberalization, it was soon followed by the first opposition gubernatorial victories as well as the first widespread opposition domination at the municipal level. Within a decade opposition from the right (the National Action Party, or PAN) would control a half-dozen state governorships, while that of the left (the Party of the Democratic Revolution, PRD) would control the crucial Federal District mayoralty.

But this was also a decade of tremendous economic transformation. The economic collapse of the de la Madrid (1982–8) *sexenio* was followed by a package of economic reforms that in their totality amounted to the abandonment of the state-led development strategy that had prevailed since the 1930s. While Mexico joined the General Agreement on Tariffs and Trade (GATT) in 1986, the massive privatization of public enterprises was carried out by Salinas after 1988. Similarly, the former regime of import licenses and strong protection was replaced by rapidly falling tariffs as Mexico imposed its outward-looking reforms. Perhaps most fundamentally, the constitution was amended to simultaneously end the process of agrarian reform and permit the privatization of large tracts of agricultural land long held in collective forms of tenure (*ejidos*). The process of external opening culminated with the ratification of NAFTA in 1993. In social terms the effects of transformation were catastrophic – wages fell dramatically in real terms as the state attempted to stabilize surging prices and formal sector employment collapsed, while in the countryside price supports for virtually all agricultural products were abandoned (save corn and beans) and access to credit curtailed. Indeed, the effect of the crisis in the already impoverished countryside was, if anything, more severe than in the cities.

How could the Mexican regime square the circle of allowing dramatically increased political competition after 1988, a time during which it was imposing tremendous economic hardship? Moreover, while doing so, how did it manage to retain power for so long? In the Chilean case, we saw that posttransition conservative parties were able to construct a strong political base for neoliberal policies in the form of a sandwich coalition of upper-class winners from liberalization and the atomized and economically dependent rural-sector losers from the same process. This has also taken place in Mexico. The long-governing PRI maintained its hold on power throughout the transition not because it has continued to control politics in urban centers where beneficiaries of reform were concentrated, but rather because it is still overwhelmingly – and paradoxically – dominant in the rural areas.

Some would not consider this sectoral domination particularly surprising. After all, the PRI has been hegemonic in the Mexican countryside since the suppression of the Cristero rebellions of the 1920s and 1930s and the initiation of the agrarian reform. Indeed, since its creation in 1938 the Confederación Nacional Campesina (CNC) – the corporatist arm of the PRI in the countryside – has been the mediator of rural social control, using its privileged access to the state to channel, fragment, and control rural demand making. While this is true, it cannot account for PRI domination in the countryside in the 1980s and 1990s. First, economic liberalization eliminated or dramatically reduced the pool of resources available for distribution through clientelist channels like the CNC. Moreover, the end of the agrarian reform removed perhaps the most useful tool the CNC had at its disposal – a monopoly on access to redistributed land (Bartra 1985). Indeed, even the limited (and delayed) social welfare efforts initiated under Salinas had as their goal the bypassing of this traditional apparatus of rural social control.[6]

The answer, I contend, is similar to that found in the Chilean case. Marketization in agriculture produced social consequences that undermine the practice of democratic political competition – limiting the ability of alternative perspectives to reach, or be expressed, there. One caveat is very important here – with respect to liberalization and political opening, the transformation of the Mexican countryside is less advanced than that of Chile; and implementation has been far more geographically uneven given the realities of a federal institutional structure. Nevertheless, free market policies in Mexico have produced similar patterns of atomization, disorganization, fragmentation, and economic dependence that has rendered peasants vulnerable to the pressures of the governing party and (depending on location) its allies among the rural elite. There are, however, differences. Most importantly the political monologue in the Mexican countryside is not entirely cemented by the absence of organization in civil society, but by the fact that much of the political space in rural areas is already *occupied* by organizations linked to a dominant neoliberal party (by the 1980s, the PRI). The presence of such groups creates incentive structures that, when combined with the severe collective action problems induced

---

[6] And these policies, at least on their face, were compatible with if not directly supportive of substantial levels of autonomous local social organization. For an insightful discussion of the variegated implications of Salinas-era social welfare policies, see Fox (1994).

by marketization, permit little autonomous political organization or participation. And increasingly the PRI has become dependent on the strength of this rural base.

To assert, however, that free market democracy is stabilized in an unlikely elite-peasant coalition does not explain *why* neoliberal economic reforms make this possible. It is to that crucial task that I turn in the second chapter.

2

The Sectoral Foundations of Free
Market Democracy

> Despotism, by its very nature suspicious, sees the isolation of men as the
> best guarantee of its own permanence. So it usually does all it can to
> isolate them.
>
> Alexis de Tocqueville (1969, 509)

Given the inequalities and distributional conflicts free market reforms usually engender, how can politicians render them compatible
with democratic politics? The answer outlined in this chapter differs
markedly from both the historical treatments of democratic regime
formation in Europe that emphasized agrarian class structures and
political coalitions (Moore 1966; Luebbert 1991) and from the contemporary emphasis on institutional structures and elite interactions
in the literature on "third wave" democratization (O'Donnell et al.
1986; Gunther et al. 1995; Mainwaring and Scully 1995; Linz and
Stepan 1996). Instead, the argument made here borrows from both
literatures, emphasizing the importance of social coalitions founded
in the countryside, but situating them in the neoliberal institutional
context of the third-wave democratic transitions. The contrast with
elite-centric, voluntaristic approaches is more stark: I contend that the
structural and institutional conditions examined here in large measure
define and strictly delimit the terrain on which political "bargains"
can be struck. My approach is in one sense an extension of the civil
society/social capital arguments (Putnam 1993, 2000). The difference

is that associational life is an intermediate step in the argument, one that I explain rather than take as exogenous.

Works on earlier Latin American episodes of democratic regime formation have productively focused on patterns of working class mobilization and incorporation into politics (Collier and Collier 1991; Rueschemeyer et al. 1992). But in contemporary underdeveloped contexts like Chile and Mexico, democracy depends not so much on how a mobilized labor movement is incorporated into politics, but rather on how neoliberal elites go about the construction of a mass electoral base for free market policies – this time among demobilized and economically vulnerable peasants. This unlikely coalition of winners and losers can be constructed, however, because of the *specifically rural* social atomization, dependence, anæmic political competition, and constrained alternatives engendered by economic liberalization. Neoliberal elites in this context establish a rural electoral dominance that gives them a stake in the much more competitive national political arena, and enough seats to ensure a legislative veto over policies threatening to fundamental interests. Free market democracy is thereby consolidated, if partial.

As we saw in Chapter 1, the problem of free market democratization is how to open up political competition in a new neoliberal context, without reigniting the mobilization, redistributive demands, and populist politics that drove the initial wave of authoritarian seizures in the 1960s and 1970s (O'Donnell 1973; Linz and Stepan 1978; Collier 1979). The answer that this book provides, that sectoral defects in rural democratization are the foundation for its national-level stability, is based in three broad theoretical claims. First, the nature of democracy under neoliberalism is in fundamental ways different from the challenge of democratization in statist economies. Second, the crucial political dynamics are properly analyzed at the subnational – sectoral – level, and it is in aggregation that national outcomes can be understood. Third, free market economic policies have political implications that are specific to rural sectors, and make possible the political dominance therein of neoliberal elites despite unfavorable material outcomes.

The remainder of this chapter explicates these theoretical claims. I begin with the notion that the threat to meaningful democratic practice in economically liberal contexts hinges critically on failures of interest aggregation and political participation. By contrast, in statist contexts it was the questions of the autonomy of civil society from the state and excessive politicization that were central to democracy's fate. The second section examines the role of subnational variations in explaining national outcomes, in particular that political dynamics in the countryside are characteristically different from those in urban centers.[1] It is the defectiveness of rural democracy that makes the consolidation of national democratic institutions possible. Finally, and most crucially, the chapter makes the theoretical case for sectoral-level linkages between free market economic policies and democracy. Of course, the implication of these claims is troubling, because it would suggest that efforts to deepen democracy in the countryside may reduce its overall stability.

The paradoxical outcome – competitive national-level democracy based in part on conservative hegemony and peasant quiescence in the countryside – hinges on the effects of free market policies on specifically rural social relations. The central contention is that structural features of agricultural production combine with the dramatic disincentives for collective action and expression induced by economic liberalization in such a way as to block independent political participation by the rural lower classes. Marketization in agricultural settings induces the destruction of communities and long-standing patterns of residence, social fragmentation, and severe economic differentiation, and economic dependence on local elites. The results are dramatic problems of collective action and interest fragmentation that vitiate the possibility for meaningful political participation by peasants. Without historical stocks of social capital, community ties, institutional infrastructure (formal and informal), and external supports (from, e.g., labor activists, religious groups, or political parties), autonomous peasant political action in the face of economic dominance by neoliberal elites hovers between the irrational and the impossible. But without precisely such action, which would place the interests of peasants onto the political agenda, the political monologue of rural political elites remains unchallenged and substantial threats to their electoral support

---

[1] This is an insight that was formerly prominent in scholarship on politics in statist economies, but has been little recognized in the literature of neoliberal era democratization. See, for example, Scully (1992) and Loveman (1976).

generally do not materialize, whatever changes in material conditions that may occur.

This unevenness in the practice of democracy – despite uniform institutional rules at the national level – is the paradox of free market democracy. Rural anomie and elite domination make democracy safe for capitalism at the national level, but are an expression of its inadequacy at the sectoral level. And these are problems not easily corrected, for to do so can undermine the stability of democracy. Because Chilean and Mexican elites lack a strong normative commitment to democratic politics, they are unlikely to remain loyal to the regime without some mechanism to guarantee them a share – or effective veto – in the making of policy outcomes. The advent of the much-needed normative commitment to democracy is, unfortunately, an issue for the decidedly long term, as the experiences of the young and old Latin American democracies alike that succumbed in the authoritarian wave of the 1970s demonstrate.

THE FIRST STEP: UNDERSTANDING DEMOCRACY IN THE OPEN ECONOMY

In an odd disjuncture, the comparatively vast literature on the relationship between economic liberalization and democracy has been built on a foundation drawn from the identification of the weaknesses of democracy that emerged from examination of the statist polities of the 1960s and 1970s. Less attention, if any, has been focused on the possibility that the barriers to democracy's consolidation may be qualitatively different across developmental strategies. Arguments about the benefits of economic liberalism for democracy highlight ways that the former mitigates the features of statism that have long been held to undermine democracy (e.g., the clientelistic use of rents, populist and inflationary excesses and inefficiency, and stop/go growth cycles). Whatever the potential longer-term compatibilities between economic reform and democracy, however, most scholars have also contended that the process of transition is quite difficult. Liberalization, it is feared, may unleash uncontrolled mobilization, radical distributional demands, and may even provoke the resort to centralized authoritarian practices (from actual seizures of power to quasi-constitutional episodes of decree rule) as part of the effort to implement painful changes. But these are the very problems of corruption, polarization, and political order long identified as causes of democracy's collapse.[2] These are important insights, but they are heavily shaped by the economic contexts in which they were developed – and almost all of these were states pursuing statist and inward-looking economic strategies. But under neoliberalism, I argue, the challenges facing democracy are different: a dearth of participation and social disorganization become more important than the threat of mobilization and redistributive populism.

Any standard definition of democracy has among its requisites the possibility of meaningful, autonomous political participation by individuals and groups (Collier and Levitsky 1997). But this aspect of democracy is also a problematic point of intersection with the prevailing economic model. In different ways both statist and neoliberal development paradigms can undermine the autonomous participation that is the hallmark of liberal democracy. In the former case the pervasiveness of the state's intervention in the economy can create dependence on the part of political groups, as well as patronage resources used by elites to purchase electoral support. By contrast, market-based policies can raise such severe collective action problems as to prevent social and political organization altogether, typically among the most underprivileged strata of society (Garretón 1983; Schmitter 1992)

Thus, in free market economic contexts, the crucial political issue is how the basis for collective action, and by extension political participation, is transformed. Democratic competition requires the presence of social groups – both parties and secondary associations – to help aggregate interests, provide alternatives, and ensure accountability. But as markets penetrate, the incentives to act politically facing individuals

---

[2] That is, this literature has emphasized the avoidance of populism (Dornbusch and Edwards 1991), the perils of hyper-mobilization (Huntington 1968; Linz 1978), and tradeoffs between demands for consumption and needs for investment (O'Donnell 1973) that induced polarization and collapsed democracy across the South American continent in the 1970s. More recently scholars have emphasized how regime characteristics (Lijphart and Waisman 1996), electoral rules (Siavelis and Valenzuela 1996), and elite pacts (Gunther et al. 1995) reduce polarization and induce centripetal political competition, stabilizing democracy. These are important insights, but the argument here is that they do not address the crucial problems of free market democracy, which are located in the realm of participation and organization, not popular mobilization and polarization.

may be dramatically reduced in a sectorally bounded fashion. When national-level free market policies and institutions interact with the social and structural realities of agrarian life and urban life, contrasting patterns of social relations emerge. In the countryside, autonomous political mobilization is blocked by high barriers to collective action as well as the vulnerability of peasants to local elites. As a consequence, associational life is underdeveloped and democracy anæmic. In urban areas the challenges are not as severe, and political competition is often vigorous. This is particularly the case because urban liberalization produces fewer severe economic dependencies than in the countryside and because urban civil society is less disrupted by the economic transformations themselves.

By contrast, under statism the formation of organizations is usually much less problematic – indeed, it is often directly encouraged in both urban and rural sectors – but *autonomy* from the state is a constant dilemma.[3] Here is where neoliberalism has paradoxical implications. By removing public economic intervention, reducing rents, and privatizing formerly political decisions it inherently increases the autonomy of political actors from the state. And this may be the key reason why many scholars and political figures consider free markets inherently democratizing. My argument is that, in the countryside, it simultaneously changes the resources, incentives, and structure of interests of potential actors in ways that prevent them from forming organizations and participating in politics.

It should be clear that I do not claim that either developmentalist or neoliberal economic policies are "more fertile" ground for democracy's implantation. Instead, each poses distinctive challenges as well as displaying features that facilitate democracy's success. The difficulty has been that scholars have taken the problems of interest group autonomy and political polarization – which were crucial to understanding democracy's instability in the era of statism – and have attempted to use them as an optic in the examination of free market democracy. But the political vices and virtues of statist and neoliberal approaches to

---

[3] Where the state controls a large proportion of economic resources and engages in their discretionary allocation, its leverage over private interests can become so severe as to undermine meaningful political competition. Obviously, the epitome of such a situation is the authoritarianism of state corporatism.

economic governance are largely opposed, and understanding the latter necessitates a focus on collective action not on political order and group autonomy. In the following section I set out the characteristic dilemmas of statist and free market democratization, and explore the causes of the latter's consolidation in Chile and Mexico.

Democracy and the Economy

Statist development tends to reduce the *group autonomy* that is so essential to pluralist democratic competition. In its state socialist and corporatist forms it most obviously had this effect – public power over the economy was used to organize, control, and depoliticize civil society (Friedrich and Brzezinski 1956). The more common mixed-economy cases have also been criticized because of the degree to which public action is distorted by a large state presence in the economy – particularly the organization of political life around the quest for rents (Krueger 1974; Olson 1982). Others disagreed to the extent that they accept that democracy can survive in such contexts, though they still raise the questions of the lack of group autonomy and inverse problem of state capture by rent-seeking interests – both of which would vitiate meaningful democratic competition (Crisp 1998). It is the virtue of free market policies that they necessarily undermine this state tutelage over groups by privatizing or deregulating the economic decisions that had provided the necessary leverage for political elites to impose outcomes.

On the other hand, the virtue of statism is that it encourages the aggregation of and expression of interests.[4] Why does statism facilitate group formation? This is in part true because organized social agents are not nearly as threatening from an elite perspective under import-substitution than they can be under open-market conditions. In economic terms, the forms of redistribution typically demanded by such groups are not inimical to growth at least in the short run – indeed they form the backbone of the third-world variant of the fordist compromise. During the early phases of import substituting industrialization (ISI), increased wages for the working class (and occasionally peasants)

---

[4] Indeed, this is precisely the source of its economic inefficiency according to Olson (1982).

can be paid for because these same workers are later the consumers of
the products made by domestic producers (Hirschman 1968). Politically, populist leaders pursuing nationalist/developmentalist strategies
have powerful incentives to promote the organization of interests –
especially among the usually underrepresented poor and working-class
groups – both as a counterweight to traditional elites and as a source of
legitimacy (Kaufman and Stallings 1991; Waterbury 1999). In this way
the state solves the collective action problem that historically prevented
the expansion of domestic demand.[5] But twin perils lurk: that the demands of class and sectoral interests can spiral out of control, or that
they are incorporated under state tutelage in varieties of authoritarian
corporatism (Huntington 1969; Schmitter 1974).

By way of example, the central criticism of the highly statist pre-
1973 Chilean democratic regime was that it was *too inclusive*. Politics
was pervaded by an enormous number of conflicting interests placing
intense and often contradictory demands on the state (Valenzuela 1978;
Piñera 1990, 1991; Büchi 1993). Even in the Mexican case, where societal organization along corporatist lines had been seen as a mechanism
of social control since the 1940s, frequent outbursts of political demand making recurred both within and without the official apparatus
of the state and party during this period. But merely because free market policies undermine the ability of states to pursue these forms of
social control does not imply that the reforms are democratizing *in se*.

Here is the crux of the issue: if the challenge to democratization
under a statist developmental regime hinged on the *autonomy* of organizations in civil society and the tendency for polarized politics to
emerge, the problem under neoliberal conditions is the *formation* of
groups representing differing societal interests. As much as the existence of interventionist state institutions (from labor laws, to regimes
of social provision, to agrarian reform) promoted the formation of concrete interest groups in society and made politics central to everyday
life, their privatization reduces such incentives. As a result, problems
of collective action loom large and in sectors where they undermine
autonomous social organization or interest aggregation they become
problems of democracy.

---

[5] While many would agree that such strategies *qua* economic policy are self-defeating
in the long run, almost all concur that these sorts of political incentives are present.

It is the goal of this book, then, to reexamine the linkage between markets and democracy in light of the problem of collective action. Only then can the all-too-typical assumption of civil society's resurrection in the wake of authoritarianism (O'Donnell and Schmitter 1986, 48–56) be transformed into an empirical question. And in so doing we will gain insight into the foundations of meaningful democratic competition and the meaning of free market democracy.

THE SECOND STEP: THE IMPORTANCE OF SUBNATIONAL DYNAMICS

Scholarly examination of the consolidation of third-wave democracies has focused analytical attention almost exclusively on the national level.[6] This is in part derivative of the emphasis in this literature on institutional variables (e.g., electoral rules, presidential versus parliamentary systems, party systems) that are uniform nationwide. While a productive approach, the national focus has also served to obscure crucial sectoral level variation in political outcomes – a variation born of the structural linkages between patterns of social organization and institutional dynamics (Snyder 2001a). Thus, the perspective here moves beyond an examination of the incentive structures embedded in institutions and instead focuses on the varying social foundations of political behavior as they manifest themselves in the context of new economic and political institutions.[7]

The effort to understand national outcomes in relation to sectoral politics has a long and productive history outside the contemporary democratic consolidation literature. Indeed, different patterns of rural social organization and their political consequences have been crucial components of explanations of regime dynamics (Moore 1966; Paige 1997), social revolutions and peasant politics (Banfield 1958; Wolf 1969; Paige 1975, 1997; Scott 1976, 1985), the historical instability of Argentine politics (O'Donnell 1978), and the collapse of democracy in

---

[6] See, for example, Linz (1990); Linz and Stepan (1996); and the contributions to Mainwaring and Scully (1995) and to Domínguez and Lowenthal (1996).

[7] For an elaboration of the notion of structural linkages and an examination of how a focus on the linkages between state institutions (not necessarily political ones) and society shape the dynamics of political mobilization, see Houtzager and Kurtz (2000).

Chile (Loveman 1976). Indeed, some of the best examinations of earlier democratic regimes in Latin America discussed their political development in terms of sectorally grounded conflicts (Hirschman 1958;
Mamalakis 1965; Frieden 1988, 1991).

The effort here is to examine national-level political and economic
institutions as they interact with sectoral social dynamics – that is,
the focus is on the structural linkages between state and society, not
on either institutional dynamics or social coalitions considered alone.[8]
In particular, I argue that rural and urban democracy – under neoliberalism – constitute what Schmitter (1992, 427) has called "partial
regimes." While a single set of institutional rules in theory governs
political competition, in practice the character and quality of representation and contestation vary dramatically. I will argue that it is in the
aggregation of these two sectoral regimes that the dynamics of national
politics in Chile and Mexico can be understood.

Why the Rural Sector Is Different

It is not a coincidence, however, that rural political dynamics are often quite different from urban patterns. There are systematic reasons
why this should be the case, particularly in developing countries, and
not simply because of peculiarities of two that are at the center of
the present study. Two features of rural society are most critical. In
economic terms, production and employment are inherently seasonal
and uncertain. In societal terms, populations are typically scattered,
remote, and difficult to organize beyond the village level. While atomization occurs in both city and countryside under free market economic
policies, both the social and the political consequences are less severe
in the urban sector.

Most important in this regard is the question of stability. Across
an enormous variety of agricultural products, one of the hallmarks
of modern production is the impermanence of labor force demand.
Whether this involves migratory labor flows as in fruit and vegetable

---

[8] The effort is to build on recent efforts that have emphasized the interactions between
state institutions and society in explaining political outcomes, either building up from
the society side using social capital (Putnam 1993, 2000; Fox 1996), or out from the
state-institutions arena (Evans 1996).

agriculture in the United States and coffee production in most of Central America, or a combination also involving the underemployed populations on microsized peasant holdings, production at a technological level sufficient to gain entry into export markets frequently demands great quantities of labor but for only short periods of time. Indeed, one of the characteristic effects of agricultural modernization in Chile and Mexico has been to dramatically heighten the seasonality of agriculture through the widespread introduction of short-term labor contracting.

The other hallmark of agriculture is simply that it occurs far from urban centers and the employment alternatives that they represent. This is crucial, for as liberal theorists have long pointed out it is the ease of exit from labor relations that undergirds the freedom of workers. But this holds true only as long as workers do not reside in quasi-monopsonistic settings (from a hiring perspective), where economic dependence *can* be translated into political dependence through the absence of local employment alternatives. In a countryside dominated by a small number of local elites, where employment opportunities are low, and the capacity for political monitoring is high, the imperative to stabilize income over the entire year can induce a meaningful political dependence.

One solution for small producers and agricultural laborers would be to organize in order to mitigate the effects of unstable employment and elite dependence (e.g., through cooperatives and unions). But as Bates (1981, 87–8) has noted, the size distribution firms and the physical geography of agriculture make rural collective action problems unusually severe. Rural elites, by virtue of their small number and economic concentration, are comparatively able to act together to defend shared interests. By contrast, large numbers reduce the individual marginal payoffs to collective action for peasants while geographic dispersion raises individual costs of participation, making interest group politics among the rural poor difficult enough to organize even before the opposition of powerful local elites is considered. Moreover, outsiders are unlikely to aid in the mobilization of rural producers and workers, because in poor countries these make poor allies. The high price to be paid for successfully forming an alliance with such a coalition partner – for example, a rise in domestic food prices – makes them particularly unattractive to potential nonelite urban allies who spend a substantial proportion of their total income on food (Bates and Rogerson 1980).

The Historical Importance of Subnational Political Regimes

It must be recognized that while the contemporary literature on democratic consolidation largely ignores sectoral differences, more historical treatments found them to be central to understanding national political dynamics. Indeed, the most prominent body of work that has emphasized sectoral differences can be found in the literature on clientelism (Scott 1972). This has in the American context taken the form of discussions of urban machine politics, and in the Latin American context more often centered on discussions of rural patron-client arrangements.[9] The key point is that in this literature it is assumed that, whatever the national-level political rules, the practice of politics in the sector covered by clientelist relations is different – and implicitly or explicitly less authentically democratic – than in the rest of the nation.

Indeed, the dynamic of one subnational regime – specifically rural clientelism – has long been seen as central to explanations of the historical stability of Chilean democracy (1932–73) and, ironically, of Mexican authoritarianism as well. In Chile, traditional patterns of labor recruitment and social organization (until the 1960s) left peasants dependent and captive constituents of the landlords who controlled the overwhelming majority of productive land in the country. Elite dominance was based in the system of *inquilinaje* – labor service tenancy – that relied on the absence of a functioning labor market. In exchange for access to a small parcel of land, peasants were expected to provide labor for landlords. These family tenancies were customarily heritable and with them came a landlord obligation to provide minimal health and old-age security. But these customary rights were framed by an obligation to provide political support to the allies of the landlord, and the reality of expulsion and blacklisting where landlord authority was challenged (Bauer 1975). Unsurprisingly, rural electoral

---

[9] Weyland (1996, 38 and fn. 31) treats clientelist relations as a problem bedeviling the poor throughout Brazil, but admits that such domination is more prevalent in the countryside. Loveman (1976) and Bauer (1975) have shown how such practices made elites hegemonic in the Chilean countryside until the social reforms of the 1960s, and Hagopian (1996) has shown how rural clientelism remains central to contemporary Brazilian politics.

results provided overwhelming majorities for conservative candidates in Chile's otherwise highly competitive democracy until the emergence of a rural welfare state in the 1960s broke the elites' stranglehold over social provision and employment – after which peasant support for conservatives evaporated.

A similar dynamic is apparent in Mexico during the statist era (1940–88), this time mediated by the rural face of the governing party instead of traditional landlords (though these were sometimes the same). The control of the governing party, the PRI, over the countryside was channeled through its rural corporatist organ, the national peasant confederation (CNC). Domination of rural politics hinged on two axes: the CNC monopoly over access to land and capital. The contextual difference is that the land in question was land for redistribution using the revolutionary agrarian reform. Large numbers of landless peasants in the Mexican countryside had a legal or political claim for land redistribution (*derecho a salvo*) under the constitution. But since the end of the Cárdenas *sexenio* (1934–40) these rights had only intermittently and selectively been enforced by the state. And enforcement – and thus the opportunity for peasants actually to receive land through the formation of new *ejidos* (land reform cooperatives) – depended on one's standing in the eyes of the CNC. Similarly, for peasants already in the large reform sector, continued access to a host of vital inputs, but most importantly credit provided through the rural development or *ejidal* banks, depended on CNC intermediation. As unpopular or authoritarian an organization as it might be, the CNC was vital to rural life until the 1980s because of its control over both social mobility and access to the means of production in rural Mexico. And it was crucial to political stability because of the overwhelming rural electoral majorities it was able to deliver to the PRI.

THEORY: NEOLIBERALISM AND DEMOCRACY IN THE COUNTRYSIDE AND THE NATION[10]

To argue that under neoliberalism the practice of politics varies widely in urban and rural sectors is somewhat paradoxical when it is remembered that the economic policies themselves were explicitly designed

---

[10] This section relies heavily on Kurtz (1999b, 277–8).

in part to reverse long-standing urban and industrial bias of statist development. Indeed, a central tenet of the reforms was sectoral neutrality – letting markets, not states, decide the proper loci of productive investment. Yet this uniform set of national policies produced severely atomizing social consequences when implemented in rural areas. In Chile and Mexico, to the extent to which reforms were implemented, the deregulation of land, labor, and commodity markets produced a form of social disarticulation that has stabilized the dominance of the modernized agrarian upper class. But how was this accomplished?

In political terms, neoliberal reforms undermined the quality of rural democratic competition by: (1) selectively constricting the national policy agenda in ways that exclude issues of importance to the countryside, (2) fragmenting peasant interests and producing steep barriers to their aggregation and expression, and (3) dramatically reducing the access of rural dwellers to urban allies or alternative information. In essence, neoliberalism has vitiated rural associational life, and with it the independent capacity of most peasants to articulate interests and aggregate them in a politically meaningful way. It made the cooperation that is essential to political participation impossible by creating an anonymous and atomized rural sector, where peasant collective action is framed by one-off interactions, low levels of information and trust, and by a large number of players. And, not surprisingly, in such contexts participation almost never emerges (North 1990, 12).

Neoliberalism and the Structure of Interests

But why exactly does rural neoliberalism have such corrosive effects on associational life, and how do they produce conservative political outcomes in the countryside? The problem begins with the redefinition of the boundaries between public and private spheres under neoliberalism. Core neoliberal principles of market-based allocation and defense of private property rights have the effect of removing nearly all of the issues historically considered crucial to rural political competition from the political arena. During the period of statist development in Mexico and Chile, public intervention or direct control was crucial in the setting of commodity prices; the marketing and distribution of crops; the access to and cost of credit and insurance; and for provision of crucial mechanical and petrochemical inputs. As a consequence, political participation and intermediation were a fact of life for peasant producers. But as neoliberalism redrew the boundary between state and economy in a way that made the provision of these goods and services a strictly private affair, the salience of politics declined almost to nonexistence. When coupled with a commitment to property rights that precluded consideration of questions of land tenure and agrarian reform – perhaps *the* quintessential agrarian issues – politics, democratic or otherwise, became materially irrelevant. Peasants were not excluded *ex ante* from democratic competition by neoliberalism, but their issues were.

Perhaps even more crucially, neoliberalism transforms the interest-based foundations of collective action and political participation in the countryside. To begin with, market-oriented reforms induce a differentiation of peasant interests as public institutions, formerly loci for interest aggregation and expression, are transformed or abolished. For example, guarantees of property rights and the end to agrarian reform in both Mexico and Chile removed a powerful basis of common interest and spur to political participation from the peasants – a legally enshrined but practically unenforced obligation of the state to provide land. Similarly, legal institutions like the 1967 peasant labor code in Chile had made all rural workers – landholding and landless alike – legally entitled to join the same unions, which had a geographic base. They did so in large numbers, forming a common identity and set of grievances in the process. The subsequent neoliberal labor code of 1979 (and its 1992 reform) instead fragmented workers by type of employment (year-round, temporary, multiemployer, single-enterprise, and independent) or by property (workers on geographically discontiguous farms were forced into separate organizations, even where the farms had a single owner); and permitted multiple labor organizations even within a single enterprise and a single category of workers. The structure of interests soon began to mirror this institutional fragmentation.

Framed in terms of the literature on social movements, what this did was create an unfavorable political opportunity structure. By removing the public institutions – labor law, social provision, agricultural extension and service, and land reform – that had formerly provided incentives for peasants to enter politics in the 1960s, the groundwork was set for their exit in the 1980s and 1990s. While the clientelist domination of the 1950s was not recreated after marketization, the withdrawal of the public sector from the countryside removed peasant issues from politics. Instead of mobilization around the agrarian side of the national issues of the day in the statist era – social reform, land redistribution, and developmental assistance – the challenge facing peasant politics under neoliberalism is redefined as the *introduction* of rural issues into a national political arena that *a priori* largely defines them as illegitimate. By their nature, agrarian issues challenge the very definition of the boundary between state and market embodied in the neoliberal model. But the feat of transforming the national political agenda, without allies, could only be the product of large-scale and sustained collective pressure.[11] And it is to the possibilities of this that I turn next.

Why Is Rural Neoliberalism Corrosive of Organization?

The pursuit of free market developmental strategies typically has far more disruptive social implications in agrarian sectors than in cities. The most notable aspect of this comes in the definition of individual property rights and the creation of markets in land. Unlike cities where firms and properties have typically long been privately owned and widely transacted, even in the heyday of statism, agrarian property rights are different. Where they were privately held, patterns of ownership concentration were frequently so extreme and sale of properties so uncommon and socially restricted as to fail to constitute a meaningful market (on Chile, see CIDA 1966, 172–3; Zeitlin and Ratcliff 1988, 155–8). Alternatively, as in Chile and Mexico during the process of agrarian reform, agricultural land may be held in inalienable collective tenure or subject to severe restrictions on ownership, use, and parcel size.

Consequently, the creation of land markets first required the delineation of individual property holdings (and rights to transact), and

---

[11] This is not in principle impossible. In the Brazilian case the peasantry has had some success at accomplishing precisely this. But it is also instructive that this has been true precisely because the institutional and economic transformations of neoliberalism have largely *not* reached rural Brazil. For a comparative examination, see Houtzager and Kurtz (2000).

then the formation and maintenance of actual land markets (since these did not exist or were underdeveloped). This is an inherently conflictual process – akin to the enclosure movement in England – that in Chile was completed in the late 1970s, and has made only slow progress in Mexico despite nearly a decade of efforts (Jarvis 1992; Cornelius and Myhre 1998). Socially, the effects of individualization of property rights are also profound, striking at the long-standing links between peasant communities and the land embedded in law, collective owner-ship, and/or customary practice.

The transformation of such a system necessarily undermines the social bases for peasant collective action. Privatization and individual-ization of land ownership bring with them the destruction of long-standing communities, the entry of new community members, the expulsion of surplus population, and a spiral of socioeconomic dif-ferentiation.[12] As some community members acquire land (or new en-trants from without purchase it), and others lose land and experience downward mobility, strong conflicts of interest *within* the community will develop. This is exacerbated by the fact that outsiders – particularly capitalist farmers – have advantages in knowledge and access to credit that allow them to out-compete peasant producers (Carter and Barham 1996). Their entry not only induces community class differentiation and a fragmentation of material interests, but also undermines the in-formal bonds of knowledge, trust, and reciprocity that emerge only over the passage of time.

In collective action terms, incentives to act decline markedly. The underlying structure of interests in rural communities becomes frag-mented (by land ownership and economic trajectory). The individual-ization of social mobility gives peasants alternatives to collective action (even if *upward* mobility is unlikely). And crucially, the ability to moni-tor and sanction free riding declines precipitously. As villages are razed to construct individual farms, the stocks of social capital they embody – norms, personal bonds, trust, and local organizations – go under the

---

[12] Rural communities have long been seen as reservoirs for surplus labor that lacks productive insertion into the broader economy and helps keep urban wages low (de Janvry 1981, 38–9). With the individualization of ownership in postagrarian reform settings, peasants who do not receive land are often expelled as their traditional or collective rights to residence are abrogated.

bulldozer as well. As collective property is sold (e.g., water rights, agricultural implements) the community structures that governed their use disappear as well. But all these are precisely the resources that peasants have historically used as building blocks to aggregate interests and support mobilization.[13]

Liberalization brings with it not only the creation of the first real land markets, but in many cases meaningful labor markets as well. Two characteristics of the neoliberal agricultural labor market stand out: (1) there is typically a massive imbalance between labor supply and demand as peasants are expelled from previous "low productivity" forms of tenure, and (2) employment opportunities are heavily seasonal in nature. The result is a highly competitive labor market that by its structure tends to make organization and collective action difficult, and that provides employers strong economic levers with which to control employees. Workers rely on growers' goodwill to gain access to employment, and just as critically, to extend the period of employment as long as possible over the course of a year. Alternatives, by virtue of agriculture's inherent geographic isolation, are limited.

The Structure of Political Opportunity

It is well known from the literature on social movements (McAdam 1983, ch. 3) that characteristics of a group by itself are not the only factors shaping the emergence or absence of collective action. Rather, patterns of political competition, contending actors, the availability of allies, and vulnerability or dependence can also shape the possibilities of political participation. And the Chilean experience in the 1960s and 1970s bears out the central role of reformist parties of center and left as well as the labor movement in supporting and helping initiate collective action (Petras and Zeitlin 1967; Scully 1992). The argument here is that neoliberalism consistently closes the political opportunity structure, specifically for peasant actors. While market-based economic governance does not have this effect in as pronounced a way in urban areas – neoliberal and reformist forces compete over a host of issues there – in the countryside they generally offer nearly identical positions

---

[13] Examples abound, from Southeast Asia (Scott 1976), to the American West (McNall 1988, 10–19), China (Perry 1980), and Latin America (Mallon 1983, 268–307).

on the issues of importance to peasants such as land tenure, protection and price supports, marketing and distribution, and credit. Opportunity for collective action is restricted because expectations for success by peasants are reduced, and on rural issues, elites are not divided (Tarrow 1998, 77–8).

Peasants are thus in a dual dilemma under neoliberalism: their internal resources for collective action are at a nadir while external resources and potential allies are unlikely to be forthcoming. But why don't reformist parties compete strongly with neoliberals for support among the peasantry? If reformist parties have made a commitment to the broad outlines of the free market model, the problem is that they will have few issues that they can use as a wedge to enter rural political competition. Commitment to private property precludes land reform, while commitments to freedom of prices and private provision prevent large-scale price support, input provision, credit subsidy, and insurance protection formerly provided by the state. While reformist parties could certainly take positions on these issues designed to build rural support, to do so would necessitate abandonment of core features of the neoliberal model – property rights, eschewing a public-sector role in production, and the avoidance of distortions of relative price signals.

In many ways the Brazilian case contradicts this notion – a powerful left party (the Workers' Party, PT) campaigns there in part on a program of land reform and agrarian revitalization. Moreover, the countryside supports a substantial peasant movement. But this rural mobilization has weakened as Brazil's tardy entry into the process of neoliberal reform has taken hold, and it was very crucially built on a massive rural *corporatist* institutional infrastructure that survived the democratic transition (Houtzager 1998). It is precisely because rural neoliberalism is underdeveloped in Brazil that large-scale peasant organization and participation is still possible. It is also notable that upon election, even Brazil's new PT President has gone to great pains to reaffirm his commitment to market-friendly economic policies. And even in Mexico there is variation: in a few states where subnational governments rebuilt corporatist institutions in the wake of national liberalization, rural disorganization was not necessarily the outcome (Snyder 2001b).

Resources, internal or external, are not the only factors that go into the making or breaking of collective action and political participation.

The dynamics of local political competition and the power of local elite opponents also shape autonomy and action. Conservative rural elites – strongly opposed to autonomous peasant political participation – often sit in a powerful position relative to rural actors. Their economic dominance, and their ability to employ it for political ends, is a further barrier to real political participation.

It is certainly true that neoliberal policies can sometimes generate high levels of growth in agriculture; but they also have the characteristic social effect of inducing economic dependence. Among the most severe is a strong tendency to make labor demand markedly seasonal (Barham et al. 1992, 53, 65). And in the countryside, unlike even low-paid urban employment, alternative sources of employment are exceedingly limited. Once labor market regulations and customary practices that had formerly stabilized the employment relation are stripped away, the economics of seasonality induce a severe dependence among peasants. Intense competition emerges over access to the scarce and valuable year-round jobs. Meanwhile temporary employment comes with disincentives to economic and political collective action – activists are unlikely to receive permanent employment, and because their employers often change year to year, investing individual energy in improving conditions on a particular farm is irrational. Reformist political activity, on the other hand, is a ticket to dismissal, blacklisting, and downward mobility, especially in rural contexts often far removed from effective legal oversight.

It is important to note that this vulnerability to elites is not a recreation of the clientelistic practices that were widespread in the past. It is not a broad-based and diffuse dependence rooted in the traditional village, but rather a market-mediated inequality that survives because collective action problems inhibit "voice" on the part of peasants, and the absence of economic alternatives undermines "exit." It is a domination that conveys a marked advantage to local elites, but not political hegemony. This is an advantage they can take with them into the rural electoral arena. It is, however, also a threat to rural democracy when it undermines autonomous political organization and interest articulation. By contrast, atomization and economic vulnerability do not have such substantial political consequences in urban areas. Here the barriers to self-organization are lower, employment alternatives are far greater, and issues of political relevance *are* actually on the national agenda.

The result is emphatically *not*, however, a system of coerced quiescence. It is both more and less restrictive than that. Instead, market forces in the countryside serve to fragment peasants, isolate them from competing interpretations of contemporary reality, undermine the salience of political participation, and raise practical barriers to the formation and articulation of interests. In the place of the political dialogue and debate more characteristic of urban politics, rural democracy is an extended monologue performed by local political and economic elites. It is a low-intensity democracy that is enforced even though votes are secret and the police are often nowhere to be seen.

Aggregating Up: Understanding Free Market Democracy

Democracy is about an institutional structure in which the rules for the selection of government are fixed and fair, while policy outcomes are inherently uncertain (Przeworski 1986, 58). Democratization, however, is often about placing important limits on the range of possible outcomes in a posttransition regime – limits that prevent policy outcomes threatening to elites capable of reversing the transition. That is, it is about moving toward democracy using somewhat undemocratic means. The most obvious manner in which this is accomplished is using the "constitutional choices" that structure electoral competition and the scope of politics in the incoming democratic regime (Munck 1994, 370). But as I have argued in the preceding text, economically induced social transformations can equally and in interactive fashion accomplish similar restrictions on political outcomes. The transformations of economic liberalization (both within the state and within the economy) affect both the interests of rural social actors, and their ability to successfully aggregate them. By undercutting the very formation or conception of certain particularly threatening interests, and by making their political articulation extremely difficult, a wide range of policies are kept outside the agenda of the democratic area, without recourse to obvious institutional restraints.

What does this say about free market democracy? If the electoral rules and the voting are fair and free, isn't that all that's required? In a sense the answer to this question is trivially "yes." The key, however, is that one cannot judge whether the rules are fair and free in a vacuum. The actual political effects of the "constitutional compromises" made by transition elites cannot be understood without reference to the social basis of politics as it is constructed in different sectors (Schmitter recognizes this point [1995, 24]). Indeed, historical patterns, the distribution of partisan allegiances, and the level and scope of organization all impinge on the effectiveness of any set of democratic institutions. And if the quality and deepening of democracy is at issue then the sectoral-level effects of economic transformation on democratic practice are crucial (for a positive example, see Heller 2000). There can be no single institutional "recipe" that guarantees vigorous pluralist democracy, a fact that is highlighted by the wide variety of institutional arrangements, all considered democratic, found in the industrialized west. Whether a particular set of institutions functions in a democratic fashion depends on its interaction with the social and political context within which it is suffused.[14]

If neoliberal economic and social policies can have the positive effect of facilitating the opening of a transition to competitive politics – through their politically demobilizing, and sectorally heterogeneous effects – what influence do they have over the potential for democratic consolidation? This is a complex question, which depends heavily on what is meant by "consolidation." If consolidation simply means the creation of a competitive political system in which highly polarized political conflicts do not emerge, nor are any actors tempted to defect from participation in the democratic regime, then economic liberalization is quite conducive to the consolidation of the gains of political liberalization. Indeed, this may be a key reason why the free market democracies of the underdeveloped world tend toward political stability, while the statist and developmental democracies of the 1970s frequently succumbed to authoritarianism.

But this is the paradox of free market democracy. The very aspects of free market economic organization that facilitate the consolidation of national democratic regimes serve to undermine the practice of democracy at the sectoral level. Alternatively, measures aimed to increase autonomous rural political participation could undermine the electoral base of neoliberal elites in the countryside and with it their

---

[14] None, for example, would consider deeply clientelistic or machine-oriented political systems fully democratic, whatever the formal institutional rules governing elections and politics.

contingent – but essential – support for democratic politics. The demonstration of just such a trade-off is perhaps the signal contribution of this volume.

One potential escape from this dilemma occurs when a true normative commitment to democracy emerges. But this is an inherently long-term development, and such commitment is simply absent in most of the underdeveloped world (Bellin 2000). Even in Chile, despite a forty-year history of peaceful democratic competition, elite commitment to democracy in the early 1970s evaporated in a heartbeat in the face of unwanted policy changes. A similarly thin commitment to democratic practice can be seen in the actions of contemporary Venezuelan elites, despite a four-decade history of open competitive politics. Moreover, the process by which such a normative commitment emerges is poorly understood (for important efforts, see Rustow 1970; Mainwaring 1992; Lawson 1993).

Progress toward democratic consolidation continues in Mexico and Chile. And massive polarized political conflicts do not emerge in the countryside despite high levels of material deprivation.[15] In neither case do the institutional rules of the electoral system present a severe formal barrier to participation or mobilization, but the neoliberal reorganization of rural society and economy vitiates the potential for vigorous democratic contestation. Privatization has tended to remove issues of special importance to the peasantry from the national political agenda. Emergent atomistic and competitive social relations have both dramatically fragmented rural interests, and have rendered their expression through organizational intermediaries very difficult. Finally, political competition requires alternatives, and the access of competing political forces to information outlets in the countryside is highly uneven. The alternative avenues of information dissemination available in the much more dense and vibrant urban civil society simply do not exist in the countryside. The pessimistic concluding question

---

[15] The 1994 Zapatista rebellion is an exception that proves the rule. It took place in one of the areas most removed from neoliberal economic transformation and among a social group that had long-standing communities and a strong locus ethnic identification at odds with the atomization and fragmentation prevalent in the more marketized agrarian settings in much of the rest of the country. Moreover, the rebellion has shown no signs of expanding into equally impoverished but more economically transformed parts of the country.

is, could free market democracy survive its real establishment in the countryside?

What Is to Come

To evaluate the propositions posed here, this book begins with an examination of the Chilean experience with free market democratization. In the first of three chapters, the political economy of agrarian liberalization is examined. The results show how over the course of two decades a mobilized and radicalized peasantry was reduced to near total quiescence and political conservatism that long survives the brief but intense period of physical repression of the mid-1970s. The second examines the way in which economic reform has restructured rural associational life, and tests many of the theoretical propositions laid out in Chapter 3. The third examines the political behavior of urban and rural interests, with an eye to understanding the role of the countryside in securing the national democratic transition. The final two chapters of the book analyze this agrarian thesis in comparative evidence taken from the Mexican experience and elaborate on the broader theoretical implications of the present effort to "bring society back in" to the study of democratic consolidation and the politics of economic reform.

ADDENDUM: CONCEPT AND DESIGN

It is the intention in this study to stay strictly within the confines of an institutional definition of democracy (Dahl 1971; Collier and Levitsky 1997). In so doing, I do not reject the concerns that have inspired more expansive definitions of democracy. The conceptualizations of democracy that involve an extension of its meaning to include socioeconomic outcomes have been created out of a real concern that the actual practices of democratic competition in cases fitting the strictly institutional definitions are in an intuitive sense quite different from prototypical understandings of democracy.[16] But widening the definition of democracy

---

[16] Harding and Petras (1988) and Jonas (1989) both contend that a certain degree of socioeconomic equality is essential to democracy. Huntington (1989, 16–20), by contrast, has argued that the existence of a market economy and a certain degree of wealth and income inequality are definitional of democracy.

to include distributional outcomes is an inappropriate response to this concern as it precludes the empirical examination of the linkages between patterns of economic organization and democratic politics (Karl 1990, 7).

Instead, a more careful operationalization of the conceptual core of the instituitonalist notion of democracy would, I believe, resolve part of the conflict between different understandings of democracy. The key issue to be examined in this context is the role that secondary associations and interest-group competition play in comprising what pluralists would recognize as a democratic regime. In an earlier phase of theorization, when pluralist scholars were very concerned with distinguishing democratic regimes from "totalitarian" ones, a focus on associational life was a central part of the meaning of democracy. In fact, the very emergence of democracy was linked to the conflicts between and among various autonomous interests and the state. As Lipset, Trow, and Coleman (1956, 15–16) point out:

> Democratic rights have developed in societies largely through the struggles of various groups – class, religious, sectional, economic, professional, and so on – against one another and against the group which controls the state. Each interest group may desire to carry out its own will, but if no one group is strong enough to gain complete power, the result is the development of tolerance.

The key point here is that democracy in very important ways depends on the ongoing process of interest group competition in civil society. This is cast in opposition to control by the state over interest groups – a defining feature of totalitarianism – but nonetheless makes the *actual practice* of social organization and political competition – in terms broader than elections – critical to successful democracy.

Dahl, another principal architect of this earlier understanding of democracy that has become the bedrock of the present institutional approaches, brings this understanding explicitly into his definition of polyarchy. Among the institutions that he sees as "necessary to polyarchy" are:

> an *effectively enforced* right to form and join autonomous associations, including political associations, such as political parties and interest groups, that attempt to influence the government by competing in elections *and by other peaceful means.* (1989, 233, italics mine)

It appears then, that the right to association may not be a simple juridical entitlement, but might depend on the actual existence of such groups, and their competition in ways that go well beyond simple suffrage.

Here, however, is the rub. The pluralists made the assumption – quite rational in terms of a comparison between Leninist regimes and the advanced industrial democracies of the West – that such autonomous organization and interest-group competition would be the inevitable result of the liberalization of state control over organization and civil society. As Dahl (1989, 219) put it,

A further concomitant of the greater size of the political order . . . is the existence in polyarchies of a significant number of social groups and organizations that are relatively autonomous with respect to one another and to the government itself: what has come to be called *pluralism*. . . . (italics in original)

The difficulty here is that the emergence of contending interest groups in civil society has been treated as an assumptional issue by scholars using an institutional definition of democracy. But in the extraordinarily liberal economic contexts that have only recently begun to emerge on the South American continent, such assumptions must be treated as empirical issues. Moreover, because an extensive and convincing rational choice literature has pointed out the inherent difficulties in constructing and mobilizing large groups, the assumption of automatic participation is even more problematic. And because the actual existence of a multiplicity of competing groups is essential to democracy, then we cannot simply be satisfied that no legal prohibition or de facto state repression exists to certify a regime as fully democratic. If, as I contend in this study, under certain very specific circumstances highly liberal forms of social (dis)organization impede the formation of autonomous secondary associations, the democratic character of political competition is seriously compromised, even given a strictly institutional understanding of democracy.

The recourse to the inclusion of income distribution or levels of welfare in the definition of democracy misses this fundamental insight. Without the ability to organize – whatever the reason – a fundamental aspect of democracy – public contestation – is threatened. But many societies in which this ability is not seriously impeded remain inegalitarian, class stratified, and poverty stricken. This does not make them any less democratic. Lipset, a scholar who for obvious reasons remains very concerned with the earlier understandings of democracy that tended to highlight the role of secondary associations, put it this way:

> If citizens do not belong to *politically relevant groups*, if they are atomized, the controllers of the central power apparatus will completely dominate society.... Citizen groups must become the bases of – the sources of support for – the institutionalized parties which are a necessarily condition for – part of the very definition of – modern democracy. (1993, 12, italics mine)

Pluralism makes assumptions about the role of secondary associations, but institutional definitions of democracy in the recent literature have tended to neglect this aspect. Rather than recognizing them as a core attribute of democracy, they see them as a natural entailment of the liberalization of authoritarian controls. It is the point of this study to examine this as an empirical relationship, and explore the conditions under which associational life does indeed flourish and those in which it does not. The latter speaks volumes about the assumed compatibility of economic liberalization and political democracy.

The Design

This study is built on an explicitly multilevel research design. The first portion develops hypotheses and elaborates a causal model based in the comparative historical analysis of two countries across time and sector. The second employs within-case quantitative testing of the specific theoretical entailments of the arguments developed in the comparative analysis in two extensive local-level ecological datasets. This design is structured to take maximum advantage of the strengths of comparative analysis in the elaboration of core concepts and the isolation of complex causal processes while at the same time subjecting key hypotheses to rigorous quantitative evaluation. The quantitative analysis using within-case variation at once subjects the hypotheses to hard tests while at the same time avoiding the problems of measurement validity that frequently bedevil large-scale cross-national data analysis.[17]

---

[17] The extensive and unresolved debate as to the appropriate cross-national indicators of such basic concepts as democratic regime type or level of economic liberalization suggest the difficulties in pursuing this strategy (for a recent summary and discussion, see Munck and Verkuilen 2000). By restricting the quantitative analysis to the cases

Why were Chile and Mexico selected? First, the theory developed here addresses the medium-term implications of economic liberalization for the consolidation of democracy. That is, it concerns a process whose dynamics cannot be directly observed until the short-run effects of the process of transition have largely come to a close. Chile was the first country on the Latin American continent to launch a sustained and coherent neoliberal economic reform, having begun the process in the late 1970s (Silva 1996; Kurtz 1999a). Mexico began in earnest somewhat later, but has consolidated the reforms with the ratification of the NAFTA agreement in 1993. The contrast between Chile and Mexico also permits an analysis of the dynamics of sequencing and simultaneity in the construction of free market democracy. Chilean neoliberalism was imposed and consolidated in the context of a brutally exclusionary authoritarian regime, while Mexico has successfully pursued much more simultaneous political and economic opening in a far less brutal (and improving) political context. Given the prevailing concern in the literature on economic reform with the consolidation of policy change before loosing political controls, it makes sense to examine whether increasingly open politics undermines the dynamics of reform or whether the stabilization of free markets and democracy actually responds to other causal factors.

Finally, the design explicitly compares cases that are at a similar level of economic development, that have important historical legacies of statist economic governance, and that occupy a similar position in the international division of labor. Particularly the first is crucial because many scholars have pointed out the robust relationship between democracy and the level of economic development (Diamond 1992) or at least between development and the avoidance of authoritarian reversal (Przeworski and Limongi 1997). The Chilean case is used to develop and explicate the central theoretical contentions, and is thus more well developed. The argument is then extended to the Mexican context.

The quantitative examination of the overall causal hypotheses as well as key intervening portions of the explanation is a crucial test of the

about which much is known, but using new data for the hypothesis tests, rigorous testing can take place with greater confidence that the measures employed are appropriate indicators for the theoretical propositions under examination.

comparative historical findings, validating them in new data with dramatically different methods. In both countries, detailed municipal-level aggregate data sets were constructed that contain a host of electoral, social, and demographic variables. Ecological inference techniques (Achen and Shively 1995; King 1997) are used to match the aggregate data with the individual-level processes described by the theory.

PART II

THE CASES

3

Neoliberalism and the Transformation of Rural Society in Chile

The military government that seized power in Chile (1973–89), bringing to a brutal end Salvador Allende's experiment with democratic socialism, is well known for having engineered one of the first and most thoroughgoing free market economic transitions on the South American continent. While the economic consequences of this process of economic reorientation have been much discussed, the *political* implications it had are decidedly more opaque. It is the central thesis of this book that these political effects were indeed profound, but in equal measure they were socially heterogeneous.

Indeed, the implementation of national level neoliberal policies in rural Chile meant nothing less than the establishment of agrarian capitalism in a sector of the economy where it had not before existed, and was in any event well along in the transition from traditional landlordism to cooperative socialism. This post-1973 free market "great transformation" in agriculture thus not only redefined prevailing patterns of economic activity, but also the building blocks of rural social structure. The contrast with the urban effects of liberalization is stark. In the cities economic reform meant principally the freeing of long extant and comparatively well-functioning markets. By contrast, in the countryside the foundations of a market economy – individual and alienable property rights, free labor contracting, and free price setting – had to be built largely from scratch.

In the process, rural social and associational life was transformed, and a formerly organized and mobilized peasantry descended into an atomization, dependence, and quiescence that lessened not at all with political opening in 1989. In urban areas, by contrast, reasonably robust and competitive democratic practices reestablished themselves quickly once authoritarian controls were lifted. By no means was the level of organization and mobilization in urban areas similar to that of the period before military rule and economic liberalization. Nevertheless, it was sufficient to underwrite a competitive politics notable by its absence in the countryside.

In short, neoliberalism unmade the peasantry as it remade rural politics. The fierce repression of the first few years of military rule had brought nearly a decade of mobilization and broad-based peasant organization to a standstill, a depoliticization that later became permanent as neoliberalism removed rural issues from the national political agenda, replaced negotiated public provision with private markets across the spectrum of agrarian activity, and destroyed the historical foundations of peasant society. In creating markets, peasants were expelled from their parcels and homes, communities were razed to create individual farms, and geographic mobility became more the norm than the exception. As markets were created, so were *individuals*: shared interests and collective action were replaced by organizational decay, conflicts of interest, social differentiation, and the emergence of a peasant *homo œconomicus*. Neither an end to repression nor a return to economic growth has stemmed the decline in peasant self-organization and political expression.

The key issue, then, is how the seemingly neutral and nondiscriminatory policies of the neoliberal developmental model have served to weaken the basis for specifically rural democratic political participation. Because neoliberalism consists of polyglot components, I examine the political effects of liberalization separately across four crucial markets: (1) trade opening and commodity price liberalization, (2) the privatization of both productive enterprises and traditional governmental services, (3) the creation of an agricultural land market, and (4) the creation and integration of a rural labor market. Neoliberal policies in each of these arenas had important political consequences for the rural sector, principally in terms of how they shaped incentives for, and barriers to, collective action.

The contrast in the countryside with the period before military rule cannot be drawn starkly enough. In the years leading up to the coup of 1973, Chilean peasants were involved in a process of upheaval and peaceful but radical political mobilization unprecedented outside the comparatively rare instances of social revolution. Parties of the left and center were engaged in a political bidding war for the support of peasant voters and organizations, whose actions had long since spiraled out of their control. By the early 1970s, this mobilization – demonstrations, strikes, and land seizures – had become sufficiently widespread to threaten the very viability of agrarian private property as an institution.

How in general did neoliberalism provoke quiescence in this formerly organized and highly mobilized peasantry? First, and most critically, it undermined the associational networks (both formal and informal) that had historically characterized rural community life. This transformed the question of group political participation and interest aggregation into a one-off prisoner's dilemma – and free riding replaced cooperation as the order of the day even where shared interests survived. Second, marketization reshaped the very structure of rural interests – latent or organized – by fragmenting social groups into conflicting strata and removing most historically important issues from the national political arena. Third, neoliberalism and the commitment to it among nearly all posttransition political parties transformed the political opportunity structure within which peasants operated. Not only did peasants face dramatic new problems of self-organization, but the reliance upon or formation of alliances with external, reformist forces was largely precluded in a way that was not true for the urban popular classes. Finally, opponents of peasant organization among the local elites were empowered by economic liberalization. The result was sterile terrain for meaningful, autonomous rural popular-sector political participation.

In subsequent chapters, I examine directly the effects of neoliberal reforms on social life and the associational foundations of political participation as well as the consequences this has had for posttransition political competition. In the remainder of this chapter, I set forth a theoretical account of how an unlikely rural conservative bastion was created during the course of economic reform among a formerly mobilized and radicalized peasantry. The key issue is how free market reforms – across a variety of arenas – created an organizational and participatory deficit in peasant society: contemporary politics suffers from the near impossibility of autonomous organized rural participation. This is, however, a defect in Chilean democracy that is the mirror image of its pre-1973 tendency toward excessive polarization and mobilization, and it is a feature that has helped to stabilize the overall democratic transition. The lack of competitiveness of rural politics – and the conservative orientation it underwrites – has underpinned the commitment of powerful elites to the democratic regime and helped to ensure its survival. At the same time it undermines its quality.

Because economic liberalization is about the freeing of critical markets, in the following text I examine its political implications across the four that are most critical to the countryside: international trade, privatization of state enterprises, land, and labor.

FREE TRADE AND RURAL POLITICS

The opening of the highly protected Chilean economy to foreign imports proceeded in two waves – the first, from 1973–5, reduced tariffs to more manageable levels but was not designed to provoke economic reorientation. It was the second phase of trade opening (1975–9), culminating in the uniform 10 percent tariff and nearly complete import deregulation, that began the radical restructuring of the Chilean economy and rural sector. The effect of trade policy, by the early 1980s, was to lay the foundation for a new social structure in agriculture that would eventually provide an important basis of economic and political support for the neoliberal model. Traditional large-scale grain producers along with new capitalist agro-export elites became diehard backers of neoliberal politicians, while their local economic dominance eventually helped bring along substantial peasant electoral support. It was the social disruption entailed by trade liberalization that was a crucial factor that made peasants vulnerable to agrarian elite political influences.

Trade opening exposed Chilean agriculture for the first time in generations to international prices. The comparative advantages thus revealed helped to create a new class of capitalist export-oriented agribusinesses (largely in fresh fruit); at the same time other rural social actors came under intense pressure, including laborers and domestically oriented food producers (both large scale and peasant). Thus while the initial liberalization of trade was designed to reorient the agrarian economy it clearly would not serve by itself to construct even an upper class base for neoliberalism. The military addressed this problem in the 1980s, making moves to reach an accommodation with the segment of the agrarian elite that relied on the domestic market. When the economic collapse provoked by the international debt crisis hit Chile in 1982, the military was forced to reintroduce limited protection for domestic *capitalist* producers in a bid to reestablish rural political support and help confront increasing domestic opposition. Overall, however, this did not undermine the free-trade thrust of economic policy, nor were peasant-produced crops included in this protection. Instead, agrarian elites and liberal markets were relied upon to deliver political support in the countryside. But how did trade help to build such a coalition?

In the immediate wake of the coup in 1973, political conditions became more favorable for agricultural producers (especially for large landholders). In addition to a crucial guarantee that halted further land expropriations, the Minister of Agriculture, Colonel Sergio Crespo, promised an end to rigid agricultural price control and that adequate supplies of vital inputs would be assured. The announced goal of agricultural policy was substantial increases in production for the domestic market (*El Mercurio* September 28, 1973). The agrarian policy of the preceding socialist government (1970–3) was criticized as providing "political prices" that were too low to allow profitable investment in agriculture (ODEPLAN 1974, 139). And with the end of price control, producers anticipated a windfall.

The costs of trade liberalization were initially not severe at least for large producers. From Table 3.1 it can bee seen that tariff rates, while beginning to decline steadily, were still quite high through mid-1977.

TABLE 3.1 *Exchange Rates and Tariffs (pesos of 1977 per dollar of same year; percent)*

Period	Exchange Rate	Maximum Tariff	Average Tariff
October 1973–April 1975	23.52	>220%	94%
April 1975–July 1977	29.52	120	52
July 1977–June 1979	20.67	45	22
June 1979–June 1980	23.43	10	10
June 1980–1982	20.87	10	10

Source: Ffrench-Davis (1980).

In addition, over the same period the Chilean peso was devalued by nearly 25.5 percent. This helped to compensate producers for the decline in tariff protection. Further compensation to large growers for the decreases in tariff protection came from the free-fall in wages.[1] By 1977, the ratio of an index of wages to the wholesale price index (1970 = 100) had fallen to 52.6 (Foxley 1983, 69). In a very inflationary context, commodity prices were rising much more rapidly than wages. Cortázar and Marshall (1980) have also shown how official inflation indexes were deliberately falsified in order to engineer such a decline in real wages (because nominal wages were fully indexed to inflation throughout the 1970s). Finally, international wheat prices – Chile's staple crop – had more than doubled by 1973, helping to further reduce competitive pressures on this, the most important food crop, that was predominately produced on large farms (UN FAO 1975).

Indeed, even as tariff reduction proceeded, care was taken to protect the larger capitalist farmers. The price supports for their most important crops, wheat, sugarbeet, and rapeseed, were maintained until 1979, after which they were gradually phased out. They persisted far longer than any other special protections were permitted to continue (Crispi 1982, 489; ODEPLAN 1979, 47), highlighting the political import of the agrarian sector.[2] The crops most commonly produced by peasants (e.g., beans, rice, and potatoes) were much more quickly exposed to international competition (ODEPLAN 1977, 84).

Free trade had not yet, however, successfully induced export orientation (Kurtz 2001). While in the heyday of the import substitution,

---

[1] This was *particularly* true of the rural sector where wages declined for two reasons. Until 1981 wages in all of Chile were indexed to a consumer price index that substantially underreported the real price level, causing a sustained erosion of real wages until 1978 (see Cortázar and Marshall 1980). Second, soon after the coup the Junta decreed that up to 50 percent of the minimum wage could be paid in kind in the agricultural sector, superseding an earlier law that required cash payment of the entire minimum wage. Traditional in-kind payments (*regalías*) were in addition to this cash payment (E. Valenzuela 1979, 59). Finally, in its account of 1974 inflation, two components were reported – the "repressed inflation" from the previous years of price control, and that inflation actually due price movements of 1974. Wages were indexed only to the latter, inducing a "splicing error" that produced a substantial real-wage decline (Jarvis 1985).

[2] In 1986–7 Echenique and Rolando (1989, 59) report that 78.1 percent of wheat, 90.4 percent of rapeseed, and 68 percent of sugarbeet production was produced in the nonpeasant sector.

1960–4, agricultural products unsurprisingly accounted for a mere 4.92 percent of exports, during the first phase of military rule (1974–8) they expanded only marginally to 5.86 percent (calculated from Banco Central de Chile 1989). It was not until 1976, and in earnest only after the reforms of 1979, that real reorientation of agricultural production, and hence exports, took off.

Still, the liberalization of agricultural prices and the opening of trade had important political implications that would persist even into the postauthoritarian regime. Before 1973, the prices paid for agricultural commodities were set by the relevant state purchasing boards (*Empresas de Comercio Agrícola* [ECAs]). This made the setting of prices part of a politically mediated bargain that was squarely at the center of the democratic arena. Leaders of the military regime contrasted this with the "neutral" pricing that would be generated through integration with the international market.[3] Whether international prices were any more "neutral" is an open question, but this move decisively changed their political relevance: they were no longer a public issue.

Trade opening disrupted not only the long-standing political and developmental bargains that had historically underpinned agricultural commodity prices, but also those that defined the gamut of rural markets: credit, equipment, and chemical inputs. All three had been dominated by public provision through parastatal firms, and typically prices were set well below international levels. This was part of the compromise that made cheap food and intermediates available for industrialization – subsidized inputs made possible artificially low crop prices. Trade opening (and privatization) destroyed this bargain, but more importantly it destroyed the very ability of the state to negotiate over these issues – producers had become subject to international prices over which the state had little if any influence, even should it have decided to intervene.

Thus, when international opening reached a peak in 1979, a predictable set of pressures emerged in the Chilean rural sector. After a series of extremely slow and painful transitions, central valley agriculture

[3] Particularly in commodity markets, it is hardly clear that international agricultural prices are neutral, because they reflect differences in income elasticity of demand relative to manufactures (Prebisch 1959), imbalances of power (Sanderson 1985), and massive first-world protection and dumping.

was transformed into a nexus of high-value fresh fruit export, while the uncompetitive traditional grain sectors of the center and south underwent a crisis of unprecedented proportions. But precisely because these changes were the consequence of international price pressures and not domestically defined "political prices," the military government could escape much of the responsibility for them. By letting the impersonal international market determine agricultural prices, issues that had formerly taken center stage in national politics were "privatized." Having decontrolled trade, any demands for improved agricultural prices would appear to be demands for a special subsidy, paid for by the Chilean public at large.

In economic terms, near-complete trade opening by 1979 (coupled with currency overvaluation between 1979–82) put tremendous competitive pressure on Chilean agriculture. Falling international prices for key commodities after 1975 exacerbated the dilemma. To make matters worse, first-world dumping and international price trends drove the real price of wheat – Chile's staple food crop – down from $163 a ton in 1979 to $109 in 1984 (FAO 1985; Sanderson 1985; deflated using U.S. wholesale price index). To add insult to injury, liberalization in Chile had ended most antidumping provisions in the trade laws that might have provided some compensation. Finally, producers suffered disproportionately because of the substantial imbalance in power between oligopsonistic processing and marketing industries in relation to the very numerous growers (Llambí 1991, 41). The effect on output was severe. By 1981 agricultural exports[4] totaled 387.6 million dollars. Imports, however, had soared to $764 million, with nearly a third of this total due to imports of a single crop – wheat (calculated from Gómez and Echenique 1988, 300). While wheat imports soared, Chilean production plummeted, with land planted in wheat declining 25 percent between 1979 and 1982 (Banco Central de Chile 1989).

Geographic Differentiation

What were the political effects of this set of trade policies? The impact was quite uneven in the rural sector, and in the end, I will argue, served

---

[4] This includes crops and ranching, both as primary goods or processed, but not forestry products.

to divide and weaken large-producer organizations and eventually to atomize and depoliticize the peasantry.[5] The first major axis of division created was regional – between the Central Valley (Regions IV through VII) and the South (Regions VIII to X).[6] The Central Valley possesses a natural comparative advantage in the production of fruits and vegetables for export.[7] The South has traditionally been a cereal and ranching area whose climate is unsuitable for export fruit agriculture. As a result, the policies of trade liberalization did successfully favor the expansion of fruit agriculture as a substitute for grain production in the Central Valley, but this was not possible in the South. Between 1979 to 1982 the area planted in cereals declined 22.4 percent in the Central Valley. In the South over the same period it declined 27 percent. At the same time there was a 28.3 percent expansion in land area devoted to fruit production in the Central Valley (calculated from Banco Central de Chile 1991, 40–2). The problem was that there was little into which southern agriculture could profitably shift its production; instead it faced decapitalization, low crop prices, and declining output. This tended to create a political division between southern and Central Valley capitalist producers.

The geographic differentiation in the potentialities of Chilean agriculture was mirrored in a political division between organizations representing capitalist producers in both regions. The traditionally hegemonic *Sociedad Nacional de Agricultura* (SNA – National Agrarian Society) came to represent dynamic Central Valley exporters, and its politics were almost an extension of those of the military government. Indeed, in the crisis years between 1979–83 it was led by Germán Riesco, who had been the director of the Agriculture Ministry's planning agency (Oficina de Estudios y Políticas Agrarias [ODEPA])

---

[5] On the increasing divisions within landowner organizations, see P. Silva (1992).

[6] Chile is divided from north to south into thirteen administrative regions. The XIIIth is the Metropolitan Region of Santiago, and is in the Central Valley. Regions I to III in the far north are nonagricultural. Regions XI and XII are suitable principally for ranching and forestry.

[7] Two principal reasons exist for this. First, central Chile possesses a mediterranean climate similar to California's central valley. Second, its location in the southern hemisphere means that its harvests come in during the winter in the industrial core countries. Thus, it does not normally compete with first-world agriculture (and for this reason does not face prohibitive trade barriers) (Ministerio de Agricultura 1987, 8–9). Finally, the comparatively low wages of Chilean producers, especially in comparison with other southern hemisphere producers, was critical (Crispi 1982, 512).

immediately prior to taking office as president of the SNA. Several SNA presidents subsequently served as Ministers of Agriculture under General Pinochet. But SNA leadership of the agricultural capitalist class was challenged nationally by the *Confederación de Productores Agrícolas* (CPA – Confederation of Agricultural Producers) and regionally by the *Consorcio Agrícola del Sur* (CAS – Agricultural Consortium of the South). These latter two groups tended to represent domestically oriented, more traditional, producers (Gómez 1986, 10–17; 1987, 19).[8]

Once economic crisis struck agriculture in 1981–2 these groups entered into strong conflicts with each other and at least between the CPA/CAS and the state. When the military regime was rocked by urban protest between 1983 and 1986, this dissention among potential supporters became quite risky. But rather than make concessions to mobilized opponents in the cities, the military moved to reintegrate the home-market sector of capitalist agriculture into the governing coalition. Without much fanfare (and justified on national security grounds), the military reintroduced protection and limited import substitution in the crops most vital to this sector. It was a far cry from the response southern dairy farmers had received from the Ministry of Agriculture to their complaints about the dumping of foreign milk on the Chilean market in the 1970s during the process of socioeconomic restructuring: *que se coman las vacas*[9] (cited in Gómez 1987, 24). But with forced democratic transition a possibility, the importance of assembling a positive neoliberal political coalition rose dramatically, becoming so great as to provoke the contravention of liberal norms in the effort to regain rural upper-class support. Indeed, the military's willingness to reintroduce protection for agriculture signals the absolute centrality of solidifying the support of the agrarian upper class.

Class Differentiation

For the rural popular sectors, the story was different: it was a tale of fragmentation, political marginalization, and downward mobility not

---

[8] The CPA was the successor of CONSEMACH, the union of agricultural employers created in one of the corporatist provisions of the 1967 peasant unionization law (Ley 16.625).

[9] This translates as "let them eat their cows."

buffered by an eventual accommodation with the state. Even in the relatively well-off Central Valley that possessed substantial comparative advantages in export production, few producers were able to take advantage of them, given the substantial capital requirements and long gestation periods for the transition (Carter et al. 1996, 40–1; Gwynne and Ortiz 1997, 29). Profit rates on their domestic food crops were too low to provide sufficient capital, and agricultural credit was unavailable or too expensive. Export crops also utilize expensive imported inputs to meet first-world consumer, health, and phytosanitary standards, which are beyond the means of most small producers (Sanderson 1985, 54).

The combined effects of prevailing international conditions, full opening to imports, and exchange rate overvaluation after 1979 were predictable – peasant incomes plummeted without a compensatory shift into new products. The average production of wheat tumbled from 10.2 million quintales (qq.) over the 1976–9 period to 6.4 million qq. during 1980–3 (Banco Central de Chile 1989, 65). Industrial crops (sugarbeet, sunflower, and rapeseed) and peasant-produced food crops (beans, lentils, potatoes, etc.) suffered major output declines and imports drove down prices. The interests of the bulk of the rural sector were thus sacrificed for two goals: the reorientation of the Central Valley toward export production, and the control of inflation by using international prices as a hard constraint on domestic food price increases. In terms of these goals, the military was largely successful. Fruit production for export expanded rapidly in the Central Valley, and by 1981 inflation had bottomed at 9.5 percent (CIREN-CORFO 1987, 19; INE 1992, 4).

In this context of an already-restructured agricultural sector, in 1984 limited protection was reintroduced for three crops: wheat, sugarbeet, and rapeseed. This protection was enough to guarantee continued production of these crops for the domestic market, but not sufficient to divert substantial resources into the sector. The peasantry, remaining excluded from the governing coalition, continued to produce unsubsidized wage foods such as beans, corn, lentils, and potatoes. The dictatorship was either consciously or unconsciously taking advantage of the tendency of peasants to continue or expand production in the face of declining crop prices (Crispi 1982; for a detailed discussion see Ellis 1988, ch. 6). This, of course, facilitated the provision of cheap food for urban workers (which in a very competitive labor market allowed the payment of lower wages), without necessitating such traditional mechanisms as input monopolies, purchasing boards, or other obvious state "interventions."

What were the political implications for peasants and agricultural workers of this set of purportedly neutral trade decisions? The privatization of input suppliers, the legalization of agricultural input imports, and the abolition of the state marketing boards forced relative prices for agricultural commodities to reflect domestic and international market conditions.[10] They were no longer a discretionary element of state policy. This immediately removed them from the political agenda what had been one of the most important issues in rural politics since the 1930s (Carrière 1981; Wright 1982). All rural producers, but especially peasants, now faced a price structure wholly beyond their influence, and (seemingly) beyond the influence of the national state.

Advocating changes in crop prices, then, became tantamount to rejection of the neoliberal model writ large; a decidedly more difficult position to take. The neoliberals in the military government argued that any sectoral policy favoring agriculture would amount to a special subsidy causing higher food costs for the mass of consumers, and particularly disadvantaging the most defenseless sectors. More specifically, with regard to agriculture, the central thrust of neoliberal thinkers was that the *avoidance* of sectoral policy was critical because it was precisely the market interventions of the past that they believed had so seriously undermined earlier agricultural growth (ODEPLAN 1987, 57; CEP 1992, 174).

The opening to the exterior created political divisions *within* each of the different class strata of the rural sector as well, making the presentation of unified demands nearly impossible and even fragmenting underlying interests. Within the agrarian elite, producers were sorted into traditional and nontraditional sectors by levels of capitalization and geography, in turn leading to splits in their respective representative

---

[10] Of course, transforming public monopolies into private oligopolies does not necessarily mean markets begin to function efficiently. In political terms it puts price decisions outside the arena where democratic contestation applies, and into the economic arena where dollars (pesos) and not votes are counted. On the oligopolization of input, credit, and marketing industries see Dahse (1979) and Gómez and Echenique (1988).

organizations (Gómez 1986, 1987; Silva 1992). Within the peasantry, division occurred between those with land, those in the process of losing land, those permanently employed, and those only able to obtain work on a seasonal basis.[11] Thus, without any unity, the clamor for protection, price support, or new credit policies became even more blatantly the cry of a narrow interest for special favors. This cast the neoliberal, anti-interventionist position in the enviable position of defending "equal treatment" and "justice" against the favoritism and rent seeking of special interests.

PRIVATIZATION: REDRAWING THE BOUNDARY BETWEEN PUBLIC AND PRIVATE SPHERES

During the socialist government of Salvador Allende (1970–3) the number of major firms under direct control of the Chilean state expanded from 67 to 529, while between 1965 and 1973 the public sector's share of GDP rose from 14.2 to 39.0 percent (Sáez 1993, 79). Indeed, the first steps along the "Chilean road to socialism" involved a massive expansion of the state's direct control of key sectors of the economy. Virtually the entire banking system, the large mineral concessions, a substantial portion of manufacturing, and nearly 52 percent of agricultural land were nationalized, statized, intervened, requisitioned, or expropriated.

Almost immediately upon taking power, the military regime dedicated itself to shrinking the state's role in the economy (for justification see Junta Militar de Gobierno 1973b, 131–3). The general process of privatization in Chile proceeded in two distinct stages and its political and economic impact in rural areas was quite different from that in urban areas. This section addresses the social and political effects of the turn toward state subsidiarity in rural areas. The intervention of the state in agriculture (particularly through social service provision) has long been held to have ended the era of clientelist domination that prevailed before the 1960s, and it is against this background that its withdrawal must be evaluated (Loveman 1976; de la Cuadra 1991).

---

[11] This is marked contrast to the tendency in the precoup period toward a homogenization of conditions among rural cultivators (peasants and workers) (Schejtman 1971).

In addition to constricting the national political agenda, the moves to privatize crucial services like education, health, pensions, and technical outreach left peasants in a vulnerable and individualized position with respect to rural elites. While mediated in an altogether different manner, elements of this situation parallel the peasant dependency so characteristic of the *hacienda* period (1924–64). Whereas the expansion of the state into the rural sector in the 1950s and 1960s, particularly as a service provider, had a critical side effect in fomenting the expansion of meaningfully democratic social relations, its exit recreated dependent relations though not of the clientelistic sort that characterized the earlier era. Because of the different history and economic structure of urban areas, the expansion of the welfare state was not, in that sector, historically tied to the process of democratization. When the neoliberal transformations of the late 1970s extracted the state from most of its former welfare-providing roles, it once again left the peasantry to confront the agrarian upper class from an individualized position of extreme vulnerability. The difference is that this is a vulnerability born of atomization and economic weakness organized by impersonal markets; it is not the diffuse and personalistic attachment of traditional clientelism.

Inputs and Services

The dismantling of state productive enterprises with connections to the rural sector has implications for rural democratic contestation in terms of the way it narrows the framework for legitimate democratic contestation. The state had, since the 1930s, entered the rural sector, both in a typical role as the provider of public goods, as well as direct producer of the gamut of necessary agricultural inputs. This public-sector expansion was driven by both the political bargain underlying the 1932–73 import substituting developmental model as well as by efforts to democratize the countryside by breaking clientelist dependencies. Whatever the economic costs of precoup public interventionism, it provided alternatives for peasants seeking access to key services and gave them leverage – through the unions and the parties allied to them – over the prices that structured their life chances.

After the coup, the state moved rapidly to privatize the input-providing and commodity-marketing enterprises under its control.

Particularly important in this respect was the sell-off of the banking system and the abolition of commodity price caps and supports. Between 1965 and 1972, state-supplied agricultural credits had expanded by some 834.3 percent (calculated from Crispi 1980, 14). The public seed supplier – Empresa Nacional de Semillas (ENDS) – and the agricultural machinery service – Servicio de Equipos Agrícolas Mecanizados (SEAM) – provided critical inputs at low prices and on subsidized terms (Silva 1987, 204). After the coup the market for inputs was opened to foreign competitors and the agricultural equipment in state hands was rapidly auctioned during the 1974–5 recession.

As a result, the control over these vital input monopolies passed into the hands of a small number of privileged economic conglomerates, practically the only conceivable buyers in the midst of the recession (Kay 1981, 572). This transformed a series of public, nonprofit monopolies into private profit-seeking oligopolies (Dahse 1979). In the process, a formerly national-level system of negotiated agricultural price determination was replaced by a widely dispersed, private set of highly unequal economic transactions between peasant and capitalist producers and their input and credit suppliers. Increasingly peasants faced pressures of social differentiation, and intrapeasant competition in their struggle to mitigate their structural weakness vis-à-vis the suppliers of these inputs.

With respect to the formal private-sector credit market, after 1975 the smallholding peasantry became effectively excluded. Because of difficulties in risk assessment and because of the costs of loan administration, private banks are reluctant to lend to smallholders. For those lucky enough to obtain credit, real interest rates for those without access to international credit markets reached usurious levels, sometimes in excess of 40 percent in real terms. Thus those "lucky" peasants who did borrow more often ended up losing their land than managing successful adjustment to new conditions (ICIRA 1979). More commonly, the lack of bank credit forced peasants to purchase inferior seeds (non-certified) from their ex-landlords using very expensive in-kind loans. Not only did this reestablish powerful vertical dependencies, but it also represented a serious capital drain (Olavarría 1978, 23).[12]

---

[12] "Interest rates" on these seed loans generally amounted to 100 percent between planting and harvest. That is, one bag of seeds at planting was repaid with two at harvest.

Similar problems resulted from the elimination of the agricultural marketing boards (ECAs). With the abolition of the ECAs, most agricultural prices were liberated. This move, initially cheered by representatives of at least the larger rural producers, did not produce the substantial increases in wholesale commodity prices that were expected with the end of "political pricing."[13] In fact, a transition to supposedly neutral market mechanisms had a negative impact on domestic commodity prices in general, and a disproportionately negative effect on peasant producers. The simultaneous privatization of input suppliers and food-processing facilities during the severe postcoup recession led to an enormous concentration of ownership in food-linked industries. Gómez and Echenique report substantial oligopsony in sugar, oils, milk, fish, fruit, and vegetable processing (1988, 181). Similarly, even large holders had constant and bitter complaints about concentration in the wheat-processing (flour) industry (Gómez 1986; Silva 1987, 222–3). The result was an increase in consumer prices that was not necessarily passed on to growers. For example, bread prices increased at the same time that wholesale wheat prices declined to exceptionally low levels.

This situation of downstream oligopsony affected both large and peasant producers. But peasants, even when their output was not subject to further transformation, generally faced the added burden of marketing their crops through very unequal relationships with middlemen and without access to credit markets. Consequently they were forced to sell their crops at harvest time, when prices are lowest, in order to meet payments on usurious in-kind loans from local elites. At the same time, cooperatives for collective marketing, which had helped eliminate distributional middlemen and raise rural incomes, had disintegrated after 1975 (Silva 1987, 223; Barría et al. 1988, 195–205).

What are the political implications of this state of affairs? With the withdrawal of the state from crop pricing and distribution, political bargains no longer mediated rural living standards; the latter were now determined by private markets linking peasants, middlemen, and the processing industries. What was formerly a collective political conflict over the "fair" price of a crop was transformed into

---

[13] See, for example, the editorials in the Sociedad Nacional de Agricultura's newspaper, *El Campesino*, April 1974 (cited in Gómez 1986, 28).

an individual, and highly unequal, private economic exchange. The simultaneous shift from cooperative to individual land tenure and the destruction of cooperative organizations in agriculture was essential in setting the background for this system, as it individualized producers and set them in competition with their fellows. No longer would the state or private organizations provide a counterweight to the political and economic influences of rural elites.

Privatization, then, generated an effective transfer of resources from peasant producers to processing industries and food consumers, but without any direct state presence in the rural sector. It set off a vicious cycle of self-exploitation, where as the prices of peasant-produced commodities fell, output expanded.[14] Planting by capitalist farmers plummeted – their signal crop, wheat, was grown on 902,000 hectares (Ha) in 1968–70, but on only 598,000 Ha by 1980–1. By contrast, the planting of typically peasant-produced crops (*chacras*) expanded substantially despite deterioration in prices and the general unavailability of reasonably priced inputs and credits – from 240,000 Ha planted in 1968–70 to 415,000 in 1980–1. This seemingly irrational behavior from a capitalist point of view makes sense in a peasant economy where family labor is a fixed cost, with a near-zero opportunity cost, reflecting the absence of local employment alternatives. Of course the added production only continued the downward pressure on prices.

This leaves peasants in a difficult and confusing political situation. A change in the extremely unfavorable structure of prices would require either the intervention of the state, or some sort of collective power in the face of the oligopsonies in marketing and processing. The former was foreclosed not only because the Chilean state (under the military) had renounced any substantial sectoral policy, but also because the necessary institutional capacity to carry out such policy had been dismantled by the military. To attempt to better their situation through the now-dominant market mechanism would have required strong collective organization among peasant producers, something prohibited not simply by the national-security policies of the military, but by

---

[14] This is generally seen as the result of a peasant desire to generate a minimum income (subsistence), rather than to maximize profits. As prices decline, labor inputs and production by the peasant family increase to compensate.

the very differentiation and atomization produced by the neoliberal model. Without the state to provide necessary incentives to limit problems of free riding, peasant self-organization was exceedingly unlikely, and the existing infrastructure of peasant organization declined rapidly (Bengoa 1983a; Barría et al. 1988).

Social Service Privatization

The organization of social service provision in the Chilean countryside has a very different history than that of the urban sector. From the implementation of the 1925 Labor Code onward formal sector urban workers could count on national pension and health systems (Foxley 1979, 125). During the period of clientelism (1932–64) the provision of these services in the rural sector remained in the hands of the landlords. The private monopoly that landlords held over access to old-age security, health care, and even basic education helped to undergird their political and social domination within the confines of the traditional hacienda (for descriptions see Bauer 1975; Bengoa 1990). It would also deliver the political support of the peasantry on election day.

Beginning after 1958 and taking off with the election of Frei in 1964, the state intervened in the rural sector to become an alternative provider of these social services. This severed a key link of dependence and vulnerability between *inquilino* (traditional service tenant) and landlord, making it possible for the first time for meaningful rural democratic competition to emerge. Clientelism required a discretionary monopoly on the provision of vital social services to enforce its political agenda – without such leverage, landlords lost political control over their employees.

But the state's presence as a rural-sector social provider was to be short-lived. As part of the "seven modernizations" of 1979 and thereafter, pensions, some of the health care network, and substantial parts of the post–primary educational system were privatized (see Vergara 1994, 237–62). This converted minimal social provision from a social right into a privately mediated purchase basically dependent upon income and employment. As with the privatization of productive enterprises, it removed a set of issues historically critical to rural-sector democratization from the political agenda. This left few alternatives with regard to social policy to the highly targeted approach to social

welfare favored by the military regime.[15] Indeed, means testing introduced serious new social divisions among peasants and rural workers. The most desperately poor were dependent on an underfunded
state system, others had precarious access to private services through
their employment, and still others were denied access to social services
altogether.

Perhaps more importantly I contend that social service privatization
produced a set of vertical dependencies and intrapeasant divisions that
both unbalanced the playing field for future democratic competition,
and meaningfully reduced the salience of the democratic arena for the
rural lower classes. These social reforms, coupled with the distinctive
structure of rural production, reduced the potential for broad-based
political organization or identification among peasants and agricultural
workers. Finally, the privatization of crucial services helped to define
a new axis of division within the peasants, giving the fully employed
a vested interest in the success of the private financial sector (which
managed their retirement funds), and indirectly of the broad outlines
of the neoliberal developmental model.[16]

What were the political motivations behind the privatization of the
long-established public social security system? According to then Labor
Minister José Piñera, the architect of this reform:

The basic problem of the [old] system of distribution lay in its collectivist conception of man and society . . . a mistaken ideological notion about the nature
of behavior of human beings. The system of distribution underestimated varied evidence on the behavior of human beings, according to which men show
greater effort when this effort is related to a specific compensation. . . . As a consequence, the great lesson for the design of the new system was not to neglect
the free choice and decisions of individuals, nor to break the indispensable tie
between personal effort and compensation. (cited in Raczynski 1993, 54)

Two elements of this striking quotation are crucial. First, the system
was designed to correct the collectivist "defect" of the old pension

---

[15] This approach provided minimal supports to the very poorest elements of the peasantry, often in the form of direct cash transfers. These supports were in turn paid for
through a highly regressive tax structure, in effect redistributing income from middle
sector and working class employees to the very poor. As a result, formal and informal sector rural workers are divided politically, and the basis is set for a sandwich
coalition between the wealthy and the very poor.

[16] On this point, see Foxley (1983, 106).

system. It had as a *central* goal the individualization of beneficiaries. The old system relied on political processes to make distributional decisions that Piñera believed must be inherently individual (and therefore private). Second, the level of benefit is tied to "effort" (read that as "income"), which is viewed as a free choice. This makes the pension one receives, at least in ideological terms, a product of one's effort. If it is insufficient, the blame is one's own. For the state to intervene would not only be unjust (essentially stealing from those who exert more effort), but also a restriction of personal choice (an essential freedom in the eyes of the developers of the neoliberal model). Politically, the goal was to recast social provision in apolitical terms, and to delegitimate redistributive claims.

As a consequence of reform social insurance coverage has declined markedly; only for year-round salaried workers is participation in the new private-pension system compulsory. For the rest it is both voluntary and unlikely. In a study in 1988, Gómez and Echenique found that 53 percent of temporary workers[17] belong to no pension system, 32.9 percent were – often only occasionally – contributors to a fund, and 13.2 percent were grandfathered into the old social-security system. Previously, the old collection of public pension plans managed to cover nearly 75 percent of economically active and retired workers, and even in rural areas coverage reached 68 percent (Raczynski 1993, 18). This indicates that rural workers are now on the margins of being able to obtain minimum pension or health coverage. Few, even of those who do contribute, given low rural wages, manage to save enough for a meaningful pension.

How has the privatization of the pension system helped to conservatize and depoliticize the rural sector? The private provision of pension services does so in part because it makes the level of pension benefits a function of personal investment, which cannot be altered in obvious ways as a result of political pressure on the state, or through action in the democratic arena. This is in marked contrast to the operation of the previous defined-benefit system. In fact, political action was generally essential to the access of peasants to

[17] This is a sample of workers from the Central Valley, which is among the most dynamic regions of Chilean agriculture. It is reasonable to assume that levels of coverage are inferior to this in the less dynamic and more remote areas.

state-provided social services. Such pressure was frequently used to force landlords to make their legally required contributions to the social security service. As such, political parties and unions were important mediators in the obtaining of pension benefits for rural workers (for an example of this political mediation see Aylwin 1967; Loveman 1976). In general, the precoup public pension system was divided into separate funds with different benefits according to very broad occupational classifications. This provided an obvious incentive for broad-based collective organization around shared interests shaped by the structure of the state welfare institutions. With the destruction of these institutions,[18] the incentive for collective organization and the facilitating conditions for collective identification erode. Moreover, the relationship between individual peasant contributors and fund managers is highly unequal given the prevailing asset concentration in the industry.[19]

Because workers in the new system are entirely responsible for making the premium payments for their retirement funds (employers have no contributory role), a social conflict around which peasants historically organized was fragmented. Coverage under the old system was largely a function of the capacity to engage the state to compel landlords to make legally required contributions, a role taken up by peasant unions and reformist political parties. Under the private system, unions can have no role in this process, nor would political leaders have any way of interceding on behalf of peasants. Coverage in a pension fund is mandatory only for permanent, formal-sector employees – and even there it is merely a compulsory savings scheme. For all others, including the bulk of the agricultural labor force, participation is entirely an individual decision. Such workers must balance pressing current consumption demands with the need for long-term security, generally opting not to join. Thus, a former class conflict between peasants and landlords has (1) been displaced from the political to the economic

---

[18] It is both ironic and instructive that the single exception of this privatization of social provision was the (still) state-administered fund for the military and national police (Carabineros).

[19] The top-five funds had by 1988 already controlled 83.7 percent of affiliates, a level of concentration that is even higher when measured at the level of conglomerate group, each of which can own more than one fund (Banco Central de Chile 1989, 440; Foxley 1983, 106).

realm, and (2) displaced from its former locus between workers and owners to workers and very distant third parties (the pension funds). This in turn further atomizes rural workers, by removing a historic basis of collective identification.

Despite the fact that employers are not responsible for paying for social security benefits, the privatized pension system does build in strong dependencies on one's employer. In the countryside, making the required premiums necessitates access to a year-round job (as the data on low coverage for temporary workers indicates). But agricultural work, unlike much of industry, is inherently seasonal, and modern agriculture much more so than traditional (Rodríguez and Venegas 1988). If the continued access to social services requires continued employment, it adds quite substantially to the risks involved in entering into a conflict with one's employer. This is particularly true because most of the protections against unfair dismissal have been removed.[20] Particularly in the rural sector, engaging in conflicts with one's employer risks not only job loss, but also access to a variety of important social services if one is in the more privileged formal sector.

The political implications of this organization of welfare provision are also atomizing. Given the coverage rates mentioned, and the "freedom" to choose among different pension plans, it is likely that in any agricultural enterprise many of the workers will be uncovered by a pension plan (Administradoras de Fondos de Pensiones [AFP]), and those that are may be tied to different AFPs. Thus, any conflicts that arise about pensions will involve only a fraction of the workers in a firm. And the sorts of issues that will be considered important will differ. In any event, the conflict will never be of a clearly horizontal or class-based character as the employer is not the entity responsible for social provision. In short, the very foundation that must underlie collective action – latent common interests – has been seriously disrupted. Whereas in the earlier period there was a homogenizing dynamic in the productive enterprises, under the current system there is an increasing degree of social differentiation. Workers are very clearly *not* all in the same boat, and their present conditions and life trajectory depend far

---

[20] The 2001 reform of the labor code has reinstated some protections against arbitrary firing.

more than in the past on the characteristics of their households and their individual- and family-level survival strategies (Venegas 1987, ch. 12).

THE COMMERCIALIZATION OF AGRICULTURAL LAND

The creation of modern, capitalist agriculture in Chile progressed in a decidedly uneven fashion, ending with the emergence of a strong regime of individual private-property rights and the domination of the sector by medium- to large-scale capitalist agribusinesses. Market-based agriculture, however, could equally have produced a small-to-medium farmer-dominant outcome.[21] The large-scale dominance that developed in Chile was thus in important ways a consequence of choices made by the military government during the process of reform – and it was in part shaped by the political goal to constitute a social base for neoliberal policies in the countryside. Establishing agrarian capitalism in the Chilean context was no mean feat – it entailed the creation of land and labor markets from scratch. And as a consequence, liberal transformations had qualitatively more severe effects on rural social and economic life than they did in urban areas.

The military's starting point was not, however, auspicious. It inherited a rural sector with an upper class that was at once thoroughly discredited, more feudal than entrepreneurial, politically weakened, and economically devastated.[22] And, as a result of the land reform (1967–73), the state had direct ownership of over 40 percent of the best agricultural land in the country, while stringent legal constraints hemmed in the remaining private properties. Thus, the social fabric within which the neoliberals of the military government sought to introduce market relations had three critical characteristics: it lacked a preexisting agrarian business class; it was characterized by collective, nontransferable property rights; and it was organized in a village residential structure largely incompatible with individual private farms.

---

[21] De Janvry (1981) outlines the two paths of agrarian modernization and their sociopolitical implications.

[22] By 1973 nearly every farm large enough to be subject to expropriation under the land reform (and many which were too small) had been transferred to the reform sector. In addition, the residual "reserves" granted during the Allende administration to expropriated landlords tended to be small if they were granted at all.

Land markets could hardly be created without enormous implications for rural social relations.

The transformations wrought in the rural sector also had a broad, noncontroversial economic goal in the creation of a modern export-oriented sector. But beneath this economic priority – ironically shared with the preceding Allende and Frei governments – were three crucial political goals linked to the institutionalization and consolidation of a neoliberal political base in the 1980s.[23] First, rather than attempting to build a support base in the discredited traditional rural upper class, the regime endeavored to create a new social group – export-oriented agricultural entrepreneurs – that would be politically supportive of the neoliberal project (before and after any democratic transition). Second, it aimed at permanently weakening and depoliticizing the rural lower classes by facilitating rapid social differentiation, intrapeasant economic conflict, and by individualizing avenues of upward and downward social mobility. Finally, it generated a social geography inimical to the collective organization of even fragments of the peasantry, helping to create not only the political isolation of rural producers and workers, but their geographic isolation as well. In the process it also heightened their dependence on, and vulnerability to, large growers and marketing agents.

Land Markets

It is possible to make sense of the politics behind the organization of agrarian land markets in part by examining the policies that the military regime did not pursue in the wake of the coup, as well as those that it began but then aborted. At the time of the coup, the state not only controlled agricultural input and crop prices, but also owned or controlled an enormous stock of capital goods (e.g., tractors, irrigation canals, and storage facilities) and distribution channels and cooperatives.[24] Simultaneously, it had control over most of the best agricultural

---

[23] It is important to differentiate the institutionalization of the authoritarian project from the consolidation of permanent military rule. The idea behind the project was to assure the continuity of a particular economic and social order regardless of the political regime that held sway.

[24] Because the threat of expropriation gutted private agricultural investment, virtually all purchases of capital goods in the 1970–3 period were made by the public sector.

land in the country. But in a marked departure from policy imposed almost immediately (1973) in the urban sector, there was no wholesale reversal of the expropriations of agricultural properties carried out during the administration of President Allende. In the urban sector, most firms "statized" or "intervened" during the Allende administration were simply returned to their old owners or sold at auction (Sáez 1993, 80–1). But rather than reject the 1967 land reform outright as an illegal interference by the state with property rights, the military government proclaimed a desire to take the process to its "logical" conclusion.

The 1967 agrarian reform legislation, passed during the Christian Democratic Frei administration (1964–70), had envisioned a three-to-five-year transition period of state management of expropriated farms after which the definitive assignment of cooperative (collective) or individual land titles would occur, according to the residents' preference (Law 16.640 of 1967). Until military rule, such assignments almost always ended with the creation of collective, inalienable property. According to Renato Gazmuri, a post-coup Subsecretary of Agriculture, the military's initial effort involved a commitment to carrying land reform to its legal conclusion, though land assignment would now be permitted only in the form of individual peasant parcels, not cooperatives (*Ercilla* July 30, 1975, 30).

This was obviously not yet a move to create large-scale capitalist agriculture. While property was to be assigned individually, the state would favor the cooperative organization of the reform-sector peasants into *Sociedades de Cooperación Agrícola* (SOCAs, or agricultural cooperation societies). The SOCAs were to be organizations for the management of collective goods (machinery, irrigation water, buildings), as well as channels for public credit. The principal sponsors of this corporatist form of organization in 1974 were the Ministries of Agriculture and Labor, under the control of the elements of the military government that initially had a more corporatist orientation toward state/society relations: the *Carabineros* (national police), and the Air Force (O'Brien and Roddick 1983, 47; Silva 1987, 157).

Thus, the initial political aims of the military regime were twofold. On the one hand it aimed at consolidating the support of a successful and capitalist peasant middle class, by protecting it against the territorial claims of the ex-landlords, as well as from the proponents of bringing more peasants into the reform sector. The old agrarian upper class, despite being a central opponent of the Allende administration, was forced to be content with a partial land restitution, up to the maximum 80 equivalent hectare reserve contemplated in the 1967 agrarian reform law.

Peasant political support for military rule was to be organized through the SOCAs, and this, it was hoped, would provide a bulwark against leftist infiltration in the countryside. This approach was short-lived, because after the ascendance of neoliberal policies of economic "shock treatment" after 1975, the goal of providing support, and facilitating organization of the peasantry disappeared; and with it the SOCAs. By 1978, only 30.3 percent of parceled-land reform co-ops had resulted in the creation of a SOCA, compared with 50.9 percent in 1976. Of these, 56.1 percent existed only on paper, performing no actual functions (ICIRA 1977; ICIRA 1979, 26–7).

It was in the subdivision of the agrarian reform co-ops[25] that the beginnings of neoliberal policies in the rural sector became clear. From the beginning, the neoliberal faction within the military government argued for a turn toward large-scale capitalist export-farming (CEP 1992, ch. L) and away from farmer agriculture. This was hampered, however, by the fact that in 1973 peasant agriculture controlled roughly 63 percent of the arable land. For them, then, the crucial step to be taken was the formation of a vibrant land market that would reallocate this factor of production to those (capitalist) farmers most able to compete internationally. Notably absent from this strategy was a policy of generating political support among the peasantry, or facilitating their adjustment to an increasingly open economy. As we saw previously, peasants were systematically denied access to the reasonably

---

[25] These are the *asentamientos* (settlements) and *sociedad agrícola de reforma agraria* (agrarian reforms societies, or SARAs). The former is a transitional form of cooperative organization contemplated in the agrarian reform law of 1967, while the SARAs represented permanent cooperative ownership of reform property. For a period of between three and five years after expropriation, peasants would work collectively in the *asentamiento* to learn the necessary skills to run the farms autonomously. After this period, they would opt between a collective (SARA) or individual form of property ownership. During the democratic period (1967–73) definitive titles were almost always assigned to cooperatives. Under the military, they were assigned only as individual private property.

priced inputs or long-term credit necessary to facilitate any successful integration into international markets.

To reach this end, then, two preconditions had to be met. A juridical structure for the land market had to be created and lands held by the state had to be privatized. With respect to the former, the provisions of the existing agrarian reform law were clearly inadequate. Private landholdings of over 80 basic irrigated hectares (BIH) were prohibited, as was the alienation or rental of reform-sector land.[26] Even corporate ownership of agricultural land, rental, or subdivision of large holdings was banned. By 1979 the military regime had changed the institutional context by legalizing holdings of over 80 BIH, making land-reform parcels fully alienable and rentable, abolishing the agrarian reform law and with it the threat of expropriation, and permitting corporate land ownership (Decree Law 2247 of June 1978; Decree Law 2405 of December 1978; Jarvis 1985, 30).

The most important single step in the process of agrarian restructuring was the privatization of much of the reform sector into individual peasant parcels, and the vigorous land market that the sale of these parcels sparked. The policy of privatization was three-pronged. The original land reform law contemplated a "reserve" for the former landlords of 80 BIH of an expropriated property. Any landlord who received less than this amount of land, or whose property was deemed "illegally" expropriated received a partial or complete restitution, respectively. These so-called "normalizations" involved 27 percent of the land in the reform sector. A further 51.6 percent of the reform-sector land was divided as individual peasant parcels. The remainder was either transferred to other public agencies or sold at auction (Departamento de Economía Agraria 1980, 25).

The resulting initial structure of land tenure can be seen in Table 3.2 (Kurtz 2001, 8). From 1973 onward, the evidence shows a clear trend toward transfers of land from the peasant sector to the capitalist sector. It is important to note, however, that the earlier

---

[26] The BIH is a unit that makes agricultural land of different quality comparable. It renders the physical area of an agricultural property into the value equivalent of highly fertile, irrigated land in the Central Valley through a series of conversion factors contained in the agrarian reform law and its accessory regulations.

TABLE 3.2 *The Reorganization of Land Tenure under Military Rule (percent of agricultural land in basic irrigated hectares)*

Farm Size Stratum	1973	1976	1979[a]	1986	1990s	1997[b]
Minifundio	9.7	9.7	13.3	14.0		
Family Labor Farm	13.1	24.9	29.0	26.0		
Reform Sector	40.6	18.1	4.0	3.0		
PEASANTS	63.4	52.7	46.3	43.0	39.0	27.7
Capitalist Farms	36.6	43.4	36.3	31.0		
Large Agribusiness	0.0	2.9	16.9	26.0		
CAPITALIST	36.6	47.3	53.2	57.0	61.0	72.2

[a] These data were calculated by Jarvis working backward from property-tax assessments, making the assumption that the value of a basic irrigated hectare was $78,000 pesos. For a justification, see Jarvis (1985, 10–21).

[b] It is crucial to note that these data are not strictly comparable to the other columns in the table. The Agricultural Census of 1997 from which they are taken no longer measured land in basic irrigated hectares. Thus, in the construction of this table, data on absolute size distribution of landholdings were used: those between 0 and 20 Ha were considered peasant sector, those between 20 and 200 Ha were considered capitalist. Those over 200 Ha were considered principally ranching or unutilized properties and were excluded from the calculation as they would bias the results dramatically.

Sources: For 1973, see Cereceda and Dahse (1980, 135). For 1976, see INE (1975). For 1979, see Jarvis (1985, 10). For 1986 see Jarvis (1992, 199); for 1990s see World Bank (1995, 35); for 1997 see ODEPA (1997). Table adapted from Kurtz (2001, 8).

massive and inefficient land concentration of the prereform period was not being recreated. Rather, a stratum of large and medium capitalist farms has been created, at the expense of both the peasant sector and of the huge holdings of the past.[27] Among the peasantry, the parcelization of reform-sector lands through 1978 created an enlarged stratum of family smallholders, but one whose control over land was tenuous and often brief.

The aggregated character of this data tends to mask some of the very intense processes of social differentiation initiated among the Chilean peasants once the sale of reform lands became legal. The data show that family farms between 5 and 20 BIH in size declined under the military's economic liberalization (see Table 3.2). These data, however, still seriously understate the extent of peasant-farm decomposition. The

[27] It is important to remember that the size category of greater than 80 BIH in 1965 contained farms that on average were *much* larger than this cutoff point. In the wake of the military coup, this large-holding segment is much more concentrated in the vicinity of 80 BIH.

military's own studies suggest that by June of 1978 roughly 36.8 percent of newly created parcels had already been partially or completely
sold, generally to nonpeasants (ICIRA 1979, 114–23).[28] Thus, the sale
of land-reform parcels does not mark as much a process of social differentiation among the peasantry, as a severe process of social decomposition. This is not as clearly demonstrated in the land tenure data
because a single capitalist producer may own several farms in the size
range of 5–20 BIH, each of which would be recorded separately and
appear as small peasant farms.

What has emerged, then, from this radical restructuring of rural
social property relations is an increasingly heterogeneous rural sector.
While no segment of the rural peasant and working classes is in a
particularly stable position, neither is there a clear tendency toward
homogenizing proletarianization. Table 3.2 outlines the changing class
structure of the rural sector. Two features stand out. First, while the
share of agricultural land held by the peasant sector has declined since
1973, the absolute numbers of landholding peasants have increased
slightly (see Tables 3.2 and 3.3). Thus, there is a tendency toward
land loss and subdivision at work. Second, the rural wage labor force
has increasingly become dominated by temporary employment. There
has been virtually no growth in permanent (year-round) agricultural
employment since the coup.

Land Tenure and Politics

What exactly is there about the creation of land markets that was
political? On one level the land-marketization policy was no more
than the logical extension of a neoclassical economic model to the rural sector; one that had been pursued in different ways during both
the Alessandri and Frei administrations (1958–70). On another level
choices were made by political leaders that selected economic winners
and losers, limited the terms of political debate with regard to agricultural policy, and fragmented long-standing interests so severely as to

---

[28] This was not, however, a process of social differentiation among peasants. Rather,
only 6.5 percent of these sales were to other peasants. Indeed, 89.3 percent of the sales
went to the emergent capitalist segment consisting of marketers, capitalist farmers,
urban professionals, and public-sector functionaries (Cereceda and Dahse 1980, 117).
They began to constitute the new capitalist, agro-export class fragment.

raise insurmountable barriers to collective political expression. Land marketization can be accomplished in a variety of different ways – with vastly different social consequences. The particular set of structural reforms enacted by the military, however, was highly unfavorable to the survival of small-scale peasant landholdings. In the accompanying process of class differentiation and decomposition, the social basis for peasant political interest aggregation and organization was very seriously undermined (Silva 1987, 163).

In a very real sense the Chilean military regime brought the process of land reform to completion, and with it the salience of this political issue. For decades the central issue in rural politics was the restructuring of land tenure to overcome a level of backwardness and underdevelopment that was seen as hindering the progress of the nation as a whole (CIDA 1966). The justification for profound interferences with property rights was based on the need to modernize a very backward agricultural sector, and received support across the political spectrum. The political competition of the 1960s and early 1970s was largely circumscribed by debates about how to best carry this out (see especially Kaufman 1972).

With the parcelization, "normalization," and auction of land reform properties in the mid-1970s and the capitalist modernization that ensued, the justification for new interferences in land tenure patterns were undermined. The issue of agrarian reform is now off the agenda – the politically illegitimate and economically inefficient large landlords of the past are gone, and they have been replaced by a sector of highly successful capitalist agribusinesses. In this narrow sense the land reform was both successful and completed, even if most of the land is still not in the hands of its tillers. The abolition in 1978–9 of the state agencies in charge of reorganizing land tenure, and the constitutional limitations on any future attempts at large-scale property transfers (Ley Orgánica Constitucional de Expropiaciones 18.932), have destroyed the institutional capacity to enact serious reforms even should the issue somehow force its way back into national politics.

In addition to this obvious narrowing of the public sphere's effect on everyday life, the very creation of a land market, as carried out in Chile, seriously constricted the arena of future political debate. While neoliberals argue that markets are neutral devices for the allocation of resources, for them to function efficiently they require a set of rules enforced by the state (Chaudhry 1993). These rules have an important effect on who wins and who loses in the marketization of land. Carter and Mesbah (1992) have convincingly argued that the distributive patterns that emerge from the functioning of a land market depend heavily on the initial conditions, supplementary legal and institutional norms, and economic context in which it operates. Here is where the political goals of military-era land-market creation are revealed.

The first two years of the military regime (1973–5) began auspiciously enough for landholding peasants, as steps were taken to ensure that they would be able to confront the operation of free input and product markets. This was part of the corporatist tone of social and economic policy of this period. Credit and technical aid continued to be publicly provided through the state bank and the Instituto Nacional de Desarrollo Agropecuario (National Institute for Agricultural Development or INDAP), while the SOCAs were organized to channel this credit and distribute technical support. The beginnings of a "farmer road" to the capitalization of agriculture may have been in the making (De Janvry 1981). Certainly, this was the central thrust of the political rhetoric of the military regime during this period. But as the parcelization of the reform sector progressed, and the neoliberal policy makers became increasingly predominant within the government, the rules created to govern the nascent land market and the conditions under which peasants confronted it changed to their marked detriment.

Indeed, by 1979 the privatization of reform parcels had become part of a strategy to manage the transfer of lands out of the hands of the peasants in a way that would simultaneously divide them politically and keep some of them open to political appeals from the right. The linchpin in this policy was the parcelization of the land reform under conditions that made it extremely difficult for the peasantry to retain the land it was granted during the "completion" of the land reform. I argue that this policy was largely a success as it gave rise to long-lasting intrapeasant divisions, and placed the blame for failure to survive economically squarely on the land recipients *as individuals* and not on their situation, seen in collective terms. In a sense the peasantry was given its historical chance, but under conditions in which it was sure to fail.

What were the politics involved in the termination of the land reform? In the first place the distribution of reform-sector properties really only included land. The provisions of the land-reform law were reinterpreted to permit the expropriated landlords to remove capital equipment from the *fundo* and take it to their reserves (Law 16.640 of Agrarian Reform, 1967). This created a substantially undercapitalized reform sector and a relatively highly capitalized private sector. In addition, the critical mechanical equipment owned by the state either through CORA (*Corporación de Reforma Agraria*, the land reform administration) or the SEAM (the agricultural machinery parastatal) was not distributed to peasant beneficiaries, but rather auctioned at very low prices during the 1975–7 recession to the private agricultural sector, contributing to its transition to efficient capitalist management.

Politically, this very inexpensive transfer of public assets to the new agribusiness class amounted to a massive side payment for some of the most ardent supporters of the military coup. Foxley (1983) has shown that purchase prices were roughly at 50 percent of the real value of the goods at auction. Finally, the military-appointed managers of the land-reform co-ops (and their predecessors) ran up substantial debts in the mid-1970s that the co-ops had to finance through the sale of whatever capital equipment they owned at the time of dissolution, eliminating one final source of access to critical productive means for the parcel recipients, and providing artificially cheap capital goods for the nascent capitalist sector (Jarvis 1992, 194).

It was crucial to establish land markets and the transition to agricultural capitalism by allowing land to *pass through* peasant hands. Simply to recreate the old, inefficient patterns of extremely inegalitarian land tenure would keep alive the issue of land reform in future political debates. Instead, the military brought the process of land reform to its "natural" ending point – it distributed the remainder of the land in technical compliance with many of the terms of the 1967 agrarian reform law. Any subsequent dynamics of land concentration, however, could not then be decried as the result of undue political power, as they resulted from private, individual, and "voluntary" transactions. If peasants sold their land it was because they failed as farmers. By establishing the legitimate ownership of land in the hands of peasants in 1978–9, the military provided for the legitimacy of changes in ownership patterns emerging through subsequent land transactions. Indeed, just this sort of private transaction was elevated to the status of a civil right by the military regime. Of course, institutional and world-market conditions made subsequent transfers out of the peasant sector and into the capitalist one inevitable.

Atomization and Competition

The most important effects of the creation of land markets, however, had to do with the way it restructured the practice of politics and social organization within the cultivating classes. The process of land parcelization and the rules that were developed to govern the emerging land market left little doubt as to the eventual trajectory of land tenure in the new liberal era. Crucially, in political terms, three mechanisms helped cement the disorganization and demobilization of the losers from this process – peasants and agricultural workers. First, it created a set of social divisions and conflicting interests among a formerly much more homogeneous set of rural cultivators. Second, while obvious means to collective advancement through political and economic organizations were shut down, pathways of individual social mobility were opened. But they were opened in ways such that upward mobility for peasants came largely at the expense of other members of the same social stratum. This heightened the antagonisms generated in the initial set of social divisions marked by the parcelization of the reform sector. Finally, it helped to generate a social environment where the traditional appeals made by the political left were of little practical relevance, and that left open important avenues through which the right could develop a rural base of political support.

The initial subdivision of the reform sector was anything but the neutral technocratic process described in the rhetoric of the military regime. The allocation of reform-sector lands was based on a point system, subject to an exclusion of all individuals who had participated in a land invasion (Decree Law 208). This immediately introduced a severe penalty for a form of political action that had been commonplace in the 1970–3 period. A minimum of 1,700 land invasions occurred between 1970 and 1972, with only roughly 5,000 large properties existing in the country (Marín 1972). Most importantly, the verification of this apolitical behavior was a required letter from the expropriated landlord of the farm in question. This process of exclusion was

subject to much abuse, and excluded peasants were denied a mechanism of appeal or even the knowledge of their accusers.[29] Thus the
first social differentiation introduced during the "normalization" of
land tenure was the assignment of land only to "apolitical" – read that
as "conservative" – peasants. It also sowed the seed of serious internal
conflict within the peasantry.

The inequities and intrapeasant competition engendered during the
land reform extended well beyond this exclusionary mechanism. The
parcelization of the reform sector involved roughly half the land that
had been expropriated in the previous two administrations. And given
the comparatively large size of the plots handed out a fierce struggle
ensued among reform-sector peasants to obtain access to land. In the
end only slightly more than half of the *asentado* (land-reform co-op
member) heads of family received land, and practically none of the
adult sons (DEA 1980). The struggle to qualify for a land-reform parcel
engendered a highly zero-sum conflict among *asentados* that destroyed
what remained of the intrapeasant solidarities generated in the earlier
period of mobilization.

The actual criteria used to select beneficiaries were also very selective in a political way. In part they were designed to transfer as many of
the parcels to nonpeasants as possible, as part of the military regime's
attempt to create a new stratum of entrepreneurial farmers. To this
end land distribution was opened to nonpeasants, and very high point
values were assigned to applicants having university-level degrees in
agronomy, veterinary medicine, or having had experience in the now-
disbanded agrarian reform and outreach agencies. Similarly, high point
values were assigned to peasants who had been in positions of management or confidence on the hacienda. These were, naturally, those
most aligned with conservative rural elites. Finally, a discretionary allocation of points was allowed, determined by the administrator or
ex-landowner, that was in theory to assess the applicant's competence,
reliability, and responsibility, but that in reality often merely punished
earlier political activity (Jarvis 1985, 150). These criteria selected for
peasants with close ties to their former landlords (clearly the most

---

[29] Indeed, it has been reported that false claims were made to the military authorities
as personal rivalries, old grudges, or attempts to better one's own chances for land
became reasons to "turn in" fellow co-ops residents.

conservative segment), as well as those individuals not pertaining to the peasant stratum altogether.

For average reform-sector peasants, the only practical way to achieve point totals high enough to receive land involved ingratiating oneself with the ex-landlord, having large numbers of dependents (which would simultaneously undermine farm economic viability), and having worked in reform-sector lands for a long period of time. In this way, the peasant beneficiaries selected were clearly among the *least* likely to be able to confront the rigors of individual farming successfully. As a result of the selection process, parcel holders (*parceleros*) had low educational levels and comparatively large families to support, which made investing in modern farming techniques largely beyond their reach.[30] Given the absence of state support in the period of transition to independent farming, the high dependency ratios of *parcelero* families made it even more difficult even to retain ownership of the assigned land and avoid fragmentation during inheritance, much less begin a desperately needed process of capitalization, particularly in response to heightened international competition.

Jarvis (1985, 152) finds a basic inconsistency between the way in which land was assigned and the subsequent liberal policies imposed in the agricultural sector. To him it seems clear that this new peasantry was quite unlikely to flourish. But it is my contention that the military was uninterested in the success of these smallholders. Rather, it sought: (1) to create a new stratum of capitalist agricultural entrepreneurs that would displace both the traditional landlords of the Central Valley as well as what remained of the reform sector peasantry, (2) to permanently discourage peasant political activity by directly associating it with the loss of access to land and rapid downward social mobility, and (3) to fragment the rural cultivating classes in ways that prevented the formation of broad-based political coalitions, and left important segments open to cooperation with the political right.

The sell-off to nonpeasants of land-reform parcels served to constitute a new agrarian capitalist sector as well as the land market. This was not simply the unanticipated consequence of the national-level economic model. The decline of the reform-sector smallholding peasantry

---

[30] ICIRA (1979, 18) reports that only 18.1 percent of *parceleros* had completed basic primary education (through the sixth grade).

was no accident. Even as ardent a supporter of liberal economic policies as the World Bank (1980, 191) warned early on that given the inadequate education, experience, access to credit, and inputs on the part of the small farmers they would be utterly unable to compete with large-scale corporate farming. Mesbah and Carter (1992) point out that *even if* small and large farmers were able to compete in productivity terms, the frequent and severe economic ups and downs implicit in exposure to the world market would have the effect of transferring land to the capitalist sector – farm survival in economic downturns is directly linked to access to credit, and in a market-oriented system small producers are at an inherent disadvantage.

The parcelization of the land-reform properties and the wholesale reorganization of productive relations engendered new social conflicts not simply between those who did and did not acquire land, but also between peasant producers and rural wage laborers. Before and during the land reform, rural cultivators on the old estates were largely insulated from food-price inflation. Subsistence food needs were met either through home production or were granted by the landlord as part of the traditional labor contract. In the wake of capitalist transition and marketization, rural workers became personally responsible for their own food needs. Any increases in the price of peasant-produced foods – those most likely to be consumed by rural workers – were reflected in declining consumption for workers. Previously rural workers were at least agnostic on the issue of agricultural price increases. Now they were placed in a direct conflict of interest with peasant producers. Such a conflict of interests could not help but undermine the potential for broad-based or effective peasant-worker political cooperation or action.

Finally, the opening of land markets led to a wholesale change in both the overall direction and means of social mobility. During the land reform (1967–73), for rural workers and producers alike, there was a generalized pattern of upward social mobility. This was not, however, a function of individual progress upward through the class hierarchy, but rather an improvement in the living conditions of peasants *qua* peasants. Mobility was collective and upward, largely a product of the pressures that the new, militant peasant unions could apply. Or that state elites seeking political support could distribute.

After marketization, the position of peasants declined markedly, with the only remaining avenue for upward social mobility being individual progress through an increasingly differentiated class hierarchy. Depending upon one's starting position (smallholder or landless) the available trajectories were quite different. For parcel holders there existed the perhaps likely prospect of downward mobility through land loss coupled with the conceivable but unlikely eventuality of achieving farmer status through a process of land accumulation. The former condition helped cement the risk aversion of these cultivators, while the latter provided them a narrow means of advancement, but one inherently premised upon the misfortunes of other members of their class segment (those who lost land). It is important to remember that the parcel recipients were selected in the first place in part because of their political risk aversion. The "normalization" of the reform sector taught a very poignant lesson – that political activity was an effective way to ensure the loss of one's land. And given that individual upward mobility was premised on the acquisition of the land of fellow *parceleros* (and reform-sector smallholders), political cooperation and action were substantially undermined.

RURAL LABOR MARKETS: DISORGANIZATION AND DEPENDENCE

The widespread recruitment of agrarian labor through impersonal markets differed markedly from the labor-service tenancies and cooperative forms of organization that prevailed during the hacienda (pre-1967) and land-reform (1967–73) periods, respectively. The creation of large, efficient agrarian labor markets was socially tremendously disruptive, especially because it undermined the long-standing on-farm peasant communities that were central to labor recruitment in both earlier eras. It must be remembered that comparatively little nonresident labor was recruited before 1973, making the emergence of regional and national agricultural labor markets new indeed. Moreover, labor-market liberalization in the broader context of union repression, structurally high unemployment, a hostile state, and the inherently seasonal nature of agricultural production became a mechanism for solidifying the political and economic exclusion of the peasantry. It institutionalized a level of disorganization and vertical dependence that, I argue, would undermine the associational foundations of rural democratic competition.

Crucially, the social and economic organization of agriculture – especially in its most modern variants – is fundamentally different from other sectors. Output is not simply guided by supply and demand in the marketplace, but is also *inherently* seasonal. In the absence of deliberate intervention it will generate principally seasonal labor demand.[31] The extent to which this is true is partially a function of technology, but many have noted that increasing technological advancement, at least in many crops, tends to heighten rather than diminish seasonality. And indeed, labor force demand is overwhelmingly temporary in Chile's modern agro-export sector.

When such an inherently unstable labor market is combined with the particular social and economic conditions of the post-1973 Chilean rural sector, the political implications for the cultivating classes are profound. In particular, the liberalization of the labor market was accompanied by the closing off of the escape valve that rural to urban migration had provided since the 1940s – urban unemployment in the 1970s and 1980s reached catastrophic levels. At the same time labor law was changed to facilitate mass dismissal of superfluous workers. Finally, a long-term situation of very high rates of underemployment and unemployment prevailed in the countryside. These factors, linked together, prevented substantial (even productivity-linked) wage improvement, heightened intraworker economic competition, and generated a cross-sectional and life-cycle pattern of social differentiation that seriously fragmented lower-class interests.

In short, a structural imbalance of power was created in rural areas that perpetuates the economic and political dominance of neoliberal, export-oriented agribusiness elites. In neither the economic nor political arenas is the playing-field level, and real democratic competition cannot be joined in the latter without some redress of the imbalances of the former. It is the task of the rest of this chapter to highlight how the particular manner in which the labor market was created in Chilean agriculture generated such a politically relevant social power imbalance.

Labor Market Institutions

The creation of a functioning market for labor in rural areas required the breaking of a centuries-old connection between the peasantry and

---

[31] There are, of course, exceptions to this rule. But given the climatic and technological characteristics of Chilean agriculture, there is widespread consensus that substantially more seasonal labor than permanent (year round) is employed.

the land (Ortega 1987, 205). The hacienda system was one of an internalized peasantry, wherein all of the year-round labor and much of the seasonal labor was provided by long-standing residents of villages located within the boundaries of the landlord's farm (Kay 1971). Indeed, access to a dwelling *implied* that one worked for the landlord on a basically usufruct-for-labor basis. Thus loss of employment implied expulsion from the landlord's property and from community life. The *asentamientos* (transitional land-reform cooperatives) created by the agrarian reform not only did not break with this pattern of on-farm residence in traditional villages, indeed it brought even higher levels of year-round residence and employment (Olavarría 1978).

There were political and economic reasons why this identity between place of residence and place of employment was seen as invidious by the neoliberal planners. First, economically, it hinders the redirection of resources along the lines of comparative advantage. Wholesale transfers of population were inevitable if the reorientation of agriculture was to proceed, and with labor tied to existing productive patterns this would be impossible. Second, in political terms, it has been well established that the long-term resident workers on the haciendas were the most mobilized during the Frei and Allende years (1964–73) (Marín 1972). They were seen as politically dangerous, and were associated with land invasions, agrarian reform, socialism, and violations of property rights.

After 1975, the military regime combined its policies aimed at the creation of a land market (described previously) with the freeing up of workers to supply the nascent rural labor market. With the parcelization of the agrarian reform, a very large number of landless workers were dumped on the labor market. Conservative estimates suggest that only 33,678 families of the more than 61,159 existing in the reform sector at the time of the coup obtained land. More than 27,481 families were thus immediately thrown onto the labor market in the condition of landless workers (ICIRA 1979, 21). Assuming very conservatively that only one member of each of these families was in the labor force,[32] this suggests an increase in the rural wage labor force of nearly 7.3 percent.

While historically official unemployment rates in the agricultural sector have been very low, a variety of studies have suggested that the

---

[32] Given the size and composition of peasant families, this is an exceedingly conservative estimate.

way in which unemployment was measured hides very substantial levels of underemployment. Jarvis (1985, 89) has pointed out the highly biased weighting of different occupations in the rural employment survey is at fault. He finds a level of unemployment of 15 percent to be more realistic for 1974. Olavarría (1978, 14) suggests that combined unemployment and underemployment has historically been between 20 and 37 percent, while studies by PREALC suggest a number around 30 percent. Corvalán (1976, 22) compares the direct and indirect labor requirements of the crops produced in Chile with the actually available agricultural labor force, generating an implicit unemployment rate of 21.7 percent for 1955, declining to 13.2 by 1970 as the land reform created more and increasingly stable employment. Indeed, the mass expulsion of fundo residents that accompanied parcelization of the reform sector probably represents as much a conversion of disguised underemployment into open unemployment and cross-sectional social differentiation as the creation of "new" joblessness.[33] The freeing of this labor, and its expulsion from previous dwellings on the fundos immediately created a very important axis of social differentiation previously not widely characteristic of the rural working class – that between the fully employed and the unemployed or underemployed.

The generation of a new, mobile, employment-seeking stratum was not politically neutral. It is important to remember that a large proportion of those not receiving land-reform parcels were expelled because of Decree Law 208 that excluded anyone who had previously participated in a land invasion. Rural employers were well aware of this, and considered these ex-asentados politically dangerous, frequently refusing to employ them (Olavarría 1978, 32). ICIRA (1979, 22) shows that only 22.4 percent of these ex-reform-sector peasants found year-round employment, a further 25.1 percent seasonal employment, with the remainder in various conditions of disguised or open unemployment.[34] At the same time cash shortage and low levels of output prevented the new individual peasant parcels from generating substantial levels of

---

[33] Previously, on the asentamientos and haciendas, these levels of underemployment were generally shared within families. If not all the eligible family members were able to obtain work, at least they managed minimum subsistence and a place to dwell through residence on the fundo and the *inquilino* (labor tenant) status of the household head.

[34] This includes residing with friends or relatives who were able to obtain a parcel, work in the minimum employment program, retirement, open unemployment, etc.

nonfamily employment. Not only was a cleavage thus created, but a powerful lesson about the risks inherent in political activity was taught.

At the same time crucial changes were made in the regulations governing the hiring and firing of workers that changed the dynamics of employment in the nonreform sector as well. Severance costs were radically reduced, with mass dismissals openly tolerated for the first time since the 1960s. Immediately after the coup, landlords engineered mass firings and occasionally executions of politically troublesome workers. In addition, the auction of the capital goods of the reform sector principally benefited the private growers, leaving them substantially *over*capitalized. This excess mechanization coupled with a 7.5 percent expansion in days worked by the remaining year-round employees was a further source of unemployment (calculated from Corvalán 1976; Jarvis 1985, 69). Linked to this was a change in the composition of the labor force, moving toward a much more seasonal pattern of employment. Previously, the provision of year-round employment was necessary to assure a sufficient labor supply in harvest periods as permanent tenants were expected to provide additional family labor on an as-needed basis. The creation of effective seasonal labor markets made this arrangement comparatively costly and superfluous, allowing the consequent reduction of year-round employment. Finally, it has been suggested that mechanization levels on the private farms exceeded the level that profit considerations would dictate, being driven largely by the fears that many of these former landlords had of their year-round employees. They sought to minimize employment.

By 1979 a functioning, highly competitive labor market had been established. High levels of unemployment, declines in domestic food demand, and the liberalization of the conditions of employment generated extremely precarious conditions for rural workers. Wages plummeted, and ceased to include the in-kind payments that had provided some inflation hedge in the past. These conditions, necessary to begin the process of commodification of labor, would result in a long-run structural imbalance of power in the rural economy.

Antipolitics, Dependence, and the Long Run

In the establishment of the labor market after 1979, exceedingly harsh conditions were imposed on rural labor. It was not inevitable, however, that the imbalance of power generated between rural cultivators

and noncultivators would persist over the long run. But for the political goals of the military regime to be met, however, this imbalance
of power had to become a structural characteristic of the rural labor
market that would reproduce itself. Three features that characterize
the agricultural labor market help to accomplish this: (1) rural and
peri-urban labor markets have been linked in ways that generate an
essentially limitless supply of labor, (2) the precariousness of this labor
force is linked to the extreme seasonality of the modern agricultural
sector, and (3) migratory escape valves for surplus labor have been
closed, and new patterns of residence have emerged that reinforce the
heterogeneity and social fragmentation of the cultivating classes. The
consequence is the creation of tremendous and persistent economic
vulnerability for the agricultural labor force.

It is my contention that the application of neoliberal policies in the
agricultural sector has generated *structurally* high levels of unemployment and dependence. And for my claim that rural labor's position
is inherently fragmented and dependent to hold, it must survive even
long periods of economic expansion in the agricultural sector and indeed the transition to democratic politics as well. It is to that issue that
I now turn, examining the implications of more than a decade of unprecedented agrarian-sector growth and democratization on peasant
vulnerability, fragmentation, and dependence.

After an extended period of very high levels of unemployment, official statistics report that off-season agricultural unemployment rates
had fallen from a level of over 7 percent in 1985–6 to around 5 percent by 1991 (the corresponding figures for peak-harvest times are 5.4
and 2 percent, respectively) (ODEPA 1992, 19). I argue that these are
not very accurate measures of the true levels of rural unemployment.
Jarvis (1985, 87) has pointed out that there are substantial sources of
bias in the government measures of rural unemployment, especially in
its failure to account for substantial levels of *under*employment.[35] In
addition, the government's own employment surveys suggest that the
period of sustained agricultural growth between 1986 and 1991 did

[35] Other sources of bias include the fact that rates of labor force participation have
declined as workers become discouraged, and that the employment surveys used
tend to substantially overrepresent sectors of the rural labor force experiencing less
unemployment.

TABLE 3.3 *The Evolution of Rural Class Structure in Chile, 1966–1990 (economically active population [EAP] in thousands, and percent of total)*

Class Segment	1972		1986		1990	
	EAP	Percent	EAP	Percent	EAP	Percent
Agricultural Entrepreneurs	35.0	5.1	29.5	3.8	32.0	3.7
Rural Professionals and Managerial	14.0	2.0	8.6	1.1	14.7	1.7
Peasants, Asentados, and Minifundistas	364.0	52.6	318.5	41.0	375.4	43.1
Permanent Proletarian[a]	126.0	18.2	120.0	15.5	128.4	14.7
Temporary Proletarian[a]	154.0	22.2	300.0	38.6	321.1	36.9
TOTAL	693.0	100.1	776.6	100.0	871.6	100.1

[a] The national employment surveys of 1986 and 1990 do not differentiate between those employed on a seasonal versus a year-round basis. For 1986 the distribution of agricultural proletarians between these two categories is taken from Gómez and Echenique (1988, 64). For 1990, the assumption is made that the relative distribution between these two categories is the same as 1986. This should tend to provide a minimum estimate of the number of temporary workers and a maximum estimate of the permanently employed, given the general consensus that exists as to a continuing shift to the use of temporary workers in the most dynamic sectors of agriculture (Rodríguez and Venegas 1989).

Sources: For 1972, adapted from ICIRA (1972). For 1986 and 1990, adapted from INE (1992b).

not result in the creation of a substantial number of new wage-paying jobs (see Table 3.3).

These data suggest that despite substantial increases in output in the most wage-labor intensive sectors of agriculture, total wage-labor employment peaked in 1988 and has declined since then. Between 1988 and 1991 the value of fruit production for export surged nearly 80 percent, even in the face of price declines in all important fruit crops, and on the order of 20 percent for such crucial crops as table grapes (calculated from ODEPA 1992, 18, 21). And despite the surge in output, most of the employment gains over the period 1986 to 1991 have been in the "self-employed" or peasant category, groups not involved in export production. This is in keeping with arguments that the peasant sector functions as a "labor reserve," occupying workers in a very low-productivity activity until such time as employment opportunities might emerge in the formal wage-earning sector (Crispi 1982; Ortega 1987, 115).

Further support for the argument that low official unemployment statistics do not reflect an actual tightening of the labor market comes from Sáez (1986) who points out that wages in fruit agriculture were stagnant, bearing little relationship to profitability and rising productivity. Interviews with union organizers in the rural sector also suggest that the large-scale expansion in export production has not brought significant wage improvements. The government's own employment surveys also point to substantial levels of underemployment in the countryside. In 1986, 50.8 percent of small producers and 31.4 percent of wage laborers in agriculture reported being gainfully employed less than the official workweek. By 1991 – after years of economic expansion – this situation had changed little, with 49.8 percent of small producers and 22.4 percent wage laborers reporting the same (calculated from INE 1992, 301–37).

The seasonality of labor demand in Chilean agriculture is also likely to continue and will not be substantially altered by the operation of market forces (Armijo and Montero 1991, 11–12). In the first place, the techniques of production, largely imported from the industrialized countries, are geared toward a seasonal labor force (Rivera and Cruz 1984, 176; Murray 1997). Barring a (highly unlikely) redistribution of income within Chile, demand for traditional crops and employment in traditional agriculture, salable only in domestic markets, is unlikely to expand. Thus, as Chile continues to reallocate production toward export crops in which it has a comparative advantage, an increasing seasonality rather than a decline in instability will be experienced. Finally, improvement in the position of Chilean rural workers either through a generalized tightening of labor markets or an increase in year-round employment is hindered by the external constraints implied by operating in a highly competitive export sector.[36] Part of the comparative

---

[36] Crispi (1982, 485) argues that wages in Chilean export agriculture were below the level required for reproduction of the labor force precisely because of this seasonality. Much of the rural labor force is recruited from the labor surplus in the minifundista (microholding) segment, where small amounts of landholding produce enough food to lower the minimum amount of cash wages necessary to assure subsistence over the course of a year. Rodríguez and Venegas report (1989, 50) that a fruit worker's wages did not suffice for the maintenance of a family.

advantage of Chilean exports is based precisely on the low cost of labor. Any shift to greater year-round employment on the fruit farms would raise costs for employers that they can hardly support in the face of an increased oligopsony in international distribution and a decline in world prices for their crops (ODEPA 1992, 21). It has been estimated that in 1991 three-fourths of the agricultural wage labor force consisted of seasonal workers and that real wages had been declining, despite massive growth in the sector (Cruz 1991, 29)!

Finally, this new structure of employment and labor markets has become embedded in a decidedly different pattern of migration and residence than that which has historically been characteristic of the rural sector. Formerly farm-resident labor was expelled into informal "urban" squatter settlements, and the peripheries of nearby small cities and towns. Long-standing patterns of substantial rural to urban migration ceased, and in some cases reverse flows in the 1980s began to dominate (Raczynski 1981; Cruz and Rivera 1984).

Perhaps the most important social change to accompany the full transition to capitalist agriculture and labor relations was what has been called the "urbanization of the countryside." After the coup of 1973 nearly 120,000 families formerly resident in either the reform-sector or private farms were expelled from their traditional dwellings (Ortega 1987, 92). After the traumatic experience of political upheaval in the early 1970s both the military regime and private landlords were quick to rid themselves of the resident workers who had been the backbone of the rural mobilization.

The social result of this expulsion of labor was tremendous. After generations of stable residence on private *fundos*, rural workers were forced into "urban"[37] or informal residence with landholding peasants. It is important to note that this "urban" agricultural labor force does not on the whole reside in cities (population 40,000 and up), but rather in small, informal villages, towns, and squatter settlements (Rivera and Cruz 1984). In 1966 "urban" dwellers represented only 9.2 percent of the economically active agricultural population. By 1988 this proportion had exploded to more than 35.7 percent. It is clear that after the military coup the rural agricultural labor force stagnated or

---

[37] This is defined in all official Chilean data according to the most recent census. In the 1982 census, the cutoff for an urban area was 300 residents.

declined, while the urban agricultural labor force grew at comparatively rapid rates. Otero (1990, 21) has argued that this dynamic of
rapid expansion occurs in very small towns and is linked to technological change and the dynamics of the new labor market. The most
advanced areas of agriculture are furthest along in this process of rural
"urbanization." By 1986 Gómez and Echenique (1988, 70–1) divide
the residence of rural workers into the following categories: (1) peasant agriculture, including indigenous, smallholders, and minifundistas,
with 40.4 percent, (2) capitalist farms, accounting for 7.0 percent of
residence, (3) urbanized rural aldeas and pueblos[38] with 39.7 percent,
and (4) meaningfully urban areas accounting for only 12.9 percent.

The point here is simple. In the past, migration to large cities, especially Santiago, provided an escape valve for surplus rural population.
Peasants left rural areas in search of industrial jobs in the import-
substituting industries. With the transition to a neoliberal developmental model, these industrial jobs dried up and excess rural labor
ceased substantial migration to large cities. Rather, surplus population
was absorbed in informal squatter settlements in the countryside (the
very small towns) and on peasant family farms. The maintenance of
this large labor surplus was critical for the maintenance of structural
unemployment in the rural sector. Without such an imbalance, the
domination of capitalist growers over the peasantry would be difficult
to enforce.

To summarize, the present organization of the labor market in Chile
facilitates the atomization and internal division of the peasantry. As
a result, Chilean rural civil society was made into one of the most
politically and socially disorganized in the entire world (Cruz 1991,
30). Without the organizational infrastructure historically critical to
their success (most particularly the peasant unions), the political left
and center have had an extremely difficult time engaging in political
competition with the conservative elites who dominate the modern
agricultural sector.

The labor market is a crucial support for this upper-class domination
through the strong vertical dependencies it creates. Given the tremendous seasonality of employment in agriculture, and the effective lack of

---

[38] Aldeas are defined as having between 301 and 1,000 inhabitants, and pueblos from
1,001 to 5,000.

alternative sources of year-round employment, individual workers are placed in highly competitive relationships with each other. This competition serves to keep wages low, but also enforces loyalty to growers. This loyalty is exchanged for small individual benefits such as an extra month of employment as the harvest trails off, or a promise of rehiring for the harvest that is to come (Venegas 1987).

At the same time politically important divisions have been created among different strata of the peasantry. Lingering animosities between landholding parceleros and their more politically active former partners in the land-reform co-ops (who were denied land during the subdivision process) hinder class-wide political organization. Similarly, permanent and temporary wage laborers are in substantially different positions, and have substantially different future trajectories. Even among landholding peasants there are important differences between those who have a long history of production on marginal land, and those who were beneficiaries of the agrarian reform, and generally have much higher quality land. Finally, beneath all these strata are the rural unemployed and underemployed who find themselves in constant competition with other peasants merely to eke out daily subsistence. And they are increasingly dependent on the limited welfare services provided by the state and administered by typically conservative-dominated rural municipal governments.

CONCLUSIONS

The general contention of this book is that the agricultural sector plays a critical role in facilitating the transition to a national-level competitive political regime in Chile. In the past it did so by providing a "safe haven" for the political right, because of its clientelistic control over peasant votes. This control assured the right a veto over policies that were directly threatening to its interests, and therefore lessened the risks of incorporation of the urban working class and its left-wing representatives into politics. The restructuring of agriculture that resulted in the imposition of an extreme version of a neoliberal developmental model in Chile has by no means recreated this isolated and clientelistic organization of the rural sector. It has, nonetheless, reconstituted a base for the political right in the countryside. But this time this political domination is mediated through impersonal, highly unequal, and atomized market relations. It is my contention then, that the persistence of undemocratic social relations in the rural sector has been one of the foundations that permitted a national-level transition to democracy after 1989. The recreation of a rural base for the neoliberal right, when coupled with the institutional biases of the Constitution of 1980, reduced the risks of democratic transition for conservative elites, allowing the transition to proceed smoothly. The price paid, however, was the emasculation of rural democracy.

It has been the task of this chapter to show how national-level policies of the neoliberal developmental model interfered with the social and organizational basis for rural democratic competition. The analysis has been disaggregated along four aspects of neoliberal policy: (1) trade opening and commodity price liberalization, (2) privatization, (3) creation of agricultural land markets, and (4) the creation of a functioning rural labor market. These policies have hindered rural democratization for several reasons. First, they frequently "privatize" issues that were formerly decided in the democratic arena and are of great importance to peasants. Second, these policies have erected tremendous barriers to the formation of an organizational infrastructure of secondary associations (especially unions) that are considered critical to democracy. Finally, there is an absence of informational infrastructure that is critical in the *autonomous* formation of political opinions in the rural areas. In the chapters that follow I test empirically for the decline of rural associational life and the creation of a paradoxical neoliberal electoral base predicted by the previously mentioned analysis of agrarian transformation.

4

Social Capital, Organization, Political Participation, and Democratic Competition in Chile

> In democratic countries the knowledge of how to combine is the mother of all other forms of knowledge; on its progress depends that of all others.
>
> Alexis de Tocqueville (1969, 517)

We saw in the previous chapter that the imposition of free market policies in Chile brought with it dramatic social changes, particularly in rural areas. This chapter empirically examines the effects of these neoliberal reforms on the stocks of social capital and patterns of associational life in urban and rural areas, and across time. This is the intermediate step between the economic reforms and political outcomes, linking marketization to social transformations that inhibit peasant political participation. The results indicate that economic modernization has, in addition to engendering export growth, also raised the barriers to rural collective action and expression to near-insurmountable levels, provoking social atomization, heightening peasant dependence, and thereby limiting political competition. In the chapter that follows I examine electoral effects of this organizationally arid rural environment, demonstrating the crucial role that peasants – neoliberalism's clearest victims – have played in maintaining the viability of the political right and along with it the stability of the democratic regime.

In this chapter, however, the focus is on a critical intermediate step in the overall causal chain: the contention that as a consequence of free market reforms autonomous rural political participation is not merely absent, but rather largely precluded. Because political participation generally takes the form of collective action,[1] my analysis focuses on how market-oriented economic transformation has changed the incentives peasants face to engage in group efforts to obtain collective benefits (be they demanded from the state or internally provided). In essence, the argument here is that marketization has increased markedly the problem of free riding in the rural sector, as well as raising the costs and reducing the potential benefits of participation. The withdrawal of the state from substantial involvement in agricultural production, a changed institutional environment, and the absence of powerful potential allies have radically reduced the perceived utility of collective action and its probability of success for peasants. Conversely, the destruction of communities, institutionalization of impermanent labor relations, and the evaporation of preexisting social organizations have raised the costs of organizing collective action, as well as giving the decision whether or not to participate a noniterative character. This is indeed unfriendly social terrain in which to implant the seed of democratic competition. And as a consequence, rural political competition has been decidedly anæmic.

It follows then that if marketization debilitates autonomous political participation in the countryside, it should do so because of its deleterious effects on organization and social capital more generally. It is precisely this contention that I evaluate in this chapter, showing that: (1) a formerly mobilized and organized rural sector has been reduced to near total quiescence since the advent of military rule, but not principally for reasons of repression, (2) dramatic differences in patterns of social and civic organization in urban and rural areas are present, even controlling for their most common causes: human capital, wealth, population size, and public intervention, and (3) the remaining variations in what economic organization remains are distributed in ways

---

[1] Construed narrowly, it could be taken to imply only the mere individual act of voting. Given Chile's quasi-compulsory voting and the group character that most other forms of political participation have, I emphasize the importance of a collective notion of participation. At a minimum some collective action is crucial if individual voters are merely to have access to sufficient political information to cast meaningful votes. It is from interest groups that such information typically comes – directly or indirectly through media outlets.

that support the contention that neoliberalism is the root cause of this social decay.

The collapse of associational life and political and economic protest is rendered even more stark by contrast with the realities of precoup rural life. Instead of the stereotypical quiescence and conservatism generally attributed to peasant society, by the 1960s and early 1970s, agrarian Chile was a hotbed of radical politics, dense collective organization, and militant (but peaceful) protest. Historical legacies – and collective action repertoires – should have augured for a return to radicalism once authoritarian controls were lifted in the late 1980s. This did not occur. In this chapter, I frame the paradoxical quiescence of the contemporary era against the history of radical mobilization that preceded it.

BACKGROUND: THE PEASANTRY AND COLLECTIVE
ACTION IN PRECOUP CHILE

Even in the heyday of the clientelist era (before the 1960s), characterized as it was by the overwhelming political and social dominance of large landlords, instances of peasant mobilization and organization were not uncommon (Loveman 1976; Bengoa 1988, 1990). Widespread unionization, however, would have to wait until rural labor organization effectively became legally permissible in 1967. Between 1932 and 1946, while technically legal, official recognition of peasant organizations was blocked by administrative action.[2] After 1947, a separate peasant unionization law was enacted, but its provisions were deliberately structured to make it impossible for organizations to comply with its requirements (Affonso 1988, 11). This institutional preemption of rural organization was long part of the implicit pact that had undergirded Chilean democracy since the Great Depression. As long as labor organization and leftist politics were kept out of the countryside, the great landed elites of the era would tolerate its presence and political power in urban settings. This

---

[2] Technically, during this period peasants were subject to the same labor code as urban workers. However, except for two brief periods in 1938–9 and 1946–7, the legal registration of peasant unions was blocked by administrative decree. Similarly, formal labor demands (*pliegos de peticiones*) and strikes were generally not legally recognized.

accord structured progressive action during the reformist governments of the Popular Front era (1938–52), generally confining it to urban settings.

The election of a Christian Democratic president in 1964, with follow-on legislative victories in 1965, changed the terms of this bargain in a permanent way. As part of both a broader political effort by this party to incorporate new strata of the population into the dynamics of electoral competition and an economic strategy to expand the size of the internal market for Chilean industry, President Frei implemented radical changes to the rules governing land tenure (Law 16.640 of 1967) and peasant organization (Law 16.625 of 1967). Together these changes broke the back of traditional clientelist domination, by using state power to break up landlord control over much agricultural property and facilitating countervailing organization on the part of peasants; it opened the floodgates for a wave of rural organization and mobilization.

The 1960s and early 1970s thus represented an unusually favorable conjuncture from the perspective of peasant organization and political participation. On the one hand, legal changes had dramatically reduced the barriers to rural unionization. Indeed, the 1967 peasant labor law was considered even more progressive than the prevailing urban labor code. But just as importantly, the peasantry had access to a host of potential political allies in the effort to organize and participate in politics. For example, the Catholic Church became directly responsible for training potential peasant leaders and promoting unionization through two of its organizations: the Rural Education Institute (*Instituto de Educación Rural* [IER]) and Chilean Union Action (*Acción Sindical Chilena* [ASICH]). The state became involved in the promotion of peasant organizations under the sponsorship of the INDAP. At the same time, the Communist and Socialist political parties were quite active in the promotion of more radical unions, often leveraging their strengths in the mining sector to promote agrarian organization (Petras and Zeitlin 1967; Affonso et al. 1970).

The results were impressive. Organization exploded in the countryside, with substantial numbers being attracted to both radical and more reformist unions alike. While during the Frei presidency a majority of peasant union members were affiliated with Christian Democratic confederations, the left and center were engaged in a furious struggle to gain the electoral support of this formerly unattached constituency. It is true that peasants had historically voted for conservative candidates before the 1960s, but this was principally a function of clientelist dependence and the absence of secret ballots. Once dependence was broken by state provision of social services and enforcement of labor rights, and secret ballots were introduced, rural electoral outcomes finally became credible reflections of peasant preferences. The struggle between Christian Democrats and allied leftist political forces was sharpened because of the stable but exceedingly close distributions of urban electoral support across Chile's three main political groupings: the Liberals and Conservatives on the right, the Christian Democrats in the center, and the Socialists and Communists on the left.[3] The effect was to produce a bidding dynamic between center and left for peasant votes.

The dynamics of peasant unionization in this period – both the rate at which it expanded and the political identity of the unions – are quite telling. For the purposes of comparison, it is important to remember that within the 1967–73 period peasant organization was governed by a substantially more progressive labor law than the one that currently obtains (the 1979 labor law as modified in 1992 and thereafter). In this earlier period, however, unions enjoyed compulsory dues payment as well as institutional support from the tax-funded Union Education and Extension Fund (*Fondo de Educación y Extensión Sindical* or FEES).

The organization of the peasantry thus proceeded apace. Very importantly, a process of political polarization also set in. As the peasantry became affiliated with rural unions more and more, a greater share of the membership participated in the avowedly Marxist organizations of the left. Thus, in 1968 (see Table 4.1), 75.8 percent of union members were attached to centrist or Christian Democratic confederations. By 1970, the year in which the Socialist Salvador Allende was elected to the presidency, the center accounted for 68.3 percent of a much-enlarged unionized sector. By 1972, a year before the coup, the increasing

---

[3] The actual distribution of parties was somewhat more complicated as the Liberals and Conservatives eventually merged to form the National Party, while the Socialist and Communist parties were joined on the left by a host of smaller parties, ranging from left-Catholics to segments of the Radical Party, and splinter groups that left the Christian Democratic Party.

TABLE 4.1 *Peasant Union Organization and Partisan Affiliation, 1968–72*

Confederation	1968 Members (%)	1969 Members (%)	1970 Members (%)	1971 Members (%)	1972 Members (%)
Center/Christian Democratic					
Libertad	17,206 (22.8)	23,551 (22.9)	29,105 (21.1)	34,715 (15.9)	43,798 (15.6)
Triunfo Campesino	38,618 (51.2)	48,244 (47.0)	63,642 (46.0)	51,092 (23.5)	62,073 (22.1)
Sargento Candelaria	1,394 (1.8)	1,743 (1.7)	1,605 (1.2)	2,241 (1.0)	2,989 (1.1)
Leftist/Unidad Popular					
Ranquil	18,254 (24.2)	29,212 (28.4)	43,867 (31.7)	100,299 (46.1)	132,294 (47.1)
Unidad Obrero-Campesino[a]	–	–	–	29,355 (13.5)	39,675 (14.1)

[a] The confederation Unidad Obrero-Campesino formed out of a split within Libertad. It was politically affiliated with a leftist party, MAPU, that was a part of Salvador Allende's Popular Unity (UP) government.
Sources: For 1968–9, Provoste and Cantoni (1971). For 1970–2, Salinas (1985). Percentages calculated by the author.

popularity of more radical unions as well as a political split within the Christian Democratic confederations, brought the left's share of the total up to 61.2 percent.

The social and political context of this massive wave of peasant collective action could not contrast more directly with the free market era that was to follow. Organization in the 1960s and 1970s took place overwhelmingly on traditional haciendas whose resident populations had been stable in many cases for generations. Similarly, economic conditions long had a homogenizing social effect: the conditions of labor were quite uniform within farms, and generally declining with time. In contrast to the much more fragmented and unstable environment of the free market period, grievances were clear and widely shared and the targets of mobilization were obvious – the state and the landlord. To this must be added the intensely competitive political dynamics that erupted in the countryside in the 1960s as a reformist center and a Marxist left engaged in a furious struggle for peasant allegiances, in the process introducing urban alliance partners and organization resources into the unionization effort.

THE THEORETICAL CLAIM: NEOLIBERALISM AND ANTIPOLITICS

Why has neoliberal transformation raised such high barriers to collective action in the countryside? How were the historical legacies and collective action repertoires of the past rendered inoperative? First, the disavowal by the Chilean state in many spheres of economic activity (input production, crop marketing, land redistribution, credit provision, etc.) has reduced the scale of the collective benefits that could be provided as a consequence of political action. Moreover, the likelihood of success from such activity has also declined as national-level partisan competition over rural issues is almost nonexistent and the importance of peasant votes to reformist parties is low. And because parties no longer seriously compete on rural issues, the achievement of peasant political goals then imposes a double burden: first they must force their issues onto the political agenda, and then sufficient internal and external support must be generated to actually prevail. This is a decidedly difficult task, and is in marked contrast to the 1960s and 1970s when agrarian reform and rural development stood at the center of national political debate; indeed it topped the agenda even *before* peasant mobilization exploded after 1967. Thus, with potential rewards slim and the likelihood of success even slimmer, the absence of political mobilization in the countryside is hardly surprising.

The point, however, is to understand why the relative risks and rewards of political action have changed so dramatically. To begin, neoliberal institutional reforms – particularly in the structure of the labor law – have made organization more difficult. Compulsory union membership (closed shop) is no longer legal, nor is there exclusivity of representation (one union per coherent group of workers) or a mechanism to compel even members to pay their dues (checkoff). Without state help – as is customary in most labor laws – to penalize or prevent free riding, the organization of latent groups depends entirely on resources internal to the group or on the ability of leaders to provide selective incentives. In the past, such incentives consisted of the, typically essential, intermediation of local union leaders (who were almost always affiliated with political parties) with national government agencies to obtain nominal entitlements such as pension payments or health benefits. But union leaders cannot any longer perform such intermediation. While this may explain the overall decline in unionization across Chile, it does not account for the vastly disproportionate (and uninterrupted) decline in rural-sector organization.

Thus, the change in the legal framework governing labor organization has hurt unions throughout the country. The most important causes of the much steeper organizational collapse in the countryside, however, inhere in the ways in which free market economic transformation has changed the rules of the game by which rural political participation is structured. That is, the effects of profound social transformations have been magnified greatly by the institutional reforms attendant upon liberalization, leaving a doubly hostile environment for political action or participation. For example, the problem of free riders has always been present in rural Chile, though prevailing patterns of social organization in the pre-neoliberal era served to mitigate its effects. Before the free market transformation, the decision by peasants over whether to participate in organized action to provide village-level collective goods resembled an iterated prisoner's dilemma, a situation in which cooperation is possible (Axelrod 1984).

Critically, community membership was long-standing and very stable; economic differentiation was muted; and information necessary to monitor individual participation was widely and freely available within the village. This served to build the bonds of trust and reciprocity that are essential to maintaining group activity. It was the stability of community life and membership that gave the decision whether to participate its iterative character. Indeed, not only were communities stable, but peasants typically shared a common employer (and therefore common opponent) over their entire life course, generally residing on his property. The incentive to invest effort in improving local conditions could not have been higher. The tightness and multiplicity of intra-community social ties helps to identify defectors, as well as providing mechanisms to sanction them individually. In such a context it is unsurprising that following the removal of clientelist controls in the early 1960s collective action exploded. By the 1970s, it had reached levels far beyond what the state could control or manage (Scully 1992).

But the modernization of agriculture brought with it transformations that reorganized the game of politics along the lines of a one-off prisoner's dilemma – making the decision not to participate in labor or social organizations individually quite rational even as living standards collectively declined. First, with the disruption of community life, tit-for-tat strategies become ineffective as tools to encourage cooperation: there is no guarantee that the same individuals will face each other in repeated decisions over whether to participate in group action – community membership now changes too often. Second, as marketization tore the historical social geography of the countryside apart and communities became more fluid and anonymous, the ability to monitor and punish defection declined precipitously. Third, modern agriculture (export production of fruit and vegetables) much more so than traditional agriculture (basic grains for the local market), utilizes a highly seasonal labor force. Where this form of production dominates, not only is there little residential stability, but also virtually no occupational stability. Given the enormous turnover of labor on an annual basis, few workers would expect to receive even an individual share of any collective benefits gained through labor action – it is by no means assured that they would have the same employer year by year. In such a context, concerted action may provide something less than a collective good – it may largely accrue to those who do not provide it (workers in subsequent seasons), while at best only benefiting minimally those who produce it. There can be little more unfavorable an incentive structure for collective action.

The implications of this argument extend well beyond the realm of labor relations. Consequently, the claim that social organization and thus political participation are markedly underdeveloped in the countryside is tested here in a variety of data: cross-time comparisons of the dynamics of collective action before and after military rule, and data on the spatial distribution of different types of social and civic organizations in the new democratic era (1989–2000), both within and across sectors. Specifically, if my atomization thesis is accurate, I expect that: (1) organizational participation will be most developed in urban as opposed to rural areas, even controlling for differences of resources such as wealth, population size, education, etc., (2) the degree of isolation from urban stocks of social capital and the disruption of population geography, rather than historical legacies of peasant mobilization, will explain the distribution of the surviving rural labor organization and associational life, (3) labor organization will be strongest in the segments of agriculture *least* affected by free market transformation, not those economically most vulnerable to disruption or those profitable enough to easily accommodate employee demands, and (4) there will be a marked trend toward small, narrowly economic, and depoliticized organization where it survives.

CIVIC, SOCIAL, AND ECONOMIC ORGANIZATIONS IN RURAL AND URBAN CHILE

Associational life, and the social capital that undergirds it, is difficult to measure under the best of conditions. Conceptually, social capital refers to networks of connectivity among individuals, and the patterns of reciprocity and mutual trust that they produce (Putnam 2000, 19). To the extent that these patterns are well embedded in formal organizations, they are more readily observable. But of course, especially in less developed contexts, such stocks of social capital may have a decidedly informal structure.[4] Nevertheless, for several reasons, this analysis will focus on the distribution of formal organizations in civil society. First, the Chilean peasantry has had a substantial experience with such associational patterns, dating from at least the 1950s, and thus could be expected to reconstruct it when conditions permit.

---

[4] On the possibility of very strong social norms and institutions without formal organization, see the classic statement by Thompson (1971).

Second, it is difficult to believe consistently high levels of formal organization could be sustained without strong relations of trust, reciprocity, and experience (i.e., informal organization) underlying them. Finally, we are ultimately concerned with political participation, something that by its very nature is largely based on formal organizations.

While this book deals specifically with the decline in rural political competition, the implications of its central thesis are broader. If neoliberalism engenders social atomization, its effects should also affect even entirely apolitical forms of associational life. Indeed, it is a much stronger test of the theory to examine the dynamics of social organization in both political and nonpolitical domains – it allows for critical tests against competing explanations (e.g., repression, contentment) and increases the overall confidence in the results. Thus, my take in this chapter is broader, examining the dynamics of association across the civic, economic, and social fields. And if my theoretical expectations are correct, all these areas should exhibit marked sectoral differences in the prevailing level of organization.

I begin with the most obviously "political" organizations for which data are available on a countrywide but disaggregated basis – neighborhood councils (*juntas de vecinos*). These are legally chartered groups whose input is sought by officials on local decisions. The motivation to join is explicitly political: to influence the making of local public policy. Indeed, with the ongoing administrative decentralization in Chile, these organizations should become all the more important to citizens. But because an absence of such councils may simply reflect political apathy or contentment, it is also important to examine associational forms where the motivation to join is explicitly nonpolitical.

To this end, I also analyze the distribution of sports clubs across the *comunas* (basically municipalities) of Chile. Here collective action ought to be easiest – such groups engender no political opposition, they provide benefits only to those who participate, and should on average be equally appealing across the country. Moreover, participation makes no particular demands in terms of material or educational resources on participants. If strong urban-rural differences persist on this indicator, it would certainly constitute a "hard test" for my atomization thesis.[5]

---

[5] It should be noted that religious organizations are a frequently employed indicator of social capital; and religious activists have been central to political mobilization in other countries (e.g., Houtzager and Kurtz 2000 on rural Brazil). But given the historically

Finally, and most crucially, I examine patterns of rural economic organization (labor unions). In both urban and rural Chile, labor unions have historically had an importance well beyond their significance in the workplace. While labor unions were an important organizational vehicle in civil society that facilitated the political incorporation of the urban working class after the 1920s,[6] they were historically *even more important* for the entry of the peasantry into national politics in the 1960s. This entry was delayed, as the earliest peasant labor law (Ley 8.811 of 1948) was written in such a fashion as to preclude in practice legal recognitions (Abbott 1976, 92). In fact, it has been convincingly argued (Loveman 1976; Tapia 1982; Scully 1992) that the prohibition of rural labor organization was a critical element in the stabilization of the first (pre-1973) democratic regime, at least through the early 1960s. Indeed, the ascension to power of a series of post-depression Popular Front governments involved the negotiation of a more or less explicit commitment that its social reforms and unionization efforts would be restricted to urban areas. In the rural sector, contemporary accounts like that of McBride (1936, 158) have pointed out the highly constrained, isolated, and paternalistic character of *hacienda* life. This isolation provided the rural upper class with a clientelistic political base that underwrote its political prominence in this era (Acuña et al. 1983, 1). The effective political veto that this base in the electorally overrepresented rural areas gave the political right helped to solidify its commitment to the national democratic regime.[7] Even so, during this very unfavorable era important efforts at and instances of peasant organization and mobilization took place (Loveman 1976).

It was only with the passage of the 1967 peasant labor law (Ley 16.625) that formal economic organization in the countryside became possible. And when the government ended landlord monopolies over

---

low level of church penetration in the Chilean countryside, it is an indicator that I would expect to be biased in favor of the theory I propose to test. For that reason I have not pursued this avenue of investigation.

[6] It has been argued that the *urban* working class began to be politically incorporated into the political system with the legalization of labor organization in the 1920s (Collier and Collier 1991; Scully 1992). Indeed, it was "through strong ties to political parties [that] organized workers participated in national debates" (Collins and Lear 1995, 11). The strength of labor organizations and their political connections helped the urban popular sectors to become well established as a national political actor.

[7] On rural overrepresentation see Caviedes (1979).

social provision by extending the welfare state to the countryside, old patterns of clientelistic control evaporated and independent peasant organization surged. In this context, peasant unions became interme- diators with national parties and politics – the political affiliation of unions spanned the political spectrum, and the law explicitly assigned them status as interlocutors (Ley 16.625, art. 2, especially paras. 1, 5, 12, and 13). In the post-1989 democratic era, however, no alternative interlocutor has emerged and the rural labor movement is only a pale shadow of its former self, legally barred from direct participation in politics.

Social Disarticulation in the Countryside

An absolutely essential component of the argument put forward in this book is that neoliberal economic policies have *sectorally distinct* effects on social capital and the potential for meaningful associational life. Establishing rural-urban differences, however, requires more than simply comparing outcomes across sectors. While the level of formal organization in an area in part depends on underlying social capital endowments, it also reflects resources, available population, education, and historical legacies of organization – in short the resources and opportunities that guide individual efforts at collective action. Human capital and resource indicators, be they economic or educational, are negatively associated both with rural residence and the likelihood of collective action. This requires us to estimate whether collective action is indeed much lower in the countryside even controlling for these predictors of associationalism. While such controls are not essential to testing the overall hypothesis that the rural sector is characterized by a failure of political participation, it is crucial to establishing the link between the latter and neoliberal economic reform. The results indicate a level of social disorganization in the countryside far beyond what can be accounted for by its low levels of education, high rates of poverty, or comparatively fewer institutional incentives to act politically. What associative potential the countryside has, given its poverty and low educational levels, has been vitiated by market-induced atomization.

Testing for the associational outcomes that I expect proceeds in three steps. First, I examine the extent of associational life across rural and urban areas, controlling for the effects of other factors commonly expected to promote collective organization. The measurement of associational patterns utilizes two indicators recorded at the *comuna* level: the number of neighborhood councils (civic organization) and sports clubs (social organization). Both sets of organizations are legally chartered and thus the state maintains comparable records on their existence. Only the number of such groups can be determined, not membership or extent of activity. Nevertheless, they span the spectrum of associational purpose from civic to purely social groups.

After establishing very clear urban-rural differences in associational life, the second section focuses directly on variations in associational life in the countryside. Here the emphasis will be on the rural labor union as the indicator of organization and associationalism. As noted, this form has historically been *the* essential mediator between rural actors and the political parties and national political system; a role that has not been supplanted by any other organization. Moreover, as unionization was legalized in 1979 by the military (a full decade before democratic transition), the posttransition data on organizational distribution and membership reflect medium-term outcomes, not short-term rebuilding efforts.

Across-time comparisons of rates of rural unionization show that the advent of economic liberalization (and largely *not* military-era repression) brought with it dramatic declines in organization. These are declines that have been sustained in the countryside even after the democratic transition, while in urban areas unionization remained at higher levels and rebounded somewhat after the transition. Moreover, the geographic and sectoral distribution of contemporary labor organization conforms to expectations: it is concentrated in the least modernized parts of the country and in the least transformed subsectors of agriculture.

The Urban-Rural Associational Divide

There are many quite conventional reasons that one might expect that rural associational life is underdeveloped by comparison with urban patterns. It is, for example, well established in the social movement literature that access to resources or higher levels of human capital (such as education) facilitate the formation of organizations (McCarthy and Zald 1977; Tilly 1978). And of course the larger populations found in more urban regions should produce a greater extent of associational life – there are, quite simply, more readily available opportunities to do so.

The argument of this book, however, goes well beyond what might be seen as the "normal" and cumulative associational disadvantages of rural areas born of poverty, lower skills, and distance from the state and its institutions (Bates 1981). The point here is that even controlling for all these potent effects, as a consequence of the neoliberal transformations outlined in Chapter 3, associational life in rural areas will be further sharply reduced. The cumulative effect of these disadvantages is to undermine the stocks of social capital essential to meaningful political participation, and thereby create an anæmic and elite-dominated form of rural democracy.

Do the data bear out this claim? If one accepts the prevalence of civic and sports groups as a valid indicators of prevailing stocks of social capital, then rural areas are quite associationally underdeveloped relative to urban areas even controlling for a host of demographic and human-capital variables (see Table 4.2). Two sets of models were estimated to evaluate the core hypothesis: that rural areas, *ceteris paribus*, have low stocks of social capital. The data employed are measured at the *comuna* level, and thus permit only aggregate inferences. They speak to characteristics of the comunas, but not directly (without assumptions) to the individuals within the comunas.[8]

The dependent variable in this analysis is the number of neighborhood councils found in the comuna.[9] The principal independent variable of interest is rurality: the proportion of the comuna population resident in what are defined under the 1992 Chilean census as rural

---

[8] Indeed, because social capital and associational life are characteristics of communities and not individuals, an aggregated level of analysis is appropriate. Caution must, however, be exercised if claims are made about which particular individuals are or are not likely to participate as such inferences requires strong assumptions. But inferences about comuna characteristics are appropriate.

[9] Implicitly, this analysis assumes that all such organizations are of similar size, as no membership data are available. In reality, this is not the case – those in urban areas tend to have greater membership than those in rural areas. Thus, this indicator of stocks of social capital will in comparative terms tend to *understate* levels for urban areas and *overstate* it for rural ones – biases that run directly counter to the theoretical entailments of the argument of this chapter. In this sense the measure forms an exceedingly strong test of the hypothesis.

TABLE 4.2 *Understanding Civic Life: Neighborhood Associations[a] Unstandardized OLS Coefficients, Robust Standard Errors*

Variable	MODEL I Coefficient[b]	MODEL II Coefficient	MODEL III Coefficient	MODEL IV Coefficient
(*Controls*)				
Constant	−7.458	0.0221	−3.661	0.590
	(10.687)	(11.717)	(13.329)	(13.993)
Population in 1992	0.000307**	0.000377**	0.000311**	0.00376**
	(0.000075)	(0.000073)	(0.000071)	(0.000074)
Social Disruption (Absolute Value of Population Change Rate, 1982–92)			−10.401 (13.442)	−2.071 (13.161)
Degree of State Penetration (Inhabitants per Medical Post)		−0.000367 (0.000241)		−0.00358 (0.00227)
(*Human Capital*)				
Percent of Population with 8th Grade or Less (9.5, 91.8)	0.520** (0.140)	0.421** (0.146)	0.489** (0.157)	0.417** (0.159)
Percentage of Population on Welfare (0, 0.925)	−20.296** (9.488)	−13.584 (10.189)	−19.850** (9.567)	−13.664 (13.139)
(*Sectoral Differences*)				
Rurality (Proportion of Population Rural Resident) (0, 1)	−16.163** (6.179)	−17.075** (6.052)	−16.349** (6.074)	−17.089** (6.043)
N	247	247	247	247
R^2	0.357	0.389	0.362	0.388

[a] The number of neighborhood associations is well distributed in a range from 0 to 190.
[b] OLS estimates with robust standard errors in parenthesis.
* $p < 0.10$ ** $p < 0.05$
Sources: Population and rurality, INE (1993). The remainder, for 1996, from Ministerio del Interior (1998).

areas.[10] The most crucial control in Model I (and all subsequent models) is the population of the comuna. Because the comunas are of differing population sizes, without such a control measures of associational life would be contaminated with measures of population. Greater populations almost inevitably produce more organizations. In addition, controls are introduced for measures of human capital – the extent of

[10] Typically, these are population centers containing no more than 2,000 individuals, 1,000 if secondary or tertiary sector economic activity predominates. This is obviously a very strict definition, and would tend to count some populations centers that might otherwise be classified using more common definitions as urban (INE 1993, 18).

poverty and level of education – that, while important to the formation of formal organizations, are not aspects of social capital. The educational composition of the comunas is measured by the proportion of the adult population with at least primary education (*educación básica*) or less. The extent of poverty is measured by the percentage of the population receiving poverty assistance payments – a public benefit that is targeted to the poorest segments of society (Raczynski and Romaguera 1995, 305–6).

The results of Model I (Table 4.2) are striking. The control for population is statistically significant and in the expected direction – indeed the size of its effect is robust across a variety of different specifications. The primary education completion rate found in the comuna (mean 70.3, standard deviation 13.8) is related to the degree of associational infrastructure, but in an unexpected fashion. The greater the proportion of the population in the lower tiers of educational attainment, the greater the number of neighborhood councils (once the effects of rural composition, comuna wealth, and population are controlled). This is a striking reversal of the bivariate relationship between education and associational life, which is strong, significant, and positive. Indicators of poverty, on the other hand, perform in the expected fashion, suggesting that areas of diminished resources have substantially fewer associations than their populations would suggest. Because poverty and rurality overlap to a very considerable extent in Chile (León 1994), these factors work to the cumulative disadvantage of the countryside. It is also well established that rural impoverishment has been a consequence of the neoliberal reforms as well (Petras and Leiva 1994). Thus, the countryside is doubly disadvantaged under free market conditions – both directly because of collective action problems induced by reform and indirectly because of the poverty that is its consequence.

Further insights from the collective action literature suggest that the state – through its institutional structure – can have a substantial effect on the level of collective action or organization. Particularly if there is a local institutional presence, this increases the likelihood of a payoff from collective action, as it allows actors to pursue goods restricted to a smaller group,[11] and helps to define and shape coherent collective

---

[11] This makes the payoff to concerted action more resemble a private rather than a public good, and diminishes the barriers to collective action.

interests. Of course, good measures of the *local* presence of the state are hard to come by. The indicator used here – the number of inhabitants per medical post – was chosen because it was available for all comunas, and represents one of the few forms of broad-based public provision that was not massively privatized by the military government. In fact, aspects of the health care system were expanded in the countryside, and it is a branch of the state with which most citizens interact.[12] The expectation would be that as the number of inhabitants per post increases, the level of collective organization would decrease. That is, as the state becomes comparatively less visible and relevant, incentives to organize would be diminished. The estimate produced in Model II of the effect of state presence is in the expected direction, but fails to attain statistical significance.[13]

In Model III, a control was introduced for the level of social instability present across the comunas. The measure was the absolute value of the rate of population change across the time period between the 1982 and 1992 censuses. A commonplace in the social movements and collective action literatures is that organization is most likely where communities are long-standing and stable – because such environments foster *informal* bonds of trust and reciprocity (removing the doubts about the actions of others that drive the prisoner's dilemma). Moreover, stable populations can make the dilemma of collective action resemble an iterated rather than single-shot prisoner's dilemma, and thereby increase the likelihood of concerted action. While the result in Model III is in the expected direction, because of problems of collinearity statistical significance is not attained despite a fairly large substantive-effect estimate. And to the extent to which neoliberal reforms are driving this social instability (as theorized in Chapter 3), this finding only strengthens the hypothesis being evaluated here. In Model IV, introducing further controls, no discernable effect of the degree of social disruption on organizational outcomes is found.

What is most striking, however, is that regardless of the controls utilized (Models I to IV), the effect of rural composition is substantively large and statistically significant. To the extent to which such

---

[12] Save those affluent few who are affiliated with private medical care providers in Chile.
[13] This may be a product of the crudeness of measurement or the substantial collinearity between this indicator and several other indicators included in the model.

organizations are useful indicators of the strength of rural civil society, it would seem that associational life therein is underdeveloped indeed. This is particularly true when the disproportionate impoverishment of such regions is considered alongside rurality *per se*, making for a particularly bleak civic environment.

The finding that rural areas are comparatively associationally underdeveloped is not true simply of quasi-political organizations such as neighborhood councils. The dearth of social infrastructure extends to such strictly apolitical organizations as sports clubs. Precisely because such groups are not directly political in any meaningful sense, they are crucial to the testing of the hypotheses outlined here. It is my argument that rural collective action is so difficult as to be nearly impossible – even for overtly apolitical organizations that would face no elite opposition and that provide private benefits to members (in terms of recreation). Were only political or quasi-political organizations not present in the countryside, this could reflect a peasant disinterest or satisfaction with status quo politics. When associational aridity extends to recreational life, the claim that self-organization as a practical matter is exceedingly difficult becomes much more likely.

In the second analysis, the level of social associationalism is measured by the prevalence of sports clubs (see Table 4.3). Once again, the results are in keeping with theoretical expectations – across a variety of specifications there is a dramatically lower incidence of social organization in the countryside. Interestingly, the individual level characteristics – education, poverty – that predicted *civic* associationalism seem unrelated to the level of participation in sports clubs.

Why, controlling for population, does the relative level of educational attainment and welfare dependence seem to have no effect on the number of sports clubs found in a locality? This contrasts with fairly substantial effects found in Table 4.2 when examining patterns of civic associationalism. Two potential explanations may be relevant here. The absence of an effect may be a consequence of problems of aggregation, and certainly no definitive statement about individual propensity to participate based on wealth and education should be drawn from such estimates. On the other hand, it is quite plausible that the skills and resources for which welfare dependence and education are thought to be proxies are not relevant for participation in this *type* of organization. Participation in a neighborhood council geared toward engagement

TABLE 4.3 *Understanding Cultural Life: Sports Clubs*[a]

Variable	MODEL I Coefficient[b]	MODEL II Coefficient	MODEL III Coefficient	MODEL IV Coefficient
(*Controls*)				
Constant	7.831	15.650	17.046	20.639
	(13.251)	(12.847)	(15.174)	(14.475)
Population in 1992	0.000388**	0.000411**	0.000348**	0.00403**
	(0.000107)	(0.000123)	(0.000102)	(0.00012)
Social Disruption (Absolute Value of Population Change Rate, 1982–92)			−25.243* (13.389)	−18.200 (13.237)
Degree of State Penetration (Inhabitants per Medical Post)		−0.000384 (0.000246)		−0.000303 (0.000252)
(*Human Capital*)				
Percentage of Population with 8th Grade Education or Less (9.5, 91.8)	0.245* (0.167)	0.140 (0.156)	0.171 (0.176)	0.110 (0.165)
Percentage of Population on Welfare (0, 0.925)	−5.297 (13.449)	1.718 (13.252)	−4.215 (13.328)	1.015 (13.179)
(*Sectoral Differences*)				
Rurality (Proportion of Population Rural Resident) (0, 1)	−17.117** (7.714)	−18.071** (7.524)	−17.458** (7.680)	−18.194** (7.531)
N	247	247	247	247
R^2	0.324	0.344	0.340	0.352

[a] The number of neighborhood associations is well distributed in a range from 0 to 204.
[b] OLS estimates with robust standard errors in parenthesis.
* $p < 0.10$ **$p < 0.05$
Sources: See Table 4.2.

with issues of public policy is far more class- and education-bound in its requirements than is participation in, or organization of, for example, soccer leagues.

With respect to the variable of interest from the perspective of this book, however, the results here are striking. The variables (other than the control for population size) with the greatest substantive effect on the extent of social associationalism are rurality and the level of social instability (Table 4.3, Models III and IV).[14] And these are precisely in

---

[14] While the coefficient for the level of social disruption does not attain statistical significance in Model IV, this is likely due to problems of (multi)collinearity in this fully specified model. The substantive size of the coefficient remains quite large, even given the comparative crudeness of the indicator of instability employed.

keeping with the expectations of the theory set out in Chapters 2 and 3: neoliberalism has strong socially disruptive effects, and it heightens the barriers to collective action particularly in the countryside – both directly and indirectly. Here, even in this most uncontroversial form of organization, one that brings with it inherent selective incentives for participation and is not repressed or discouraged by local elites, we still see markedly underdeveloped associational life in rural areas.

Were Peasants Always Quiescent?

Even if we grant that there is presently a substantial divide in the level of social organization and participation between urban and rural areas, it has not yet been fully established that this is a product of the neoliberal economic transformations of the military era. Alternatively, collective organization may have historically been underdeveloped in Chilean peasant communities because of unfavorable cultural characteristics (Banfield's [1958] amoral familism), general structural characteristics of agriculture (Bates and Rogerson 1980), or the relative attractiveness of unorganized and individualistic resistance strategies (e.g., Scott 1985, 1992). By contrast, the argument set forth in this book suggests that not only should rural organization and mobilization be underdeveloped relative to urban areas, but that it should have declined dramatically relative to the period of statist development before the coup.

To examine the competing hypothesis of persistent rural quiescence, patterns of peasant union organization were compared before and after the neoliberal transformation of the economy. Rural unionization has effectively been possible only in two periods of Chilean history – from 1967 to 1973 under the reformist governments of Frei and Allende, and since 1979 when the military's *Plan Laboral* relegalized both urban and rural labor organization.[15] Data on the longitudinal dynamics of rural labor organization can be found in Table 4.4.

---

[15] Obviously, the terms of the 1967 and 1979 labor laws as they applied to the rural sector were quite different, and the former was obviously more favorable to organization than the latter. Nevertheless, union legalization was meaningful in 1979, and in urban areas made organizing efforts and even strike action possible, even under military rule. Parenthetically, rural labor organization was technically legal from the passage of the 1948 Peasant Labor Law onward. In practice, however, its requirements were so restrictive as to make organization impossible until the new 1967 law was implemented.

TABLE 4.4 *Peasant Unionization before and after Military Rule[a] (as a percentage of the agrarian labor force)*

	1968	1969	1970	1971	1972	1980	1985	1992
Christian Democratic Confederations	7.7%	9.7	13.0	11.8	14.4	n.d.	n.d	1.6
Left-Affiliated Confederation	2.5	4.3	6.1	17.9	23.4	n.d	n.d	1.3
Not Affiliated with a Major Party	0.2	0.2	0.2	0.3	0.4	n.d.	n.d	1.2
TOTAL UNIONIZATION RATE (% of EAP Agriculture)	0.4	14.2	19.3	30.0[b]	38.3	14.4	6.5	4.6
Agrarian Labor Force[c] (thousands)	734	725	715	725	734	800	863	949

[a] 1968 is taken as the starting point, because the effective legalization of rural unions occurred only with the Peasant Labor Law of 1967. The suddenness of organization reflects both the strong foundation for collective action among peasants as well as the permissiveness of the law.
[b] The sudden jump in membership for the left reflects a split in the largest Christian Democratic confederation, which joined the Left (UP) alliance after the election of Salvador Allende in 1970.
[c] This includes agriculture, fishing, hunting, and forestry employment. The vast majority of persons in this category are engaged in agriculture, but fully disaggregated data were unavailable. Thus, these are slight overestimates of the agricultural labor force.
Sources: For peasant unionization by confederation, Provoste and Cantoni (1971) for 1968–9; Salinas (1985) for 1970–2, 1985; OCAC (1980) for 1980; and Ministerio de Trabajo y Previsión Social (1992) for 1992. For agricultural labor force, see FAO (2000).

The data suggest strongly that the bases for collective labor organization in the Chilean countryside have evaporated. The first wave of union legalization after 1967 was followed by a massive upsurge in organization and mobilizational activity (Kay 1981). This activity in part resulted from promotional efforts by the state, with unions affiliated with incumbent administrations expanding more rapidly than opposition unions. But across both the Frei (1964–70) and Allende (1970–3) governments, opposition-controlled organizations were also able to make rapid headway, suggesting that the impetus for organization came not simply from the state but also had a firm foundation within community structures.

Not surprisingly, the onset of military rule and the suspension of labor rights had a catastrophic effect on peasant unionization, which fell from a high of 38.3 percent of the agricultural labor force in 1972 to 14.4 percent in 1980. This corresponded in particular to the dissolution and repression of leftist unions after the coup. Christian Democratic unions, by contrast, were instead initially "suspended" in their functions rather than dissolved and directly repressed.

What is most telling, however, is that after 1980, when repression declined dramatically and union activity was actually legalized, the level of rural unionization continued to plummet. Indeed, even though the institutional structure and political environment was becoming more permissive, the characteristics of agriculture had moved in directions unfavorable to organization as a consequence of ongoing neoliberal reforms. Most critically, the reversal of the agrarian reform was not completed until 1979, and the emergence of modernized export agriculture would wait until the mid-1980s to blossom fully. Thus, as rural neoliberalism became more consolidated, the theory advanced here would predict that unionization would decline. And indeed, despite legalization, rural labor organization fell throughout the period of neoliberal reform from its already reduced 1980 level, such that by 1992, three years after democratic transition and an end to repression, it accounted for only 4.6 percent of the agricultural labor force. This is less than a third the level it reached in 1980 in the midst of military rule. While repression obviously succeeded in reducing the level of rural organization, it was marketization that appears to have sealed the fate of the peasant unions. Were repression the key explanation of union decline, membership would have reached a nadir in the mid-1970s when it was most severe and then recovered as political, legal, and human-rights conditions improved throughout the 1980s.

The contrast between the pre- and post-liberalization periods also could not be more striking. Not only did peasants organize themselves widely in the 1967–73 period, the level of mobilization they exhibited was extraordinary. By 1970–2, this culminated in a wave of land invasions that seized over 1,700 large farms, nearly a third of all the large agrarian properties in the country (Marín 1972). Nor was organization confined to the unions. The local peasant councils (*consejos comunales campesinos*) created during the Popular Unity administration of Allende opened terrain for the representation of unorganized peasants and those who were not reform beneficiaries. These also expanded rapidly, and were frequently the site of substantial opposition representation, not simply of the leftist parties that initially promoted them (for discussions, see Maffei and Marchetti 1972; Acuña et al. 1983, 24).

TABLE 4.5 *Mobilizational Stasis under Military Rule: Strikes and Contracts in Agriculture,[a] 1984–90*

Year	Contracts	Coverage	Percent Agricultural EAP	Strikes
1984	57	2,447	0.43	1
1985	78	3,140	0.40	1
1986	103	4,428	0.54	0
1987	131	5,478	0.63	4
1988	115	5,390	0.61	7
1989	173	6,993	0.85	6
1990	178	8,967	1.09	11

[a] Actually includes agriculture, fishing, hunting, and silviculture.
Sources: Calculated from Dirección del Trabajo (1990, 1991). For agricultural EAP, ODEPA 1992 (1989–90). For 1984–9, Banco Central de Chile (1991).

Obviously military rule was not conducive to widespread urban or rural labor organization and the enforcement of collective rights, even after the 1979 labor law was implemented. As a result it is particularly telling that three years after democratization, levels of peasant unionization had declined from military-era lows. Moreover, as the data in Table 4.5 show, the unions that did form were lacking in mobilizational capacity. Over the period from 1984 through the end of military rule, the percentage of the agricultural labor force covered by a binding collective agreement never exceeded one percent, and strike activity was almost nonexistent. Thus, if the organizational capacity of the peasantry is measured by this more demanding but also historically crucial metric – unionization – a shocking low level of activity is evident. This contrasts, however, markedly with the organizational capacity that was preserved *despite* repression and economic liberalization in other sectors of the economy. Not only were copper miners able to defend their unions and wages and initiate bitter strikes during the course of military rule, they were also capable of convoking large-scale urban protests by the mid-1980s (Garretón 1986). Peasants were, by contrast, capable of only the smallest of strikes, and these only exceedingly rarely.[16]

---

[16] Indeed, were it not for the mobilizational efforts of Mapuche indian communities in the south of Chile, there would be almost no strike activity. Virtually the only organized *rural* protest during the course of military rule came in these areas, which

IS MARKETIZATION CAUSING RURAL DEMOBILIZATION?

It has been the contention of this book that the stagnation in rural associational life and the evaporation of a formerly potent peasant labor movement are consequences of the progress of free market economic reform. Previously we saw that there are very substantial urban-rural differences in organization, and that once widespread rural labor mobilization has declined into insignificance. But how can it be shown that this was a consequence of free market policies? In the following text I examine the distribution of postdemocratization rural labor organization, with an eye to testing hypotheses that would suggest organization is weakest in the most rural regions, and in those subsectors *most* affected by market transformations – that is, I use intrasectoral variation in the extent of liberalization to test key causal mechanisms. This test is made more stringent because more remote areas were a crucial locus of mobilization in the precoup period, and thus had strong preexisting repertoires of collective action. Similarly, the most reformed areas, characterized by modern agro-export production, have far greater resources to cope with any economic demands that agricultural laborers might make and are much more vulnerable to even brief interruptions in labor supply. If elite resistance to unionization should be weaker anywhere, it is here.

Making this case also requires an evaluation of several alternative hypotheses. Theories of collective action have highlighted the importance of leadership and the incentives embedded in institutional rules in explaining organizational outcomes. While I concur that such variables are typically of importance, they are of little help in explaining the paucity of organization in Chilean rural society. Collective inaction persists despite the organizational efforts of a host of peasant leaders who were trained in the 1950s and 1960s by the state or the Catholic Church and had experience in organizing collective action during the tumultuous process of agrarian reform. With respect to changing institutional structures, obviously the end of agrarian

---

are also the only regions where bases of collective identity and solidaristic bonds were not eviscerated by liberalization (see Gacitúa 1989 on the mobilizations). Ethnic solidarities could be relied upon to build organization in a way that was untrue of most of the countryside outside this comparatively small community (nationally, around 5 percent of the population).

reform and the advent of a new labor law in 1979 are of great importance. Though the former is an aspect of rural marketization, and the latter is an institutional structure identical for urban and rural workers; as a consequence, it is poorly suited to explain differences across these sectors.

Variations in Rural Marketization and Social Organization

My argument about the corrosive effects of neoliberal policies on rural social life hinges on the inability of those in the countryside to utilize *urban* stocks of social capital and sources of information. Thus, it is in those areas most removed from urban centers that the dynamics I hypothesize should be most starkly manifested. In practice, of course, rural areas are not always wholly separated from proximate urban centers in either social or geographic terms. It is this variation that allows for further examination of the liberalization/demobilization thesis. In quantitative terms, the most rural comunas showed the lowest levels of agricultural unionization. In addition, the *degree* to which neoliberalism has transformed agriculture varies substantially. Its effects should be most pronounced in the new agro-export sectors it created by displacing the traditional production system, and it is thus in those areas I expect organization to be weakest. By contrast, in areas still dominated by the production of traditional crops under less modernized conditions, organization should be strongest. This is true despite the fact that such producers are financially ill-equipped to accommodate union demands.

The first specific hypothesis to be examined is that the most rural regions of Chile will be the least organized. This is somewhat counterintuitive in light of the literature on peasant social movements that has tended to highlight the importance of autonomous communities as a crucial support for mobilization (Scott 1976, 1985; Magagna 1991) and the empirical reality of its concentration in the most remote of regions even under conditions of severe repression (e.g., Peru, El Salvador, Colombia, and Mexico). This was true also of Chile before 1973, where comparatively remote Southern areas were the first (and most extensively) mobilized agricultural regions. Of course, part of the point of this book is that rural marketization has destroyed the aspects of population settlements that could meaningfully be described

TABLE 4.6 *Peasant Union Membership and Density by Rural Population Composition, 1992*

Portion of Comuna Population Residing in Rural Areas	Total Rural Population	Number of Comunas	Union Membership[b]	Ratio of Union Membership to Rural Population[a]
0.0 to 30.0%	488,961	115	23,093	5.1%
30.1 to 69.9	1,141,835	128	15,296	1.3
70.0 to 100.0	617,200	92	4,407	0.7

[a] It would be better to measure this in terms of the ratio between union membership and economically active population in agriculture. The latter data are not available, however, at the comuna level. These numbers are directly proportional to this union density, however, as long as the likelihood of a rural resident to work in agriculture is more or less constant across comunas.
[b] The total of this column is slightly less than the sum of union membership given previously because comuna of origin could not be ascertained for a small number of rural unions.
Sources: Calculated from Ministerio de Trabajo y Previsión Social (1992) for union membership and INE (1993) for population data.

as "community" in the same sense as in the past. As a consequence, the further such settlements are from surviving urban sources of social capital and associational life, the more atomized and unorganized they will be.

Explanations of labor organization emphasizing institutional constraints might expect a uniformly lower level of organization across the agrarian sector. This is particularly the case when it is remembered that a hallmark of the neoliberal model has been the avoidance of strong sectoral or regional foci in economic policy making. But precisely the opposite is the case. Table 4.6 presents the level of peasant union density found across the comunas of Chile disaggregated by population composition.

Table 4.6 demonstrates the extent to which the peasant union membership is concentrated in the rural parts of the most urbanized comunas. It is also interesting to note that outside of the highly urbanized comunas (those less than 30 percent rural), agrarian union membership plummets. This tends to confirm the hypotheses that access to urban-based political allies or organizational support, lower levels of dependence, and more open spaces in local civil society are important determinants of the likelihood of individual peasants to organize. What is most striking is the nonlinearity of this relationship. Past a certain, quite-urbanized, threshold, unionization falls to almost zero levels. This is particularly surprising because there is cause to believe that in such highly rural areas inequalities would tend to be most starkly manifest, and "exit" options most drastically curtailed. In such a case some social movement scholarship would expect collective mobilization. Here, grievances would be most clearly experienced, leaving cultivators with no clear individual alternatives and little to lose in material terms from oppositional organizing. But precisely the opposite is the case in free market Chile.

Subsectoral Variation

Just as striking as the differences between urban and rural areas with respect to union membership are the differences in the level of organization across agricultural subsectors. The impact of the neoliberal revolution has made itself most strongly felt in the creation of modern, profitable, highly capitalized agro-export subsectors. In abstract terms, one would expect to see trade union organization most strongly formed in this subset of Chilean agriculture. It is here that modern production relations and the transition to capitalist wage labor are most deeply entrenched. The relative profitability of this set of products, their vulnerability to even short-run disruptions of labor inputs, and their amenability to increased productivity through capital investment all suggests that these growers would have both an incentive and the economic room to maneuver to accommodate the organization of their labor forces (for a analogous argument see Paige 1975, ch. 2). Their resistance should be lower than in the profit-starved, domestically oriented traditional sector. Surprisingly, however, the modern agro-export enterprises, despite being the largest employers of wage labor in agriculture – accounting for roughly 300,000 agricultural workers – are comparatively un-unionized (Venegas 1993, 46). Table 4.7 suggests that even in the export-oriented Central Valley, it is the *traditional*[17] farms that are organized.[18]

[17] The phrase "traditional crops" applies to the basic foods, generally destined for the local market, that were common before the rise of a substantial export-oriented sector. They include most importantly, wheat, corn, beans, potatoes, lentils, and sugarbeets.
[18] Only the Central Valley (inclusive of the Metropolitan Region) is here considered, because export agriculture is climatologically precluded in the South, making cross-subsector comparisons impossible there.

TABLE 4.7 *Central Valley Peasant Union Membership by Agricultural Subsector, 1992 (union membership, column percentages)*

	Central Valley (IV–VII)	Metropolitan; Region (XIII)
Traditional	8,435	7,894
Crops	(48.3)	(70.9)
Vineyards	1,885	521
	(10.8)	(4.7)
Nontraditional	2,775	1,152
Exports	(15.9)	(10.4)
Livestock	1,742	1,229
Related	(10.0)	(11.0)
Agricultural	2,638	333
Services	(15.1)	(3.0)

Source: Ministerio de Trabajo y Previsión Social (1992).

Even within the heartland of agrarian neoliberalism, the preponderance of union organization is in the least modernized productive segments. Employment in modern fruit export agriculture amounts to roughly 45 percent of the overall agricultural labor force in the Central Valley (calculated from GIA 1991, vols. IV–VII, XIII), based on an estimate of roughly 200,000 such workers. This is a conservative estimate compared to Venegas (1993) who suggests the number is closer to 300,000.[19] But, as can be seen from Table 4.7, workers in nontraditional exports comprise a mere 15.9 percent of unionized workers in the Central Valley (IV–VIII), and an even smaller 10.4 percent of those in the Metropolitan Region (XIII). It is instructive that in the most modernized areas of Chilean agriculture, it is the crops produced using traditional practices that are most strongly unionized. It is all the more striking given the tremendous emphasis that peasant union leaders have placed on organizing the workers in the new export crops, the greater vulnerability of such crops to work stoppages, and the greater financial flexibility of such employers to grant material concessions.[20]

---

[19] This estimate is derived by dividing the land area planted in fruit crops by the number of employees required per hectare as derived by various local studies.

[20] Leaders of the Christian Democratic, Socialist, and Communist peasant unions all independently emphasized this as one of their central priorities.

Organizational Form

The Chilean labor legislation in effect at the time of democratic transition defines three distinct types of organization: (1) enterprise unions, legally entitled to compulsory collective bargaining, (2) independent unions for workers not dependent on any particular employer, and (3) interenterprise unions for workers employed at more than one firm.[21] Given their larger size, more heterogeneous membership base, and lesser ability to provide selective *or* collective benefits, the latter two forms of organization ought to be the most difficult to construct, though in political-representational terms they would be the most valuable. Indeed, in structure they resemble the geographically based peasant unions that had a vital intermediating role in precoup Chilean democracy. The variations of organizational form among surviving Chilean peasant unions is as expected – where unionization has emerged in the most modernized subsectors of agriculture, it is concentrated in the least demanding enterprise form. Broader and more class-based unionism is prevalent only among less reformed, traditional subsectors.

Independent and interenterprise unions require a comparatively motivated and socially active membership base. In collective action terms, they ought be difficult to establish. They lack a clear-cut occupational grouping, have members who work for different employers, have more varied material grievances, and do not have the same potential to win concrete rewards in terms of collective bargaining that the enterprise unions can. Both independent and interenterprise unions also tend to be larger in size than enterprise unions, raising the level of personal motivation required to overcome the tendency of larger groups to experience free-rider problems (Olson 1965). The average enterprise union in the Central Valley has 45.13 members (Metropolitan Region, 45.66), while independent unions average 59.5 (61.1) and interenterprise unions 158.1 (260.1) (calculated from Ministerio de Trabajo y Previsión Social 1992). Because of their limited ability to win "bread and butter" benefits, as well as their substantially greater membership heterogeneity, these latter types of unions necessarily require more ideological supporters. With fewer material selective incentives for

---

[21] See Código del Trabajo de 1992, libro I, tit. I, cap. I, art. 5 for complete descriptions.

membership, one would expect higher levels of solidarity or class consciousness to be present in order to overcome free-rider and other problems of collective action.

This difference between enterprise and nonenterprise unions is important from the perspective of my broader argument. I have contended that labor organizations have historically been crucial mediators between the democratic system and the peasantry; they have also been vital to the expansion of democratic social relations to rural areas (Scully 1992). For example, the formation of geographically based unions under the 1967 Peasant Labor Law (Ley 16.625) provided a critical venue in civil society in which peasants could meet with each other,[22] and understand their shared interests *beyond* the confines of their isolated *hacienda* or smallholding.[23] In addition, the local unions and their parent federations and confederations provided coherent mechanisms for aggregating these interests into a force that was politically relevant on the national level (Petras and Zeitlin 1967, 581).

But it has also been my contention that the reforms initiated under the hegemony of neoliberal policy makers have undermined these democratizing features of rural labor organization. One of the explicit functions assigned labor organizations under the 1967 peasant labor law was the *political* representation of the collective interests of rural cultivators. Neoliberal labor reforms, while legalizing labor organization and narrow collective bargaining, sought to destroy the political and representational aspects of the labor movement. The socioeconomic restructuring of the 1970s and 1980s has, I believe, undermined the very notion that a coherent peasant identity even exists (Houtzager and Kurtz 2000).

As a result, I expect that the segments of Chilean agriculture most affected by the transformation of agriculture will be *least* likely to have broader geographically based forms of labor organization and will tend to be moderate or apolitical. Nonenterprise forms of organization would imply a much broader view of the position of rural laborers. This position is somewhat counterintuitive given the characteristics of

---

[22] In fact, the law imposed a requirement on employers to provide just such a venue, under the exclusive control of the workers (Ley 16.625, art. 13).

[23] Caviedes (1991, 44) finds the absence of such spaces a crucial explanation of the high "yes" vote in the 1988 plebiscite on continued authoritarian rule in rural areas.

TABLE 4.8 *Union Membership by Economic Activity and Type of Organization in the Central Valley, 1992ª (percent)*

	Union Type		
	Enterprise	Independent	Interenterprise
Enterprise			
Less Modernized Domestic Production			
Traditional Grains	13.7%	51.3	35.1
Livestock	74.6	12.4	13.4
Export-Oriented Production			
Vineyards	67.7	1.2	31.0
Nontraditional (Fruit, Vegetables)	58.6	11.7	29.7

ª Only the Central Valley is considered here as the agro-climatic conditions of Southern Chile preclude export agriculture, and would thus make cross-subsector comparisons therein impossible.

Source: Calculated from Ministerio de Trabajo y Previsión Social (1992).

agro-export production. Wages, working conditions, and opportunities for mobility are broadly similar within this subsector, while employment relations tend to be unstable and impermanent. Thus, for many of the modern agro-export industries an interenterprise organizational form would at first blush appear most logical.

The results of Table 4.8 are notable. Only the Central Valley areas (including the Metropolitan Region) have been included because only here is the production of both nontraditional and traditional crops, and hence a comparison, possible. The relevant contrast is between the types of organization prevalent in traditional and nontraditional crops. Not only, as we have seen, are the fruit crops less likely to be unionized, but they are also more likely to have the most restrictive form of organization – the enterprise union. While only 13.7 percent of unions in the traditional sectors of agriculture were of the enterprise type, fully 58.6 percent of those in fruits and other nontraditionals were of this type. Despite tremendous homogeneity in wages and work settings, the modern sector – where unionized – has the most narrow and apolitical form of organization.

Alternative Explanations

The most obvious of the alternative explanations for organizational decay is simply that there is an absence of effort being put forward to

mobilize peasants. Important currents in the literature on peasant social movements have highlighted the critical role of educated, skilled,
nonpeasant organizational entrepreneurs in spurring peasant mobilization (Wolf 1969; Popkin 1979). And the presence of a trained cadre of
nonpeasant organizers has been seen as a critical catalyst for the rapid
expansion of unions and cooperatives during the 1967–73 period by
Chilean specialists as well (Affonso et al. 1970). These outsiders provided certain crucial material and organizational resources as well as
nuclei around which unions could form. A second hypothesis holds
that the principal barrier to organization resides in the restrictive features of the national labor law. That is, it is a problem of institutional
constraints, not the neoliberal reorganization of rural social relations.
This tends to be the preferred explanation among peasant union leaders
and many Chilean analysts. Finally, it is my contention that the social
and economic consequences of neoliberal agricultural "development"
have seriously undermined the bases in civil society for autonomous
collective grievance formation and interest organization.

The first alternative can be quickly dispensed with on empirical
grounds. In fact there is no dearth of organizational effort in the
countryside. Four competing national peasant union confederations
and one provincial federation have all launched organizing drives.
Foreign-sponsored NGOs have attempted to foment the organization
of seasonal workers, especially women, as part of their developmental
projects. Several private research institutes have also launched agricultural extension programs and training projects for peasant leaders specifically aimed at labor and union issues. Finally, the Catholic
Church has been active in seeking self-reliance-oriented rural organization. It is *not* for lack of nonpeasant support that peasant unionization
has not reemerged, even if one accepts as given the inability of peasants
to self-organize. Nor have most of the peasant leaders of the past, and
the organizational skills they literally embody, disappeared from the
scene. Many remain active in the rural labor movement.

But are features of rural social organization the principal barrier
to mobilization, or is it the absence of urban-based organizational entrepreneurs that explains the increasing marked absence of collective
behavior in more rural areas? Analysis of the Metropolitan Region,
where all comunas are in relatively close proximity to the Santiago-
based peasant union leaders, suggests that the structural organization

of rural areas matters more than propinquity to an urban leadership cadre. As rurality increases within the Metropolitan Region, even in this stronghold of peasant unionization, union density declines to the level common in the South.

Adjudicating between my own explanation and the remaining alternative is difficult, and to some extent an exercise in counterfactual reasoning.[24] Many observers, though by no means all, have focused on the legal impediments to rural unionization. The stark contrasts between the labor laws applicable to the peasantry between 1967 and 1973, and after the imposition of the 1979 *Plan Laboral* have also been highlighted. After 1979, the urban and rural sectors were governed under the same legal-institutional framework. In urban areas, however, a much higher level of unionization was maintained throughout the period of military rule, and a substantial – if somewhat fleeting – expansion occurred after the transition to a competitive regime. In the countryside, however, a high level of unionization was not maintained during military rule, and organization continued to decline after the democratic transition.

While the institutional rules governing unionization do have something to do with the strength of organized labor in all of Chile, they are not, by themselves, a compelling explanation of the inordinately low level of specifically rural unionization. For this, the explanation must be rooted in the distinctive characteristics of Chilean agriculture – features that were created in the process of free market reform.

CONCLUSIONS

The point of this chapter has been to consider seriously the causal mechanisms implicit in the agrarian liberalization argument set forth in Chapters 2 and 3. There it was claimed that free market reforms have powerful political implications through the manner in which they transform rural civil society and associational life. Specifically, they make peasant collective action so impracticable as to render

---

[24] That is, the two competing explanations could be evaluated directly only if there were a substantial policy change either in the labor law, or in the organization of the agricultural mode of production.

autonomous political participation unlikely at best, leaving the rural political terrain fertile soil indeed for the dominance of conservative local elites.

This chapter has used a series of subnational, intertemporal, and intrasectoral comparisons to evaluate the empirical implications of the theoretical argument connecting agrarian economic liberalization with organizational and political demobilization in Chile. First, I have endeavored to show that patterns of peasant organization vary across time in relationship to the prevailing pattern of economic organization – statist and free market. Second, in the contemporary free market context, I show the sharp contrast between the prevalence of social and civic organizations in rural and urban areas, even controlling for the usual predictors of such participation and collective action. Finally, within-sector analysis shows that variations in the extent and depth of agrarian transformation are inversely correlated with the fortunes of the agrarian labor movement as expected.

In the chapter that is to come I move on to consider the political implications of the social consequences of agrarian marketization. That is, the overall argument of this book has been that contemporary democracy is stabilized in economically liberal settings as a consequence of the ways in which it helps to create an electoral bastion for free market parties in the countryside. Chapter 5 directly examines whether such a base has been constructed and whether its emergence can fairly be attributed to neoliberal reform and its rural social effects.

5

The Consolidation of Free Market Democracy and Chilean Electoral Competition, 1988–2000

The argument of this book has been that the success and consolidation of the Chilean democratic transition has hinged on the construction of an unlikely but stable base of electoral support for conservative, neoliberal parties in the countryside. As we saw previously, the rural social transformations induced by free market economic restructuring both undermined the previous foundations of mobilized and radicalized peasant political expression characteristic of the 1960s and early 1970s, and produced a level of fragmentation and dependence that engendered a new, market-based vulnerability to the influence of agrarian elites. Most crucially, the associational consequences of economic liberalization were so devastating for peasants as largely to preclude autonomous political participation. And thus, despite the striking and disproportionate increase in rural inequality and poverty during the course of the free market reforms, peasants in democratic Chile are among the strongest supporters of the parties identified with military neoliberalism. This in turn, however, has facilitated the consolidation of democracy.

In this chapter, I seek to demonstrate that a durable rural electoral base for the neoliberal right has been constructed that cannot be explained by the principal alternative approaches: the legacies of repression and authoritarianism, material self-interest, or even the oft-cited traditional conservatism of peasants. Instead, I have proposed that social atomization and collective action problems caused by free market policies are critical to understanding posttransition electoral outcomes in the countryside – and hence the nation. This formulation has a series of counterintuitive implications that I empirically assess in this chapter: (1) in general, electoral support for the neoliberal right should be substantially higher in rural areas than in urban ones; (2) in those comparatively rare instances in the countryside where social organization and capital have survived economic liberalization, support for neoliberal parties should be markedly lower than the prevailing sectoral norm; and (3) material interests likely shape urban voters' political behavior, but this should not be the case for peasants. That is, while poverty should be positively related to support for reformist center-left forces in urban settings, the opposite relationship should hold in the countryside – the poorest and most disadvantaged strata will be the most conservative. This is because in rural areas poverty implies much more atomization, economic dependence on local elites, and an inability to aggregate interests independently. The results are supportive of all three hypotheses. Neoliberal parties have indeed established an important political bastion among the rural victims (and urban winners) from economic reform, while by contrast the urban poor are largely supporters of the reformist center-left Concertación alliance.[1]

This is not the first analysis to suggest that some form of limitations on the range of potential electoral outcomes in a putative posttransition democratic political system are essential if authoritarian elites are to voluntarily cede power. But this "outcome insurance" has typically been seen in strictly institutional terms. The conventional emphasis in the literature on Chile, for example, has been on the role of constitutional guarantees of military autonomy, central bank independence, the presence of unelected senators appointed in part by the armed services, district gerrymandering, or the unusual "binomial" electoral system. The approach here, while rooted in on social dynamics, is in no way designed to refute these findings. Instead, it is an essential complement to these more common institutionalist explanations – and indeed one without which they would be unconvincing.

My claim is that the more typical emphasis on outcome-restricting institutions, while appropriate as a first step, often leaves us with an incomplete understanding of the emergence of these institutions, as

---

[1] More formally, the alliance is known as the Concertación de Partidos por la Democracia, or Alliance of Parties for Democracy.

well as with a need to investigate further *why* the incentives embedded in them provide advantages specifically for the neoliberal right. It is only in conjunction with an understanding of social organization and societal preferences that the political effect of institutional structures can usually be clearly defined. The focus here is thus on the factors generally taken as givens in earlier work. I provide an explanation of the social structures and dynamics within which the institutional rules and the political processes of Chilean democracy have developed.

In Chile more than in many cases, the structure of political institutions was a relatively autonomous choice made by the military government. This was true of both the writing of the Constitution of 1980, as well as the crucial Organic Constitutional Laws of 1988–9 that set the specific framework for posttransition democratic politics. An emphasis on sectoral social dynamics, however, helps render many of these choices intelligible – for example, explaining why rural areas were so dramatically overrepresented, why the unusual binomial electoral rule for converting votes into seats was selected, and why the rules governing political and campaign activity are so restrictively structured. Moreover, without an understanding of sectoral social dynamics, it is impossible to understand why these institutions provide a *durable* check on the power of reformist political forces. Electoral rules create winners and losers, but without a coequal understanding of the likely distribution of preferences (or at least votes), it is impossible to understand which political forces they help or harm.

Many of the crucial institutional choices made by the military government were designed to magnify the effects of its social base in the countryside, and thereby transform it into the foundation of a legislative veto over illiberal policy initiatives. Thus, my starting point is to examine how the military's knowledge of its new rural support shaped three crucial aspects of the organization of posttransition Chilean politics: the bias in legislative representation, the binomial electoral system, and rules governing electoral competition. Each of these institutions helps consolidate and magnify rural electoral support for free market forces on the political right, thereby purchasing their commitment to democratic politics. The binomial (two-member district) electoral system (described in the following text) magnifies the influence of the second-place political party – where the military expected the neoliberal right to be – while threatening the third-place force with legislative annihilation; it was anticipated that this would be the Social-ist/Communist left. The districts were also constructed with such an outcome in mind, and rural areas were distributed among constituen-cies to ensure that the political right was able in general to achieve at least second place, and thus usually at least one of the two seats available. Constituency borders are also not subject to redistricting to account for population changes, implying that rural overrepresentation will only increase with time. Finally, campaign rules were structured in a way that helped to continue the isolation of the peasantry from national (and specifically reformist) political parties. Under the guise of avoiding excessive "politicization," they make it difficult for polit-ical parties to reconstruct the deep ties to society and social organiza-tions that they once had. Of course, this creates political entry barriers for rural challengers seeking to compete with the locally dominant neoliberal parties and elites. But without just such allies and alterna-tives, peasants are unlikely to be able to engage in meaningful political expression.

Ultimately, the combination of free markets transition and institu-tional change has permitted the neoliberal right in Chile to construct a broad coalition of peasants, urban elites, and middle-sector voters. I contend that this unlikely outcome is only possible, however, because of the social consequences of economic reform. Thus, if my argument is correct, the *distribution* of electoral support for the right should com-port with the variations in the depth of economic reform outlined in Chapters 3 and 4. That is, at a minimum, rural support for neolib-erals ought be substantially greater than in urban areas and it must persist across time (it cannot be the result of immediate posttransition fear of reversal or the legacies of repression). Similarly, rural support for neoliberals should be strongest where the atomizing effects of eco-nomic liberalization have been most severe. Nor should material in-terest weigh heavily – while I would expect poverty to be associated with support for reformist forces, who have emphasized social welfare, only in urban Chile. I would expect the opposite in rural areas because poverty could be taken as an indicator of the very dependence and vulnerability that I hold undergirds neoliberal rural electoral support. Finally, dominance by the right cannot be a simple recreation of its historic areas of strength as I have argued that the traditional agrar-ian social order, and its associated social structure, was destroyed by the progressive (and regressive) land reforms of the 1960s and 1970s. Instead, rural support for the right is based on peasant poverty and vulnerability, as mediated by the disorganizing pressures of free market transformation.

INSTITUTIONAL TRANSFORMATION AND THE NEW RURAL ORDER

Most studies of posttransition Chilean politics have emphasized the role of institutional features of the political regime in their discussions of democratic consolidation and deepening (Munck 1994b; Rabkin 1996; Siavelis 1997; Londregan 2000). But this has bracketed two deeper questions: (1) what accounts for the particular institutional structures chosen by the outgoing military government? and (2) why do the biases built into these rules consistently work to the benefit specifically of conservative, free market parties? The goal thus is *not* to discount the importance of the institutional incentives that shape political competition, but rather to understand their origin and explain why they produce particular political outcomes.[2] The point is that the institutional "safeguards" that the Chilean military built into the structure of posttransition politics can only be understood with reference to political effects of neoliberal transformations in rural areas. Most crucially, these include the strong overrepresentation of peasants in *both* chambers of the legislature, the use of a "binomial" electoral law to translate seats to votes, and the strict rules governing political mobilization and campaigning. In each case the rules were chosen to protect and expand the right's position in the legislature and thus its ability to veto potentially threatening policy changes.

For this to be the case, however, the military must have been aware of the sectoral political implications of free market reform at the time

---

[2] The point here is that the analysis of institutional rules alone can elucidate some features of political competition (e.g., whether the rules favor small or large parties, encourage fragmentation, or the like). But an understanding of the social underpinnings of contending political forces and their capacities of organization and projection are necessary to fully understand the specifically political (or ideological) implications they have. In the present case it helps to show why and how they function as "safeguards" for neoliberal elites. Strictly institutional approaches simply take the distribution of preferences or strength of political forces as exogenous.

the institutions were defined. I do not, however, argue that free market policies were chosen because of their political consequences. Indeed, it is almost certainly the case that the Chilean military did not know when it implemented its experiment with free market economics what the precise social and political implications would be.[3] But by the latter part of the authoritarian period, it is evident that military leaders began to see the reconstruction of a rural political base as quite important, and an important part of this involved rebuilding its ties with rural elites (Kurtz 1999a, 419–23).

What is critical is that when the time came – quite late in the authoritarian period – to define posttransition politics, the military was well aware of the strength and location of its political support. This was possible because the rules governing democratic politics were not specifically spelled out in the Constitution of 1980. Instead, they were fleshed out only in the organic constitutional laws[4] enacted in late 1988 and 1989. Fortunately from the perspective of military planners this was *after* the results of the 1988 plebiscite on continued military rule were known. Not only had the population solidly (but not overwhelmingly) rejected a continuation of authoritarianism in this vote, but it had also clearly identified the location and size of the bastions of support and opposition to the dictatorship. This information was then used to help guide the selection of electoral rules (favoring the first minority) and the shape of the districts (overrepresenting the conservative countryside). The result was the creation of a credible political base for neoliberal parties under open politics, one large enough to block threats to vital interests.

It is true that the institutional "safeguards" that the military imposed on posttransition politics did not all hinge for their efficacy on the rural electoral redoubt. Most notable in this regard are the presence of unelected senators representing powerful political institutions,[5] the

---

[3] It was not even clear at the onset of military rule what the general direction of economic policy would be, much less its political effects (Vergara 1984; Silva 1996).

[4] Organic constitutional laws occupy an intermediate status between constitutional provisions and ordinary statutes. They require substantial supermajorities in both houses of the Congress to be amended, but less than the two-thirds vote required for constitutional changes.

[5] These include representatives chosen from among former leaders of the four armed service branches, the judiciary, the controller-general's office, and an ex-rector of the national university.

autonomy of the military from direct civilian oversight, Central Bank autonomy, and the presence of a powerful National Security Council with oversight functions. Tellingly, however, in the give and take in 1989 over the reform of the political institutions called for in the 1980 Constitution, the military was willing to compromise on many of the issues *not* connected to its rural base. The weight of the appointed senators was reduced by expanding that body's membership, the influence of Pinochet-era appointments to the Central Bank were reduced, and the National Security Council was stripped of its military majority and direct oversight functions. But the importance of the rural base is reflected in the rejection of demands to replace the binomial (two-member district) electoral system with traditional Chilean proportional representation, or to correct the population biases and gerrymandered electoral district boundaries, which are not subject to periodic adjustment. More recently, the conservative opposition has indicated a willingness to consider amending the constitution to remove the unelected senators (*La Tercera* June 16, 1997). But reforms that would directly affect the weight of its rural base (either through redistricting or through a return to Chile's historic reliance on proportional representation) have so far been political nonstarters (*La Tercera* December 11, 2002).

Rural Bias

The reliance of the military on the rural sector to guarantee the stability of the neoliberal order under democratic politics is apparent in the way in which it constructed electoral districts and magnified the influence of rural voters. Indeed, in many ways the weight of rural voters in national politics now parallels that period of clientelist domination that preceded the social reforms of the 1960s. In both cases, the stability of national-level democracy hinged the legislative veto that conservative parties had over threatening policies based on the representatives they could elect with solid peasant support. What has changed is not the role the rural sector plays in national politics, but the very different way that agrarian neoliberalism has helped to construct this conservative electoral base.

It is true that Chilean democracy has always tended to overrepresent rural interests in the legislature. The Constitution of 1925 established one deputy per 30,000 inhabitants, based on the census of 1930. The resultant 147 seats were distributed among twenty-nine electoral units, and within these they were assigned using proportional representation (D'Hondt system). With the exception of the addition of three deputies in 1969 for new districts in the extreme South, seats were never reapportioned to account for population changes between 1925 and 1973. Given the massive rural-to-urban migration during these decades, substantial rural overrepresentation resulted (Caviedes 1979, 51–2). Because conservative elites exercised clientelistic control over this rural population for much of the precoup democratic era, they maintained an effective legislative veto over policies that would directly affect their material security, making politics unthreatening to them (Loveman 1976; Bengoa 1983a; Scully 1992). It also explains why some policies with broad support – such as agrarian reform – were so long delayed. It was only with the overwhelming electoral victory of reformist forces in the 1964 presidential and 1965 legislative elections that the right could no longer prevent land reform and expansion of the welfare state into the countryside. These changes, however, destroyed the material basis for clientelistic control over peasants, but by the same token undermined the instrumental commitment of elites to the democratic regime. Indeed, this electoral calamity for conservatives was somewhat accidental. It occurred principally because the right opted not to present a standard-bearing presidential candidate in the 1964 contest fearing a narrow victory by the left in a three-way race. Instead they threw their support behind the reformist Christian Democrat, Eduardo Frei. In 1970 the opposite choice was made, helping to restore the right's legislative presence, but at the same time dividing the anti-Marxist vote and helping to elect Salvador Allende narrowly to the presidency.

In contemporary Chilean democracy, rural bias remains pronounced, and it is not restricted, as is the case in some bicameral systems, to the upper chamber of the legislature. During this final year of authoritarian rule the organic constitutional laws that define (and make nearly unalterable) the electoral system, district boundaries, and campaign rules were issued. The result was a gerrymander in two senses – districts of widely varying population sizes were created, and the boundaries were selected to the maximum advantage of conservative parties, given limited geographic constraints but substantial information on the distribution of voter preferences from the 1988 plebiscite (Londregan 2000, 83–4).

The gerrymander relies at its core on the support of peasants for right parties to function. Not only are the smallest-population (i.e., most overrepresented) districts the most rural, but the boundaries are structured such that in all but a few the center-left Concertación alliance would be unable to pile up large enough majorities (double the votes of the second-place list) to gain both seats available in each district. While the electoral boundaries for both the Senate and the Chamber of Deputies begin with strong rural biases, this situation will only *worsen* with time. Redistricting is not constitutionally contemplated in Chile, and amending the relevant organic constitutional laws would entail concurrent three-fifths majorities in both legislative chambers (which is unattainable precisely because of the size of the right's legislative delegation).[6]

How great is rural overrepresentation in Chile? To begin, in cross-national comparison the level of electoral malapportionment in both chambers of the Chilean parliament is severe. In a recent cross-national study, Chile is ranked as among the more disproportional cases in pure population terms in *both* upper and lower chambers (Samuels and Snyder 2001).[7] Moreover, while there are systems that in one or the other chamber violate one-person one-vote norms more severely, there is only one – Bolivia – that does so in both chambers.

It is not uncommon, however, for upper chambers to be malapportioned, and on this score perhaps the Chilean Senate is not unique. Indeed while it is (slightly) less biased than the U.S. Senate, it should also be remembered that Chile is not a federal system and the thirteen

---

[6] In the entire postmilitary period, the Concertación's best showing in the Senate has been a one-vote majority that has depended on the entry of former President Arturo Frei (a Christian Democrat) as Senator for life, and the suspension of two conservative senators – Errázuriz and Pinochet – because of their involvement in legal proceedings.

[7] For the Chamber of Deputies, Chile ranks eleventh of seventy-eight, while it ranks ninth among the twenty-five surveyed with respect to the Senate. While the latter may not seem severe, it must be remembered that Chile is not a federal system and thus has no institutional reason to maintain severe geographic disproportionality in its upper chamber. Only Bolivia and the Dominican Republic – of somewhat questionable democratic credentials – have somewhat more disproportional upper chambers in non-federal systems (Samuels and Snyder 2001).

TABLE 5.1 *Rural Bias in the Chilean Chamber of Deputies*

	Quartile	Average District Size	Turnout[a]	Rural Composition[b]
(Least Populous)	1	130,435	52.6%	39.1%
	2	174,188	52.4	25.9
	3	240,895	53.4	16.9
(Most Populous)	4	319,721	58.1	3.2

[a] This is a measure of votes cast in the 1989 elections, to the population of the districts as measured by the 1992 census. The population measure does include those below voting age, making the turnout measure valid only in relative, not in absolute terms. Because voting is compulsory for all registered in Chile, and the rural population is younger than the urban, the slight variation in turnout across the districts should not be taken to indicate a meaningful trend.

[b] This is a measure of the percentage of the population of these electoral districts classified by the 1992 census as dwelling in rural areas. Rural population settlements are defined as those having less than 1,000 inhabitants, or those between 1,000 and 2,000 in which less than half the economically active population is employed in the secondary and tertiary sectors (INE 1993, 18).

Sources: For population, INE (1993). For turnout, GIA (1991).

regional groupings out of which senators are elected are arbitrary administrative regions lacking both a long history or any elected officials – they were created by the military government in 1974. In Chile, as in the United States, upper chamber representation based on geography and not population produces a result in which malapportionment dramatically favors rural voters.

The simultaneous and substantial deviation of the lower chamber from the one-person, one-vote democratic norm is far more worrisome. From Table 5.1 we can see the extent of overrepresentation and how it magnifies the rural vote. The average population of the top quartile of districts is more than three times the size of the bottom quartile, and the ratio of largest to smallest districts exceeds 5.8 to 1. Moreover, the smaller districts are also far more rural in composition than the larger ones. The fifteen smallest (of sixty) are on average 40 percent rural (with a national average rural population of 16 percent), while the fifteen largest are a mere 3.2 percent rural. This allows peasant voters to cast a long shadow on national legislative outcomes – a shadow that is rendered even longer by the operation of the binomial electoral to which I turn.

Electoral Rules

The electoral law envisions a binomial electoral system, in essence open-list proportional representation with a district magnitude of only two, and with a requirement that the winning list double the vote share of the second-place list to gain both seats. It is quite different from that which Chile had before 1973 and from that of most other democratic regimes. In this system there are nineteen senatorial and sixty congressional districts, each simultaneously electing two representatives. Elections are then a two-step affair. First, the votes of the candidates of each electoral list are totaled.[8] If the first-place list obtains twice as many votes as the second-place list, then both of the candidates from that list are elected. If, however, this is not the case, one member each from the first- and second-place lists is elected. In this case, the highest vote getter within each elected list obtains a seat. A key feature of this system is that it can provide for the election of candidates on the second-place list who have far fewer individual votes than the second candidate on the first-place list.[9] The bias is thus in favor of the first minority list.

This rather complex electoral system was designed with the peculiarities of the historical Chilean party system in mind. At least until the coup of 1973 Chile had long been characterized by a political system divided into three roughly even ideological tendencies – left, right, and center, with the left generally being slightly weaker than the others (Scully and Valenzuela 1993). The binomial electoral system (in contrast to the previous, more familiar, proportional-representation system) is designed to overrepresent the second-strongest political force while completely excluding the third-place political force. Under the Chilean electoral law, the minimum vote share a party or list need obtain to be guaranteed at least one of the two seats in a district is simply 33.4 percent (even less if more than two lists participate). Thus

---

[8] Lists can be formed by individual political parties, or by alliances of different political parties (such as the Concertación). In either case, the list consists of only two names.

[9] A notable example of this is the defeat of Ricardo Lagos in 1989, a member of the center-left PPD, at the hands of Jaime Guzmán of the far-right Unión Democrática Independiente (UDI). Lagos quite substantially outpolled Guzmán in the Santiago West Senate district.

the political right, which the military knew to be the second strongest political force in posttransition Chile from the 1988 plebiscite results, could achieve near parity in congress even if it were systematically weaker than the center/center-left Concertación alliance across the country. Moreover, should this alliance not survive as the right surely (but wrongly) hoped, the system would have the felicitous effect of virtually freezing the left out of elective office.[10]

At first glance, however, the binomial electoral system has not had a large political impact in terms of the ratio of seats to (party) votes, the way electoral system bias is frequently understood (Munck 1994b). Rabkin (1996) argues that while the binomial system distorts outcomes more than is typical of proportional-representation systems, it performs as well or better than most plurality or majority systems. Understanding the reason for this lower level of de facto disproportionality is, however, crucial. In a fashion unanticipated by the military government, the center and center-left have been able to cooperate in the construction of a durable multiparty political coalition, the Concertación. This persistent center/left cooperation has had two effects: it has allowed the capture of both seats in a small number of (urban) electoral districts, and it has helped to elect representatives from the center-left – through pacts of omission – who would otherwise have been excluded from political competition altogether. That is, it is only through the complex political negotiations among major reformist parties that the most severe political implications of Chile's electoral law have been, in part, mitigated. Of course, the Communist Party was excluded from the alliance, and as a consequence is unable to elect even a single legislator despite a substantial level of support.

If seat-to-vote ratios are not massively distorted, in what senses are rural bias and binomial electoral rules important? Aggregated measures of party system proportionality miss the key point here: the system is

---

[10] This system did not risk excluding the right because: (1) conservatives had nationally almost always been at least the second strongest political force, and they presently held a clear plurality in the countryside, (2) the military had control over the initial definition of district boundaries, and structured them favorably (Caviedes 1991), and (3) as a result of internal divisions, ideological splits, and military-era repression, the left was likely the weakest of the three main partisan forces in most areas of the country.

biased against left parties in two ways. First, as the weakest political force of the traditional "three-thirds" of Chilean politics, it is *only* the parties of the left (Communists [PC] and their allies) and center-left (Socialists [PS] and Party for Democracy [*Partido por la Democracia*, or PPD]) that face the *impossibility* of going it alone politically. Under binomial rules as the third force in most regions the center-left would find its congressional representation decimated without the support of its Christian Democratic (PDC) allies in the Concertación. This is not a dilemma faced by the PDC, with obvious implications for the balance of power in intracoalition bargaining. Moreover, the Communists, barred from joining the Concertación by the Christian Democrats, have been forced to run independent candidate lists and thus remain entirely excluded from national-level representation despite substantial bases of local support. Thus, for the center-left PS/PPD axis to obtain substantial representation it is forced into an alliance and joint political program with the centrist Christian Democrats.[11] The alternative is legislative marginalization, the actual fate of the once-powerful Communist Party.

Thus, the binomial electoral system is effective in taking the level of support for the right – much of it in rural areas – and translating it into a large number of legislative seats as well as a set of incentives that force the center-left to choose between centrist politics and electoral marginalization. The predicted large disparities in seat-to-vote ratios have not emerged in Chile only because of the "pacts of omission" utilized by the Concertación to ensure balanced representation among its constituent parties in the legislature.[12] Rural bias and gerrymandering explains why the Concertación is unable to win both seats in many districts – enough conservative rural voters are kept in most districts in order to block the necessary doubling of the right's political support.

---

[11] The constraint imposed by the need to compromise is obvious across the range of issues of importance to the left. For example, the substantive reform of the Pinochet-era labor law was accomplished only in 2001 and only after long-drawn and tense negotiations between the Socialist president and key conservative Christian Democrats in the Senate (*El Mercurio* September 18, 2001).

[12] Under pacts of omission, in many constituencies the Concertación will not run a centrist against a center-left candidate, in order to insure the election of a member of the progressive wing of the coalition.

But the effect is still clear: the voices of the left (the Socialists and the PPD) are alternatively muted at the insistence of the Christian Democratic sector of the Concertación, or silenced through legislative exclusion (the Communists). But this particularly antileft bias in the electoral system is not simply a function of incentives embedded in its rules – the argument here is not that there are generic "moderating" influences. Indeed, given different distributions of underlying electoral preferences or changed district composition, these same institutional rules could have polarization-inducing effects. But given the realities of the rural social order, the rules create a *specific* bias against the left. But this result is only intelligible when placed in the context of a conservative and atomized rural sector gerrymandered into overrepresented rural areas that are selectively introduced in urban districts to prevent two-seat wins by the Concertación. The right is under no similar ideological constraint – at least in legislative elections – because it needn't appeal to the median voter in order to establish the necessary 33.4 percent vote share required to achieve parity representation. In the end it is the societal transformation induced by neoliberalism that has given meaning to the military's political reforms.

Maintaining Neoliberal Rural Dominance: Access and Campaigns

I have argued that elite support for democratic transition has depended on the credible and sustained legislative presence a rural bastion would provide. And I have further contended that this electoral dominance is founded on the atomization and disorganization of the peasantry induced by neoliberal transformations. If this is the case, however, one would expect the military's electoral rules to safeguard this conservative redoubt from penetration by reformist political parties who might use their institutional and human resources to organize peasants, reduce their dependence, and induce meaningful political competition. While no specific provisions of electoral law prevent reformist forces from penetrating the countryside, several seemingly general technical rules do have that particular effect. Just as with the electoral system, generic institutional rules can have vastly different political implications depending on the social contexts in which they applied.

The key outcome here is the limitation of the ability of opposition political forces to gain an organizational toehold in the countryside that might mitigate the collective action problems of peasants trying to organize themselves. The Chilean Constitution of 1980 and its associated organic constitutional laws, in theory to avoid the overpoliticization of society and the "inefficiency" that might result from it (which may have characterized the 1970–3 period), contain numerous restraints on the practice of democratic competition and campaigning. Most of these are designed to prevent the use of the media for ideological or campaign purposes outside a very narrow window around elections. For example, television, radio, and newsprint advertising for partisan ends is permitted only between thirty and three days before an election. In the event that a plebiscite is called, all campaign material must be devoid of partisan or "ideological" themes.[13]

The difficulty is that in the countryside, unlike urban areas, there are very few alternative avenues for contact between political parties and voters except through the mass media (particularly radio and television) (Caviedes 1991). But it is just this sort of access that is tightly constrained. Consider the case of television: even during the campaign period, political advertising is limited to thirty minutes a day (forty if there is a presidential election), and this must be divided among the different political parties according to their previous electoral record. Even posters and painted propaganda are permitted only in the twenty-seven-day period before an election.[14]

In urban areas, there are other means of access to voters, most particularly through the much denser network of social ties, or neighborhood and other "nonpolitical" organizations. In the countryside, where residence tends to be unstable and highly dispersed and unions are not widespread, there simply is no efficient means of reaching substantial numbers of voters except through the mass media. But this is blocked by legal provision. Indeed, reformist parties cannot even easily build on what little strength remains in the labor movement, as leadership roles in unions and partisan organizations are legally incompatible. This only further reduces the already very limited supply of local leadership. The question then becomes, how does one build a strong party organization in rural areas? How does one reach potential voters? It

[13] Of course, the neoliberal ideology of technocratic decision making and market dominance is not counted as either partisan or ideological.
[14] Ley Orgánica Constitucional de Votaciones Populares y Escrutinos 19.237, art. 30.

should be remembered that the starting point was one of rural organizational annihilation. Thus, under these extremely restrictive rules reformist parties would face daunting barriers to any effort to reconstruct a rural organizational existence.

It is not only in terms of campaigning that ties between citizens and their elected representatives were restricted. Even the traditional forms of constituent service historically practiced by Chilean legislators are prohibited by Constitutional provision or Organic Law – for example, intervention with public agencies or direct intervention in labor disputes. Indeed, competitive politics in the countryside have only a very brief history. Real political pluralism was previously practiced only between 1958 and 1973, with the bulk of the activity in the final nine years (1964–73). Because of this, the strong partisan affiliations and identities characteristic of urban Chile either never managed to form, or were likely less able to survive the years of military rule. One must ask what opinion-leading voice remains in the countryside – especially as one becomes further removed from large urban centers – other than that of the agrarian upper class?

The point here is not to elaborate a detailed model of institutional flaws in Chilean democracy – this has been done well elsewhere. Rather, this study considers the political effects of Chilean neoliberalism as it plays itself out in a rural social context. An analysis that does not consider the character of social relations will fail to make meaningful the impact of institutional structures of Chilean democracy, and will fall short of a coherent analysis of the connections between economic and political liberalization. Others have focused on the effects of Chilean political institutions directly. This study broadens the research agenda by bringing to this line of analysis a focus on rural social relations as they were transformed by marketization.

ELECTIONS AND THE PARADOXICALLY CONSERVATIVE COUNTRYSIDE

The argument of this book hinges on a simple empirical contention: that the transformations of the neoliberal era have created a stable electoral base for conservatives in the countryside. This outcome is both violative of conventional wisdom and empirically verifiable. The emergence of strong support for neoliberal parties in the countryside makes little sense from the perspective of voters' self-interest – no sector has more clearly and more persistently suffered deprivation and increasingly precarious employment conditions resulting from the free market reforms (Ortega 1987, 220; de los Reyes 1990). Nor would a simple reversion to historical tendencies predict strong support for the right: the status quo before the coup was of peasant mobilization, politicization, and electoral support for a reformist and redistributive center and left. Clearly, the precoup Chilean countryside was anything but the "traditional" or quiescent social order of Weberian and Marxian mythology.

When interrogated further, the theory here presented implies even more surprising claims. Not only should the rural sector be a relative electoral bastion for the right, but it should also evidence substantial variation in this support in proportion to the extent to which liberalization has actually atomized and made dependent peasant voters. To be specific, support for free market conservatives should be strongest where rural independent organization – especially labor organization – is weakest. Moreover, peasant dependence (and hence conservatism) will be highest where upward mobility is *least likely* – in the South where agricultural production is far less competitive and where urban-based alternatives are far more constrained. That is, the sectors of the peasantry *most disadvantaged* by neoliberalism should most strongly vote for it. Similarly, to the extent that measures of material impoverishment are reliable proxies for the extent of social disruption attendant upon neoliberal reform, I would also expect *rural* poverty to be associated with support for right parties, while *urban* poverty should be associated with relatively high levels of reformist voting (Concertación). These empirical claims, obviously, clash with expectations rooted in self-interested voting.

Given the passage of time we can also assess the durability of peasant support for neoliberal parties. This will help exclude competing explanations rooted in the legacies of military-era repression and fear. But it also permits us to examine whether a decade of governance by a center-left coalition that brought about dramatic declines in urban and (even more strongly) rural poverty has dented the right's rural electoral redoubt. What is stunning is that neither the advantages of incumbency nor the improvement in material conditions have weakened the hold of the right in the countryside. This indeed may be a critical test – it is an outcome expected only given the persistence of atomization and dependence highlighted by my liberalization hypothesis.

Peasant Conservatism

The electoral results from the three posttransition lower-chamber legislative elections support the contention that a stable base for neoliberal parties has emerged in the countryside, but one that is not tied to historical electoral affinities or the material interests of peasant voters. They are, however, quite compatible with the liberalization thesis put forward here. Broadly, parties of the right do substantially better in the countryside than those of the left, though more strongly so in the more remote regions of southern Chile than in the Central Valley where the overwhelming presence of the Santiago-Valparaíso urban axis is felt. Finally, while high levels of extreme poverty are generally negatively related to support for conservatives, this relationship reverses in the countryside. Here areas populated by the losers from neoliberal modernization are the strongest supporters of the parties that impoverished them – a paradoxical result that I have explained with reference to rural elite dominance and collective-action problems attendant upon neoliberal reform.

How big a bastion of support for the right is the countryside? If one considers the results of three posttransition congressional elections, support for the right in the countryside is far higher than in urban areas (see Table 5.2). It should also be recalled that these results derive from aggregated data, and will have a tendency to understate the size of urban/rural differences. For the purpose of analysis all municipalities at least 50 percent urban were considered "urban" while the remaining were scored rural. But for many of these areas, mixed-population composition is the rule, and this reality tends to obscure the urban-rural differences. Thus, many marginally rural or urban districts are included in each of the respective averages, making them closer than would be the case were it possible to perfectly segregate rural from urban areas. We should also be cautious, however, because it is impossible in this sort of analysis to establish with certainty that it is the rural individuals in mixed areas that are in fact the strongest supporters of conservative parties (though the opposite is quite unlikely given what we know of the political behavior of purely rural and urban areas).

TABLE 5.2 *Median Support for Parties in Chamber of Deputies by Sector and Election*

	All Chile					
	1989		1993		1997	
	Rural	Urban	Rural	Urban	Rural	Urban
Right	0.427	0.383	0.393	0.360	0.434	0.374
Center	0.282	0.315	0.329	0.315	0.222	0.246
Left	0.170	0.240	0.251	0.322	0.254	0.306
N	135	151	135	151	135	151

Notes: The unit of analysis is the comuna, and data are taken from all comunas not located in the nonagricultural extreme northern or southern areas in which the urban/rural distinction is not meaningful (286 of 335 comunas are included).

Sources: Electoral data for 1989 from GIA (1991); for 1993 from Ministerio del Interior (1996); for 1997 from Ministerio del Interior (1997). Population data from INE (1993). Urban comunas are defined as those with at least 50 percent of their population urban resident. Rural areas are comunas in which more than half the population resides in the countryside. The mixed population composition of comunas in the aggregate data does tend to obscure the urban/rural differences of interest.

Better estimates of the specifically rural support for conservative parties can be obtained using King's (1997) ecological inference techniques. These inferences (see Table 5.3) suggest much starker rural-urban differences than those uncovered in the initial analysis. In a three-bloc political system (strongly so, according to Valenzuela and Scully 1993; weakly according to Tironi and Agüero 1999; Montes et al. 2000), in the countryside the right consistently obtained in excess of 40 percent of the vote (the range is from 41 through 47 percent). By contrast, the only potential political opponents of neoliberalism on the left received between 17 and 27 percent of the rural vote. What is perhaps most striking is that the support for the right in the countryside is consistent across time. At the time of democratic transition, rural poverty rates had doubled with respect to their already high 1970 levels, yet the right scored 47 percent of the rural vote in the first post-transition election (on poverty, see León 1994). By 1997, after seven years of very strong economic growth and a halving of rural poverty under the auspices of continuous center-left government, the right *still* obtained 46 percent of the rural vote. Neither impoverishment by the military right nor improving living standards under the center-left democratic governments has dented rural support for conservatives.

TABLE 5.3 *Ecological Inferences[a] of Urban/Rural Vote Shares in Chamber of Deputies in All Chile[b] by Political Ideology and Election Year*

Party Support by Party Ideology	1989		1993		1997	
	Urban	Rural	Urban	Rural	Urban	Rural
Right	0.385	0.472	0.358	0.407	0.370	0.460
	(0.002)	(0.007)	(0.002)	(0.009)	(0.002)	(0.010)
Center	0.318	0.263	0.317	0.333	0.263	0.298
	(0.001)	(0.006)	(0.002)	(0.009)	(0.002)	(0.009)
Left	0.250	0.165	0.323	0.265	0.358	0.258
	(0.000)	(0.001)	(0.002)	(0.009)	(0.003)	(0.012)
N	286		286		286	
Estimated Right vs. Left Advantage	0.135	0.307	0.035	0.142	0.012	0.202

[a] The technique of inference employed is that of King (1997). It was assumed that the parameter for urban support for political tendencies was fixed across municipalities, while that for rural support could vary with respect to the rural character of the municipalities.

[b] The data used include all of Chile except the northern and southern extreme provinces where there is no agricultural sector (Regions I–III, XI–XII). These areas are very sparsely populated and the rural population is nonagricultural (and thus not comparable to that of the Central Valley and South).

Sources: See Table 5.2.

This is precisely the result anticipated by the theory developed in Chapters 3 and 4, though it runs counter to any notion of materially driven voting, or for that matter peasant autonomy.

When rural-urban differences are further disaggregated by region – the South and the Central Valley – the results become even more striking. In the Central Valley, where neoliberalism has been much less materially damaging to peasant interests and where more alternatives to rural employment exist (due to proximity to the principal population centers of the country), urban-rural differences are more muted and conservative support in the countryside is less substantial than it is in Southern Chile. The South, however, has a much weaker agricultural sector, one that is not internationally competitive and is more substantially isolated from urban sources of social capital. Despite these disproportionate material hardships, rural support for conservatives in the South is quite strong, between 46 and 53 percent (see Table 5.4), compared with a range of 36 to 42 percent in the Central Valley for legislative elections between 1989 and 1997. The results, however, are

TABLE 5.4 *Sectoral and Regional Estimates of Voter Support for Chamber of Deputies Candidates by Party Ideology, 1989–1997[a]*

	Central Valley[b]					
	1989		1993		1997	
Party Ideology	Urban	Rural	Urban	Rural	Urban	Rural
Right	0.400	0.390	0.369	0.359	0.380	0.418
	(0.001)	(0.013)	(0.002)	(0.014)	(0.002)	(0.017)
Center[c]	0.317	0.281	0.320	0.357	0.249	0.310
	(0.001)	(0.014)	(0.002)	(0.015)	(0.002)	(0.015)
Left[d]	0.239	0.187	0.309	0.294	0.361	0.279
	(0.001)	(0.013)	(0.003)	(0.018)	(0.002)	(0.019)
N	136		136		136	
Estimated Right vs. Left Advantage	0.161	0.203	0.060	0.065	0.019	0.139
	South[e]					
Right	0.342	0.525	0.317	0.457	0.343	0.484
	(0.005)	(0.011)	(0.006)	(0.013)	(0.013)	(0.013)
Center	0.325	0.243	0.309	0.323	0.321	0.247
	(0.005)	(0.011)	(0.008)	(0.016)	(0.006)	(0.012)
Left	0.277	0.150	0.367	0.229	0.335	0.277
	(0.006)	(0.013)	(0.008)	(0.017)	(0.008)	(0.015)
N	150		150		150	
Estimated Right vs. Left Advantage	0.065	0.375	−0.050	0.228	0.008	0.207

[a] Estimation using King's (1997) ecological inference techniques. It was assumed that the parameter for urban support for political tendencies was fixed across municipalities, while that for rural support could vary with respect to rural character of the municipalities.

[b] Includes the agricultural regions suitable for export agriculture in the center of the country (Regions IV–VI, and Metropolitan).

[c] Includes parties of the center, principally the PDC, PR (Radical), and PRSD (Radical/Social Democratic).

[d] Includes parties of the center-left within the Concertación (PS, PPD) and those on left that were not always members of the Concertación (PC [Communist], PHV [Green/Humanist], IC [Left Christian], MIR [Left Revolutionary]), as well as independents affiliated with the left.

[e] Includes southern agricultural regions, suitable only for domestic food production (Regions VII–X).

Sources: See Table 5.2.

reversed in urban areas. Here the more materially disadvantaged South is a weaker base for conservative parties, with support fluctuating between 32 and 34 percent compared to a range of 37 to 40 percent in the urban Central Valley. This only underscores the sectoral dynamic that is the focus of this book.

The advantage conservatives obtain in the countryside is crucial to blocking potential for direct threats to the fundamental interests of neoliberal elites and the military. It is this electoral "outcome insurance" that simultaneously solidifies their commitment to democratic politics. The only potential source for such threats is, however, from the political left. Historically, of course, when Chile elected a Marxist president in 1970 – the first country in the world to do so – it set off a chain of events that drove elites to reject democracy altogether and the regime collapsed. It is therefore crucial to my argument that the right's current rural base gives it a crucial edge over the electoral strength of the left. The data in Tables 5.3 and 5.4 show that this is in fact the case. In the rural Central Valley the right maintains a strong lead over the left, in the South the advantage becomes massive.

In proceeding with this analysis, I examine electoral outcomes disaggregated by the traditional ideological divisions of Chilean politics (left, right, and center) rather than the bipolar Concertación (center and center left) versus right dynamic that has characterized actual post-transition electoral competition. The key issue is whether serious challenges to neoliberal elites can emerge, which depends on the viability of a *potential* Communist/Socialist alliance that excludes the Christian Democratic party and recreates a historic coalition on the left. That is, only where the left is strong enough, independent of its moderating alliance with Christian Democracy, could Chilean politics once again initiate a radical redistributive experiment that threatens fundamental elite interests. Understood in these terms, the electoral results are rather striking. In urban areas, the left pole of the political spectrum only narrowly trails support for the right, behind by between 4 and 14 percent (see Table 5.3).[15] By contrast, in rural areas the right now has an advantage of between 14 and 31 percent – stunningly large in a three-bloc political system.

---

[15] Importantly, after the first democratic election, this gap virtually disappeared, as the right had an urban advantage of only 3 and 2 percent in 1993 and 1997, respectively.

Regional disaggregation further confirms this result, where in the urban Central Valley the right's dominance over the left declines from 16 percent in 1989 to a mere 2 percent by 1997 (see Table 5.4). In the countryside there is no secular decline in the right's advantage; it fluctuates between 7 and 20 percent. In the South, the differences are more extreme. In 1993, the left actually outperformed the right slightly in urban areas (by 0.5 percent), while trailing by between 21 and 38 percent in the rural areas. Thus, the right is dominant over the left in the areas expected by the present approach – the countryside, not the cities; the more atomized, if impoverished South rather than the Central Valley. This is a pattern of conservative support that cannot be explained by material interests. The political implications of this distribution of support are critical. First, given prevailing electoral laws, it forces the left into a continued – and moderating – alliance with the Christian Democrats.[16] The alternative would be to face the electorate independently, and almost surely to reap a catastrophic decline in the size of its legislative delegation. Second, this distribution of electoral support gives the right enough backing (given the ways the electoral law aggregates votes into seats) to impede unwanted initiatives, should they manage to emerge.

Material Interests or Market-Induced Atomization?

The neoliberal developmental model, while after the mid-1980s success in terms of the performance of certain macroeconomic indicators (most notably growth in GDP), brought with it a substantial degree of social dislocation, material suffering, and widening income disparities, particularly in rural areas (Foxley 1983; Rivera and Cruz 1984; Venegas 1993). In political terms, one might expect that these individuals that were "left behind" in the market-mediated model would tend to be supporters of the opposition to the military (that is, the Concertación and parties to the left of it). Indeed, the waves of massive street mobilizations that swept Chile from 1983 through 1986 had their bases in just such marginal urban squatter settlements (*poblaciones*) around Santiago (Garretón 1986; Oxhorn 1994, 1995).

---

[16] This also forces the exclusion of the Communist Party (PC) from both the Concertación – at Christian Democratic insistence – and by extension, from the legislature.

If, however, the atomizing and competitive dynamics described in Chapter 3 are really present in Chilean rural society, one might expect a very different relationship between poverty and electoral outcomes. If any in the countryside are affected by the competition, atomization, and dependence characteristic of agricultural neoliberalism, it is those who exist on both the margins of society and the labor market – the extremely poor. I thus expect that in those areas where the neoliberal transformation of agriculture has been most completely accomplished, and where contact with urban centers is at a minimum, high levels of poverty will tend to be associated not with support for the electoral left, but rather for the electoral right. I *do not* have this expectation for urban areas, where the reduction in living standards for the poorest strata was not accompanied by the same atomizing and competitive dynamics and relations of dependency, that have made themselves felt in the rural areas. Similarly, if there are instances where social decapitalization, atomization, and dependence are *not* found, the relationship between rural residence, poverty, and voting should reverse, as peasants are able to autonomously organize and express their political preferences.

Who are the extremely poor in the countryside? Generally, they are the unemployed, the underemployed, and those able to find only seasonal work on capitalist farms (Rivera and Cruz 1984; Rivera 1988; Rodríguez and Venegas 1991). While few in the rural sector are wealthy, a year-round agricultural worker or a peasant farm family are substantially better off than the floating mass of underemployed laborers generated by the "flexibilization" of the rural labor market and the "parcelization" of the former agrarian-reform sector.[17] This has created a political division, in which the less impoverished (more stable) segments of the rural working and peasant classes are in constant competition with, and risk falling into, a local subproletariat. The long-standing community solidarities that might in other circumstances bind these groups together and support oppositional activity do not exist in neoliberal Chile (on the role of community, see Calhoun 1983).

How would such a fragmentation work to the benefit of the political right? The rhetoric of the neoliberal right has consistently blamed the

---

[17] This was a segment of workers at one time considered eradicated, but which has of late come to *typify* Chilean agriculture (Collins and Lear 1995, ch. 12).

formal working class (especially its unionized elements) for the plight of the poor and only marginally employed. The lack of bottom-rung jobs is blamed on the "extraeconomic" monopolies that formal sector workers supposedly had on their jobs. That is, their "privileged" position is dependent on the creation of distortions in the labor market (minimum wages, employment stability provisions, collective bargaining, etc.) that hinder the creation of entry-level jobs (Piñera 1990). On the other hand, under military rule the meager social benefits that permit this marginal segment to survive were state provided, through the municipalities. These were almost all controlled by right-wing mayors until local level democratization in 1992, and many still are. It is a situation in which *alternative* explanations of rural poverty – ones that might criticize the agrarian capitalist class or the developmental model – are seldom heard. It is also one in which the process labeled "semiclientelism" by Fox (1994) in his discussion of Mexico might emerge.

In Table 5.5, I explore ecological regressions in an effort to examine empirically these specific hypotheses in the available data. It must be mentioned as a cautionary note that only aggregate inferences are drawn here, and I argue only that the results are consistent with my theoretical expectations. Direct assessment would require individual-level data that are unavailable and would likely be unreliable even were they to be collected. Nevertheless, the results are quite striking. In understanding the support for conservative parties across three lower-chamber legislative elections, as expected the more rural areas generally evidence stronger support for conservative parties (this is not statistically significant, however, for the 1993 election largely due to collinearity problems arising from the inclusion of multiple interaction terms). Similarly, for the 1989 and 1993 elections areas of extreme poverty were less supportive of the political right – a difference of 24 percent over the range of variation in the measure of extreme poverty (0 to 62).

The variations in electoral support for the right in urban and rural Chile can also be used to examine the intervening steps in the liberalization hypothesis set out in Chapters 3 and 4. The question that should be asked is what is the effect of rural residence where neoliberalism has *not* fully destroyed preexisting stocks of social capital? To examine this question I have collected data on the survival of peasant

TABLE 5.5 *Bases of Conservative Support in Chilean Congressional Elections, 1989–1997 Ecological Regressions at the Comuna Level*

Independent Variables	Dependent Variables		
	1989 Election Vote Share for the Right	1993 Election Vote Share for the Right	1997 Election Vote Share for the Right
Constant	0.411**	0.421**	0.392**
	(0.020)	(0.021)	(0.054)
Rurality	0.089**	0.033	0.097**
	(0.032)	(0.033)	(0.027)
Extreme Poverty	−0.004**	−0.005**	0.0003
	(0.001)	(0.001)	(0.045)
Rurality* Union	−0.044**	−0.037*	0.015
	(0.021)	(0.021)	(0.026)
Rurality* Poverty	0.004**	0.005**	−0.016
	(0.002)	(0.002)	(0.106)
N	334	333	318

** Significant at the $p < 0.05$ level.
* Significant at the $p < 0.10$ level.
Notes: Rurality is calculated from the 1992 census in all cases. While these data are not ideal, no alternatives exist and population shares are likely to shift only slightly within the range of three to five years. Extreme poverty is taken as the percentage of the comuna classified as in extreme poverty in the CASEN studies of 1987, except for the 1997 election, when the data used is the percentage of comuna residents receiving antipoverty assistance in the form of the Subsidio Unico Familiar (SUF) income subsidy in 1996. Union is a dummy variable coded "one" if there is a rural union local extant in the comuna, zero otherwise, in 1992, the last year in which disaggregated data are available.
Sources: Electoral results, see Table 5.2; extreme poverty, GIA (1991), except for 1996, INE (1997). Union data from Ministerio de Trabajo y Prevision Social (1992).

labor organizations. The intuition is that if a peasant union local – of any size whatsoever – is found to have survived economic transformation and military-era repression, then this is a strong indication that in these specific areas the level of atomization and disorganization more generally found in the countryside are not as severe. And with lessened dependence and a demonstrated potential for collective expression, I would expect support for conservatives, *ceteris paribus,* to diminish. Again, the data for 1989 and 1993[18] bear this out – the interaction

---

[18] Because disaggregated data on agricultural union membership was available only for 1992, it is not easy to interpret the results of the 1997 election. It is unclear whether the

between a dummy variable for the presence of a peasant union and the indicator of rural composition is of the *opposite* sign of the rural variable.

It is similarly the case that while, in general, highly impoverished areas support the right far less than wealthier ones, the interaction of poverty with rural composition reverses this relationship. It is the *more impoverished* areas of the countryside that support the neoliberal right, not the less impoverished ones. This is consonant with my expectation that these areas are characterized by high levels of atomization and dependence, and thus should evidence substantial right-party support no matter how directly this conflicts with the material self-interests of peasant voters. Where collective action problems are not so severe and dependence is mitigated by employment alternatives (however unattractive), the impoverished have the political freedom to support the reformist Concertación – after all, the centerpiece of their governing strategy has been the quite successful effort to mitigate poverty.

CONCLUSIONS

At first blush Chile seemed the most likely case for the contention that the freeing of markets and democratic transition were causally linked, mutually reinforcing phenomena. After all, Chilean authoritarianism ended only after a free market economic system had been firmly established, and the posttransition regime evinced a stability and level of consensus never present in the pre-1973 era of statist democracy. But as we have seen in the past three chapters, this surface-level harmony obscures some notable paradoxes. First, there increasingly seems to be a trade-off between the stability of democracy and its quality. At least in the countryside, the commitment of powerful economic elites to the regime has been founded on their dominance over local political agenda and the strength of their peasant support. This support has always been instrumental, however. It was replaced by calls for military intervention in a heartbeat when elites were challenged by a

distribution of union membership for 1992 is a good proxy for the same information five years later. For the other elections, the gaps are slightly more than two years and one year, respectively.

Socialist government from above and mobilized peasants from below in the 1970–3 period. Second, the electoral redoubt that peasant voters provide conservative, neoliberal elites is surprising both because it is founded on a fundamentally disorganized and politically isolated population that was a principal victim of the economic policies that it appears to support.

These paradoxes have pointed to an answer that suggests a far more uneasy relationship between free markets and free politics: the markets preserve democracy only insofar as they serve to undermine political contestation and social organization in the countryside. The critical connection hinges on the way in which free markets transform society, social organization, and state-society relationships. They can do so in ways that undermine autonomous political participation – but this effect is strong enough to vitiate vibrant democratic competition only when combined with the structural realities of agrarian life. But by helping to transform social atomization, economic dependence, and the political isolation of the countryside into a durable conservative electoral base, markets have also made vigorous political competition stable at the national level.

In Chapter 6 the generality of this thesis is assessed in a quite different context: Mexico. Here marketization and democratic transition are both to some extent incomplete, and in any event these twin processes were not substantially temporally separate. Does the rural sector play a crucial role in facilitating democratic transition just as it has stabilized consolidation in Chile? Is the countryside a critical sector for free market political parties? Is their dominance founded on market-induced atomization and dependence? It is to these questions and more that we turn.

6

Markets and Democratization in Mexico

Rural Politics between Corporatism and Neoliberalism

The central thesis of this book is that the rural sector plays a critical role in the construction of free market democracy because of the electoral base it can provide for neoliberal elites and their partisan representatives during periods of painful retrenchment. Otherwise, these actors might be compelled to impede or reverse democratization in the effort to defend their material interests from the redistributive policies of popularly elected leaders. We saw in the Chilean case that the creation of a conservative peasant base was possible because of the social atomization, dependence, and interest fragmentation unleashed during the consolidation of free market agriculture under military auspices. But this also begs an important question: could liberalization have been implemented there without the extended and heavy-handed authoritarianism of the Pinochet dictatorship?

Alternatively, was free market democracy consolidated in Chile precisely because the painful economic transformations were undertaken in the most unfree of contexts? For an answer, I turn to the Mexican experience with comparatively simultaneous economic and political liberalization. Examining the dynamics of this case of conjoint democratization and economic reform is critical on both empirical and normative grounds. Free market reforms are under way across the South American continent, but their implementation has as often as not been accompanied by the recourse to undemocratic practices justified because of their ability to circumvent "political" opposition to "essential" economic changes.[1] Examining the Mexican experience suggests, however, that economic and political reforms needn't be incompatible and that justifications for the recourse to undemocratic implementation strategies are disingenuous. The work here suggests, by contrast, that those politicians seeking free markets and democracy should spend far less time subverting competitive politics in the short term to facilitate economic reform, and more time trying to deepen the quality of rural democratic competition. It is there that the crucial problems lie.

In the following chapter I make the case that the Mexican rural sector was as vital for the simultaneous implementation of economic and political opening as the Chilean was to the consolidation of markets economics and liberal democracy in that country. Like Chile, the agrarian *status quo ante* in Mexico was a state-dominated mixed economy: land ownership was divided between the public (collective) and private sectors, the state played an overwhelming role in input and marketing industries, commodity prices were controlled, and private farmers were tightly regulated. Unlike Chile, however, neoliberal economic transformation was undertaken in the context of a polity undergoing a sustained process of political opening. Indeed, free market transformation in Mexico culminated in the 1994 implementation of the NAFTA accords, while political loosening produced an opposition majority in the Chamber of Deputies by 1997 and the capture of the presidency in 2000. In the following text we will see how the countryside was vital to the simultaneous *construction* of free markets and liberal democracy in Mexico, just as it was crucial to the *consolidation* of free market democracy in Chile.

Part of this argument is uncontroversial – few analysts would disagree that the Mexican countryside has long been an important electoral bastion for the long-governing PRI. Indeed, the stability of the peasant *voto verde* (green vote) is understood by politicians and scholars

---

[1] I take no position here on advisability of some or all of the liberal economic reforms being implemented across the continent. I note only – following such scholars as Gore (2000), Rodrik (1996), and Wade (1992) – that their advisability or effectiveness has received surprisingly little empirical scrutiny while potentially successful alternatives are often not seriously considered.

alike as the reason the ruling PRI maintained its grip on power for so long despite persistent economic crises, a dramatic shift to a neoliberal policy orientation, and a precipitous decline in support elsewhere (Gibson 1997). What conventional accounts have failed to adequately explain is *why* the PRI's rural base has survived the shocks of liberalization, even as its urban support evaporated. Most analyses have emphasized the legacies of corporatist control or new forms of neoliberal populism to explain this seemingly implausible result. They are not wrong but rather insufficient: the historically important corporatist institutions no longer provide enough critical benefits, or a monopoly over access to the state, to be effective. The new neopopulist welfare schemes lack the resources and vote-monitoring capacity necessary to explain why the implementation of very painful economic reforms was electorally viable for the PRI, but only in the countryside.[2]

Instead, I argue that rural marketization has helped create an electoral constituency among its peasant victims by increasing their vulnerability to local elites, raising steep barriers to autonomous collective action, and removing alternatives from the political agenda. This is perhaps surprising because in Mexico economic liberalization has unleashed powerful agricultural transformations that have not only *disproportionately* heightened rural economic insecurity and dramatically worsened living standards, but have also given lie to the core principles of nationalism and land redistribution that since the revolution had been a cornerstone of the PRI's claim to political legitimacy. Yet despite this, the countryside remains by far the PRI's strongest electoral redoubt.

What has happened, in a partial and more complicated way, is the restructuring of a base of support for the PRI among peasants, now based less in corporatism or neopopulism than in the disorganizing and atomizing effects of neoliberalism. These effects are perhaps not as severe or complete as in other contexts (e.g., Chile). Nevertheless, neoliberalism *has* induced massive social differentiation, recreated powerful economic vulnerabilities for peasants relative to local elites, and dismantled the institutional structures that were the historic foundations of broadly shared peasant "interests" across the breadth of the

[2] For a more general treatment of the efficacy of neopopulist compensatory schemes, see Weyland (1998).

countryside.[3] In addition to these barriers to collective action, the mobilization of peasant interests must take place within an organizational field already dominated by a plethora of existing groups claiming to "represent" the interests of different fragments of the peasantry, and with widely varying degrees of real political autonomy or legitimacy. This is an important, but additional, problem from the perspective of those peasants seeking to self-organize collective action or find a strong and autonomous political voice.

Given the severe material grievances and less arid political opportunity structure that characterize rural Mexico relative to Chile under Pinochet, what is notable is not the occasional emergence of manifestations of agrarian discontent, but rather its typically limited issue scope and narrow geographic concentration in areas *least affected* by neoliberal reforms. Indeed, the most obvious exception to the rule of peasant quiescence, the Ejército Zapatista de Liberación Nacional (EZLN) insurgency in Chiapas, has taken place in precisely the region the perspective advanced here would expect: where liberalization is *least* advanced and the social bases of shared interest and collective action can be based in a powerful indigenous identity.[4]

The alternative corporatist or neopopulist explanations of peasant support for neoliberal politicians have emphasized two different, and to some extent contradictory mechanisms: (1) the legacies of corporatist control exercised through the CNC and the other remaining developmentalist institutions in the countryside, or (2) a new form of clientelism based on the political distribution of new social welfare funds through the Programa Nacional de Solidaridad (National Solidary Program, or PRONASOL) and the Programa de Educación, Salud, y Alimentación (Program for Education, Health, and Food, or PROGRESA) antipoverty programs that deliberately bypassed the old corporatist institutions. While certainly not without merit, neither

[3] Because of at least the agrarian reforms of the Cárdenas era (1934–40), state institutions have formed a common focus for peasant grievances. After liberalization, however, the most common *targets* of peasant political action, from marketing boards to land reform bureaucracies, simply ceased to exist, taking with them the relevance of political participation for everyday peasant life. When coupled with heightened social differentiation, even latent peasant interests become fragmented as well.

[4] See Yashar (1999) for an exploration of the widespread emergence of peasant mobilization based on a politicized ethnic cleavage in the wake of neoliberal transformation across Latin America.

approach can reasonably account for the level of peasant support enjoyed by the PRI.[5]

The first perspective underestimates the degree to which (particularly rural) neoliberal reforms are at odds with the maintenance of corporatist control. Institutional decay, the withdrawal of the state from rural economic life, and the end of the agrarian reform, all undermined incentives for peasants to participate in corporatist organizations and thus the leverage these institutions have over them – they had become materially irrelevant or were privatized altogether. Snyder's (2001b) recent treatment suggests that, by contrast, in sectors where state-level governments intervene to *recreate* corporatist institutions in the wake of national-level liberalization, rural organization and mobilization expand. Alternatively, the compensations available to peasants under the neoliberal PRONASOL and PROGRESA social programs are small in comparison with the economic costs imposed upon them, and the evidence linking them to favorable electoral outcomes are based on highly aggregated or anecdotal evidence.[6] And if one accepts the contention that welfarist distribution was effective in generating rural political support, it then becomes difficult to understand why it was so manifestly unsuccessful in urban areas? Finally, conventional accounts do not well explain two critical axes of variation: organized political resistance to neoliberalism in the countryside is greatest in those areas such as Chiapas, and to a lesser extent Oaxaca, and Guerrero, less affected by the neoliberal reforms. Indeed, the peasant movements organized there also share an ethnically based foundation for collective expression that is lacking in much of rural Mexico. Conversely, those agrarian areas most dramatically transformed by the Salinas and Zedillo liberalizations evidence remarkable political stability despite having suffered the same catastrophic material hardships found in indigenous areas.

---

[5] Bartra (1996) and Ward (1993) make the case for the neopopulism/welfarism explanation. Fox (1994, 1996b) takes a more skeptical approach. Heredia (1994) points to the Mexican state's domination and fragmentation of interest representation through corporatist associations to explain how the economic reforms were made politically viable, while Ros (1994) suggests corporatist organizations were crucial to the success of the policies in economic terms (especially wage restraint). Bartra's earlier (1985) work emphasized the corporatist organizations to explain the political domination of the peasantry.

[6] This is not to argue that PRI elites did not try to use these programs for precisely such ends. They did; my only criticism here is of the efficacy of this activity.

The consequence is that in Mexico, as in Chile, a critical reason for the success of democratic transition – the maintenance of a stable electoral base for the neoliberals in the PRI in the countryside – is a crucial problem for the deepening of democratization. This sectoral heterogeneity in the patterns of political participation and organization made simultaneous national-level progress on the democratic and economic reform fronts possible for the incumbent PRI governments (leading unintentionally to the eventual victory of the conservative but oppositional PAN candidate for the presidency in 2000). It also points to a serious lacuna in Mexican democracy: the relative absence of self-organized peasant political expression and vigorous political competition in much of the countryside. Real rural democratization would threaten the very survival of the PRI and other free market parties and thus could prove problematic for the consolidation of neoliberal economic reforms. What is at stake should not be underestimated: without the rural support rooted in fragmentation and vulnerability, could a stable and viable coalition be constructed behind neoliberal reforms? Alternatively, were democratization to advance in the countryside, would neoliberal reforms encounter sufficient political support?

NEOLIBERAL ECONOMIC REFORM, THE DECLINE OF CORPORATISM, AND THE SURVIVAL OF THE INSTITUTIONAL REVOLUTIONARY PARTY

The economic crisis that shook the Mexican economy loose from its import-substituting moorings began in earnest with the August 1982 declaration of insolvency by the Central Bank. While the result was severe economic retrenchment and the eventual imposition of a broad-based and coherent neoliberal developmental model, the very dramatic unevenness of the journey is indicative of the perceived political risks of simultaneous liberalization and democratization. Indeed, the initial response to the debt crisis was anything but liberal: closure of the economy, nationalization of the private-banking sector, and fiscal austerity.[7]

---

[7] Diagnosing the problem as one of short-term imbalance, the government embarked on a program of compression of domestic demand, strict import controls (licensing was applied to almost the entirety of imports), and massive public spending cuts that quickly reversed current account imbalances. The fiscal deficit declined from

It was not until a second crisis, provoked by the collapse of oil prices in 1985–6, that the Mexican government definitively committed itself to an outward-oriented, neoliberal developmental project.

The opening of the Mexican economy began in the arena of trade, when in 1985 quantitative restrictions were removed on 60 percent of Mexican imports, overshooting the 40 percent goal only recently agreed in an International Monetary Fund (IMF) letter of intent. The following year even though GATT accession negotiations had placed an upper bound on Mexican tariffs at 50 percent, they were reduced to a maximum of 35 percent, with further programmed reductions in the works (Flores-Quiroga 1998, 15). The 1993 ratification of NAFTA only made irreversible what had already been established – Mexico had by then become an open economy. And after 1988 (though beginning earlier), a dramatic wave of industrial privatizations complemented the structural reform induced by rising import competition.

But this stylized account obscures as much as it reveals about the politics of economic transformation. In negotiating the politically charged waters of dramatic reform in the context of persistent economic crisis, two sectors received special and often quite illiberal treatment: finance and agriculture. What is interesting here, however, is that these sectors were *not* those historically most capable of imposing their interests on the Mexican state. It was the import-competing private-sector elite and the parastatal firms that had long blocked any liberalization of the economy (Tornell 1995, 54). By contrast, the countryside was the sector *least* able to articulate coherent, organized opposition to liberalization either through the official party's rural branch, the CNC, or independently. And that agricultural liberalization was slow and inconsistent is particularly odd because the creation of new agro-export sectors reflective of international comparative advantages is typically considered a cornerstone of outward-oriented models of development. Finance policy moved in illiberal directions as well, including persistent protection of (recently reprivatized) banks and exchange rate manipulation, producing results that "undermined market discipline and economic stability" (Kessler 1998, 37). In broad strokes, while Mexican trade

---

17.7 percent of GDP in 1982 to 8.9 percent in 1983, while the current account moved from an average of −9.35 percent of GDP in 1981–2 to +4.75 percent in 1983–4 (data calculated from Kaufman 1989, 117).

liberalization was extensive, other aspects of the neoliberal package proceeded in politically explicable but economically incoherent ways.

Both of these economically inefficient outcomes can be understood if one takes into consideration parallel efforts to maintain the dominance of the long-ruling PRI in the context of ever wider political opening. Kessler (1998) has convincingly shown that the manipulation of finance policy helped to produce the resources necessary for efforts to try to compensate some of the important political losers from neoliberal reform. What is less understood is the crucial role that the countryside played in the stabilization of the joint democratic[8] and free market transitions: it provided an electoral base for the governing party well beyond what its aged and decaying corporatist apparatus or new populist welfarism could accomplish. And it is a base that has persisted even through the exceedingly painful but still partial incorporation of the countryside into the neoliberal project.

The argument here is not that the Mexican countryside escaped free market reforms. Indeed, given its highly socialized starting point, agriculture is arguably the most transformed sector of the economy. Instead, the claim is that the process of rural marketization was organized in ways that maximized barriers to independent peasant political expression, created new dependencies, and fragmented potential opponents into small, competing, and ineffectual groups. In such a context the local power of PRI-linked elites (both private and in government) would be sufficient to maintain a high level of electoral support. But it did so in ways that sharply impeded rural democratization at the same time that urban political opening proceeded – indeed, it helped make the latter possible.

Making the Argument: Sectoral Reform and the Reconstruction of Rural Social Control

The historical corporatist tools that had long underwritten the PRI's control over the countryside had very substantially decayed well before

---

[8] This is not to say that during this period the PRI consciously desired full-scale democratization. Nevertheless, some degree of political opening was pursued and this eventually went far enough to permit the PRI's (unexpected) loss of the presidency in 2000.

the implantation of free market policies in the agrarian arena, however unevenly they were introduced. Starting with the Cárdenas presidency in the 1930s, rural support for the PRI had been delivered in an exchange for access to land through the agrarian reform process. Organizationally, this was mediated through the PRI's peasant branch, the CNC. The CNC effectively controlled the allocation of new reform-sector lands, delivering them to peasants on a clientelistic basis, and for some time this organization's reach into the countryside was both extensive and unchallenged.

The symmetry of this exchange, however, declined substantially as early as the 1940s and 1950s as the pace of expropriation slowed, larger private holdings were increasingly tolerated, and large numbers of certificates of inexpropiability were issued to private producers (Mackinlay 1991). Indeed, while more than 20 million hectares of land were expropriated under the government of Cárdenas (1934–40), the rate decelerated precipitously thereafter, to slightly more than 5 million under Avila Camacho (1941–6), and averaging approximately 3 million until the 1970s (Goodman et al. 1985, Table 8).[9] Moreover, the quality of the land transferred after 1940 was often marginal at best. The dramatically slowed pace of land distribution eventually provoked a crisis in the CNC's ability to mediate rural social control, leading in part to the agrarian mobilizations of the early 1970s.

The response of the Echeverría (1970–6) and López Portillo (1976–82) administrations to this new wave of peasant militancy was two-pronged, both aimed at reestablishing political control through corporatist institutions. Echeverría briefly reinitiated serious agrarian reform, creating a substantial number of new *ejidos* (land-reform cooperatives) in areas that had been characterized by mobilization. But more importantly, both administrations reorganized the rural social pact that underlay stability – instead of the distribution of land, the mediation of access to the production process became the bargain. Thus, the state dramatically expanded its role in the countryside to include the

---

[9] These numbers represent the *actual* distribution of land. Decrees declared (but did not implement) the expropriation of substantially more land, creating a large number of peasants who had "rights" to expropriated land but were caught in the torturously slow workings of the agrarian bureaucracies and were exceedingly dependent on the CNC if eventual enforcement of their rights were ever to become reality. Precisely this trap for many years provided the PRI an avenue for low-cost rural social control.

provision of inputs (fertilizer, credits, seeds, and insurance), information (price guarantees, technical assistance, and agricultural extension), and distribution (marketing channels and storage facilities). This continued the CNC's role as a mediator of valuable material resources, but also expanded the levers available to the state in establishing social control by using public agencies and public subsidy to build support (Mackinlay 1991, 143–7).[10] Beginning with Echeverría's rural development project (Programa de Inversiones en Desarollo Rural, or PIDER) and expanding dramatically with López Portillo's integrated Mexican Food System (Sistema Alimentario Mexicana, or SAM) aimed at achieving national self-sufficiency, the state's role in agriculture expanded to include virtually every aspect of production (Fox 1993). The result was to contain and "incorporate" protest through new forms of public intervention (Paré 1990, 83).

Neither old-style CNC corporatism, nor the newer production-oriented clientelism of the 1970s and early 1980s survived the catastrophic consequences of the debt crisis and liberalization. Materially and organizationally the basis for this kind of rural social control was devastated. Over the period 1980–8, public rural development investment declined 55.4 percent in real terms, representing 22.9 percent of a much-reduced fiscal pie in 1988, down from 43 percent in 1980 (Mundt and Steffen 1991, 102). And as the wave of privatization crashed over the rural sector, the very institutions that had been expanded or created in the 1970s and 1980s to promote development and incorporate dissent ceased to exist or functioned at a dramatically reduced level.

Unfortunately, peasants had adapted their limited organizational and representational resources by the 1980s to focus on improvement in the terms of production and not demands for land (both within the CNC and without through quasi-autonomous organizations). The cumulative effect was to legitimate the drop-off in land redistribution implemented by the state and to reorient what autonomous organizational activity existed around the extraction of benefits from

---

[10] This included Banrural, the agrarian development bank, as the near-exclusive credit provider for the social sector, public seed and fertilizer firms, irrigation and public works through the Secretary of Agriculture, and price support and marketing through the CONASUPO program.

developmental organizations; but in the 1980s these largely ceased to exist as well (Myhre 1994, 153). Why did these neoliberal reforms then not provoke massive peasant resistance? After all, corporatist control was collapsing alongside living standards. And indeed, serious mobilization *had* emerged earlier in the 1970s despite a far more repressive authoritarian context.[11]

Trade Liberalization, Production Support, and Interest Fragmentation

Nowhere have the effects of neoliberal reform been felt more directly for everyday peasants than in the changes made to the infrastructure of production support built up in the 1970s and early 1980s. State retrenchment in this area began at the very end of the 1980s, and was consolidated in the early 1990s. By privatizing almost the entirety of its agrarian support infrastructure the PRI also sounded the death knell for the last of its corporatist infrastructure: without the ability to exchange excludable material rewards for political support, the traditional infrastructure of clientelism has largely eroded.

In Mexico, a key element in this process was the privatization of rural credit. Historically, access to heavily subsidized agricultural credit from Banrural (the agrarian development bank) had, especially since the 1970s, been used to build the corporatist structure of the PRI in the peasantry (Myhre 1998, 40). After 1990, this was replaced by a new system of agricultural credit that both circumvented traditional institutions and fragmented recipients into distinct strata. Medium-scale private (non-*ejido*) farmers as well as commercial borrowers had access to private and publicly subsidized credit – in the expectation that they would be the bearers of agricultural modernization (Myhre 1998, 42–3). Peasants, especially those in the land-reform sector (*ejidatarios*) were left in the hands of a much-reduced Banrural[12]

---

[11] Notably, the PRI had been willing in the late 1960s to go so far as to engage in a large-scale urban massacre of dissenters (the famous student massacre at Tlatelolco in Mexico City), something clearly politically impossible in the 1980s and 1990s.

[12] Between 1988 and 1994 Banrural closed more than 50 percent of its branches, laid off 62 percent of its staff, and reduced the number of borrowers it served by more than two thirds (Myhre 1998, 42). Increasingly, peasants were left to fend for themselves

and very restricted antipoverty relief through the national solidarity program (PRONASOL).[13]

Indeed, while in the 1970s and 1980s nearly half of the peasantry received credit from public agencies, principally Banrural, after the reforms of 1989 this was reduced to a mere 20 percent, while aggregate agricultural lending plummeted 70 to 80 percent from its precrisis peak (Myhre 1994, 147). Moreover, access to credit in the 1990s became fragmented, with Banrural and private banks concentrating their very limited resources on only those producers with reasonable chances of success in a more liberalized environment and a history of prompt debt repayment.[14] The remainder were to have had access to "adjustment loans" through the credit programs of PRONASOL and PROGRESA, representing a mere 10 percent of the (already reduced) credit available through the banks and Banrural (Pastor and Wise 1998, 70). These loans were, at best, disguised consumption subsidies, providing far too little money for any form of productive readjustment to be conceivable.

Politically, the partial privatization of credit provision introduced serious fragmenting dynamics within peasant communities. Even within a single community in the social (*ejido*) sector the organizational locus of access to credit now diverged, in marked contrast to the unifying dependence on Banrural before the reforms of the late 1980s and 1990s. This fragmentation would mirror nascent class differentiation within communities. Well-off peasants with greater access to higher quality land and experience with export-viable or competitive domestic crops could borrow on the formal (private) credit markets,[15] while those with some hope for adjustment and a good repayment history might have access to the remaining resources provided by Banrural. The poorest

---

in the face of the same usurious private, informal intermediaries that the state had once replaced.

[13] Appendini (1998) points out that while this program targeted large numbers of peasants, the amounts granted were small and clearly aimed at maintaining household consumption, not fomenting economic conversion.

[14] This is crucial because part of the informal political pact that had undergirded the corporatist use of Banrural was a laxness of enforcement in debt repayment in exchange for political support. The imposition of "hard" lending criteria in Banrural further constrained the degree to which even its much reduced funds could be utilized for political purposes.

[15] These were typically private landowners. Because alienation of collective ejidal lands was not possible, these plots could not be used as collateral for private agricultural loans.

were forced to rely on the minimal subsidies available through the social welfare system. For the many peasants above marginality but below the threshold for long-run independent viability, access to formal credit is often impossible – such producers are typically forced to rely on informal credit provided by the newly reemergent local distributors and other usurious middlemen that the public interventions of the 1960s and 1970s had only recently disposed of. Critically, however, even within a typical community the institutional locus of the nevertheless widespread credit grievances was fragmented, rendering collective action around this problem difficult to organize.

Access to credit, while important, was not the only public intervention in support of production historically utilized by the state to build a base of social control. Equally vital in cementing the corporatist bargain were publicly provided price floors for key crops, import protection, as well as a vast network of marketing and distribution channels through the Compañía Nacional de Subsistencias Populares (National Basic Foods Company, or CONASUPO) system (Fox 1993). The latter was particularly important as it undermined the power of local distributional monopolists who had long bedeviled the peasantry, charging excessive prices for the transport of crops to market and taking advantage of the inability of peasants to store harvests to await better market conditions.

It is important to note that many of these interventions were removed or declined only later in the process of economic liberalization – behind the pace of reform experienced by most of the rest of the economy. For example, import licenses were required for agricultural commodities until the end of the 1980s, and CONASUPO remained a substantial purchaser of peasant output throughout the decade (Mundt and Steffen 1991, 105–7). Indeed, the CONASUPO distribution network was not fully privatized until 1996, with the sale of Bodegas Rurales and Almacenes Nacionales [storage facilities] (Rubio 1997, 27).

On the trade side, while many crops were directly exposed to world market prices, many peasants were not. From late 1987 through early 1990 guarantee prices were gradually removed from most agricultural products, with the crucial exception of corn and beans. These two crops, however, constituted an enormous proportion of the marketable peasant surplus, and the continued relative protection in this subsector simply forced a reconversion of other peasant agriculture *into* corn and bean production. Indeed, coterminous with liberalization of prices for most agricultural crops, the tariff on wheat and sorghum was raised by 10 percent in 1990, while corn and bean guarantee prices were increased in real terms (Mundt and Steffen 1991, 110).

Even within the overarching liberal context of NAFTA, Mexico was careful to maintain its strongest protection for the agricultural sector. And within agriculture, the protections sought were to prevent competition in sectors dominated by large numbers of peasant producers (basic grains), not those dominated by the politically more powerful large-scale capitalist farms (fruit, vegetables). The terms of the agreement contained provisions for the phase-in of liberalization for key peasant crops over a fifteen-year period of time, beginning with a conversion from tariffs to equivalent per-hectare cash subsidies, the latter to decline over time (Pastor and Wise 1998, 69; Bonilla and Viatte 1994/5, 25). In the short run, this policy represented a redistribution of the rents from protection from modernized agribusiness producers (who benefit disproportionately from tariffs because their per hectare production is greater) to marginal producers. The latter, of course, were the crucial peasant constituency for the PRI. Agrarian liberalization was thus structured to minimize the short-run costs to peasants.

Land Tenure and Politics

The least liberalized aspect of Mexican agriculture is clearly land tenure. Since the 1930s, tremendous quantities of arable land were incorporated into the agrarian reform in various forms of collective tenure (either *ejidal* or *comunal*). Indeed, by the time efforts to privatize the agrarian reform sector were initiated in the late 1980s and early 1990s, collective tenure arrangements covered 48.6 percent of arable land, and formed the principal means of subsistence for roughly 18 million peasants, some 21 percent of the total population (Thompson and Wilson 1994, 449).

Two aspects of the process of land privatization effort after 1992 are critical. First, it was designed to proceed in a geographically and (in practice) sectorally fragmented fashion. Second, the legal mechanisms required to convert social property to private property induce division within peasant communities long before the actual transition away from collective ownership takes place. As a consequence of this disjuncture, by the time political mobilization to defend the *ejido* (land-reform cooperative) might be necessary it would be extremely difficult to organize and nearly impossible to generalize across farms.

How was land privatization structured? It was only in 1992 that the creation of a legal market for agrarian reform lands even became a theoretical possibility, with the reforms to Article 27 of the constitution and the introduction of a new Ley Agraria (Agrarian Law). While the creation of new reform properties had slowed to a near halt by the early 1980s, moves in the direction of land privatization were delayed. In marked contrast to urban areas where economic liberalization and political opening began to take shape seriously in the 1980s, in the countryside a political countermovement can be detected. Peasant land in large measure remained firmly under the control of the *ejido* system, while the latter was "reformed" so as to increase the power of PRI-affiliated local bosses.[16] This effort to heighten local authoritarianism is unsurprising given that exchange-mediated corporatist ties were wearing thin with the end of active land redistribution and the severe declines in production support to be doled out in the 1980s.

Despite glowing predictions to the contrary, however, the progress of land liberalization once initiated has been decidedly slow and uneven. The Programa de Certificación de Derechos Ejidales (PROCEDE, or ejido rights certification program) property demarcation effort was initiated in 1993 and was to have completely mapped and certified individual ejidal plots by the end of 1994, as a precursor to privatization.[17] And despite attempts by local authorities to condition important benefits on participation in the program, only 6.1 percent of ejido land

---

[16] The crucial reform was to provide for a majority election for all parts of the ejido governance structure, including the executive, the *Comisariado Ejidal* and the oversight body, the *Consejo de Vigilancia*. Formerly, the latter was comprised of the second-place slate in the election for *Comisariado*. This had guaranteed a minimal level of opposition control within the *ejido* power structure, while direct election permitted the dominant faction – almost always PRI affiliated – to monopolize all the levers of local authority and oversight (Mackinlay 1994, 147).

[17] Land titling, it is important to note, only meant the legal demarcation and codification of individual-use rights within the collectively owned ejido. Substantial further steps – including a majority vote in favor – were required before such individually delineated plots would constitute private property that could be mortgaged or sold.

had been given clear boundaries within this time frame (Appendini 1998, 31). Moreover, progress was widely heterogeneous – one study indicates vastly different rates of participation even across comparably poor and indigenous states like Chiapas and Oaxaca (Stephen 1998, 9). Only in Chiapas was concerted peasant action to block land parcelization important – an exception that will be explored more directly in the following text. The foregoing underlines the complexity of initiating neoliberal reforms in the context of serious declines in living standards. Unlike Chile, the initial liberalization of agriculture in Mexico did not take place in a highly repressive and centralized authoritarian context. But just as in Chile, the goal was to utilize market mechanisms to make an inevitable re-concentration of land in nonpeasant hands politically palatable.

While it began as a top-down executive enactment, the process of reversing the socialization of agriculture in Mexico was deliberately constructed to proceed in a decentralized and fragmented fashion. While in Chile the *consequences* of agrarian privatization served to atomize and divide the peasantry, in Mexico the *process* of privatization is having this effect.[18] This is crucial in part because in Mexico the process of reversing the land reform – and the attack on peasant vested interests it represents – could have the potential to produce widespread and destabilizing resistance in precisely the political sector that the PRI was counting on for critical electoral support.

As written into the constitutional reform and associated agrarian legislation – the *Ley Agraria* of 1992 and PROCEDE – the privatization of social property in the countryside proceeds in two broad stages.[19]

---

[18] The sudden, universal, and generally income-reducing character of the agrarian privatization process in Chile made it a reform that had the potential to raise widespread, mobilized opposition. Its completion in the context of a period of extraordinary repression (1973–9) accounts for the lack of mobilized opposition, while its fragmenting social effects *after consolidation* have in part accounted for the disorganized and unmobilized character of rural politics (see Chapter 4).

[19] In actuality, the social (collective) property area in Mexico encompasses two forms of tenure: *ejidal* and *comunal*. The latter is a descendent of surviving indigenous corporate communities more than the product of the process of agrarian reform. The former were the land-reform collectives initiated under the terms of the postrevolutionary Mexican constitution. Only ejidal lands have been effectively targeted for privatization, with only a small pilot program that would make possible the alienation of communal lands launched (typically located in the Pacific South, especially Oaxaca).

The first involved the demarcation and certification of individual rights to land *within* the ejido. The second involved a collective decision (requiring a supermajority) whether or not to convert ejidal territory to alienable and mortgageable individual private property. Most[20] ejidos had long functioned on the basis of individual farm plots operated within the collectively owned ejido. But no clear delineation of boundaries or use rights accrued to these farmsteads, and they were in theory (though not widely in practice) subject to redistribution among the ejido members (Dewalt et al. 1994, 35). Nor were they (until 1992) alienable or rentable; though these practices were not uncommon if always illegal.

The difficulty was that each step in land privatization could and often does produce substantial conflicts of interest within and across ejidos. The very demarcation of individual rights within the ejido is a complex process, as existing family plots were not necessarily allocated on an egalitarian basis and the boundaries are frequently disputed and unclear. Indeed, by way of example, during the process of individual plot delineation in the 533 ejidos of Oaxaca, some 38 percent had by 1998 already entered officially recognized collective boundary conflicts with the Agrarian Attorney General (Procuraduría Agraria) (Stephen 1998, 10). This does not include those that also have (often long-standing) boundary disputes with neighboring private landholders or those whose internal conflicts have not yet escalated into officially recognized disputes. Indeed, a substantial number of ejidos have yet even to begin the process of titling.

The result is a trajectory of land privatization that is necessarily slow and uneven, but also structured so that coherent opposition cannot form, not at the farm level and much less so at the level of a social class. In the first place, the receptiveness of rural sectors to land privatization depends heavily on the quality of land owned by the ejido and the perceived likelihood of conversion to successful independent commercial agriculture. This is substantially more likely in the more modernized and export-oriented areas of the North, and decidedly unlikely in the more marginal, more densely populated, and more indigenous

---

[20] While ejidos were all collectively *owned*, most were farmed in large part as individual parcels, at least that part of their land not devoted to grazing. A small number were, however, operated as fully collectivized enterprises.

areas of the South. Beyond issues of timing, the likelihood of success-ful transition to commercial agriculture is also likely to vary *within* the ejido, and has been linked to divisions over whether to proceed with the reforms.[21] Those with more substantial skills or access to larger or better plots of land are likely to press for privatization, while those in a comparatively disadvantaged situation are more likely to strive to retain the collective structure as a hedge against insecurity and in the hopes of continued state support.

The privatization of the ejidos should be contextualized – the land re-form co-ops are neither generally prosperous nor internally democratic. Indeed, some have suggested that the most corrupt and backward would be the first to be privatized – because therein the relative po-litical and economic costs of collective ownership are highest (Dewalt et al. 1994, 55). This expectation is reasonable in the absence of severe collective action problems. Empirically, however, there is little orga-nized activity *either for or against* privatization, even in the most cor-rupt ejido areas and despite the fact that the state actively promotes the PROCEDE titling program. The notable exception is in the poorest and most remote parts of Chiapas. But these areas have been a basis for collective action founded on ethnic identification, not class inter-ests. Communities there have also been less affected by liberalization-induced social differentiation and interest fragmentation, and indeed the incentives to act collectively produced by public activity are greater: it is the only part of Mexico where land redistribution continues (Harvey 1996).

The results are striking – even where there is much to be gained from land privatization, there is little to pressure to support it. But equally important, in areas where privatization is likely only to bring further declines in living standards and the possibility of land loss there is little organized resistance to it. What this suggests is that material deprivation, reversal of agrarian reform, and the abandonment of the PRI's historic ideological and rhetorical commitment to peasant society has not been the key factor in explaining the political behavior of peasants. Instead, problems of organization and the absence of serious rural political competition are the key issues.

---

[21] It should be remembered that final approval of individual land titling requires a majority vote of the ejido's assembly.

The liberalization of land tenure coupled with the preexisting rural social structure has produced a dramatic degree of fragmentation in rural social geography. In Mexico, peasants have been divided among the over 28,000 ejidos, between reform-sector dwellers and the even less fortunate whose rights to agricultural land were either not enforced or not recognized, and between the regions with vastly different agro-climatic potential and infrastructural resources. Crucial to enhancing this fragmentation is the ostensibly "bottom-up" character of land privatization through the PROCEDE program. Because the legally defined initiative to begin the process comes from within the community (in marked contrast to most past practice), the state's role is in many ways that of arbiter of the process rather than promoter.

In contemporary Mexico, when inevitable conflicts within communities emerge over essential questions – such as the distribution of land, water rights, or physical capital – it is the state agrarian bureaucracy that adjudicates winners. The *initiative*, at least formally, must come from below. Ironically, this gave the PRI-dominated agrarian apparatus one final and critical lever over local politics, but one that is essentially costless: control over the adjudication of land privatization. But the uncertainties of enforcement and deliberate legal vagueness about individual entitlements to ejidal lands make the powerful role of the Ministry of Agriculture and the Procuraduría Agraria two final pieces in a political opportunity structure designed to discourage protest and mobilize support.

COLLECTIVE ACTION AND THE SOCIAL FOUNDATIONS OF MEXICAN DEMOCRACY

While it has long been taken as an article of faith that the Mexican countryside would be a bastion of support for the long-governing PRI, there are strong reasons to expect precisely the opposite. It is true that electoral support for the PRI has historically been overwhelming in the countryside (as was true of urban areas as well until the 1980s); it is equally true that the peasantry has in the past been able to mobilize politically when its interests were directly threatened, on a local or regional if not national basis. And this mobilization has often been sufficient to bring substantial material responses from the state – including a reinvigoration of land redistribution in the early to mid-1970s and the massive expansion of developmental aid to peasant agriculture in the late 1970s and early 1980s (Bartra 1985, esp. 102–12).

The onset of the debt crisis and the subsequent initiation of a neoliberal developmental strategy are well known to have produced dramatic material hardships for much of the Mexican population. They have also been associated with the decline in political support for the PRI, beginning with the near loss of the presidency in the elections of 1988 and culminating with a definitive handover of power in August of 2000. At the same time, opponents of the PRI have been able to consolidate a powerful hold on important portions of the urban electorate as well as a range of state governments and the mayoralty of the federal district. In the cities the PRI is effectively confronted politically by the PAN on the right, the PRD on the left, and a host of sectoral, class, and political movements on all sides.[22]

What is striking about the comparative plethora of urban opposition and quasi-opposition is that it represents groups that, while certainly materially disadvantaged by reforms, suffered less than those in the countryside that continue to support the PRI. Independent rural opposition mobilization, despite massive economic and social dislocations, has been scattered, localized, and in large measure ineffective. The most prominent exception to this general pattern – the EZLN in Chiapas – will be discussed in the following text. But as a rule, peasants have found it much more difficult to organize in opposition to neoliberalism, even as they have increasingly become its most obvious victims.

How bad have things become in the countryside? Would the current state of affairs lend one to expect a mobilized response? The agricultural sector has long been less productive than the rest of Mexico, representing some 25 percent of the economically active labor force but providing less than six percent of overall output (David et al. 2000, 1680). While peasants were long the most disadvantaged segment of Mexican society, the downturns of the 1980s and 1990s imposed disproportionate costs on this already underprivileged group. By the late 1980s agricultural growth rates in the aggregate had turned negative, and from 1984–9 agricultural wages dropped by 25 percent in real terms; the decline was 63 percent over the entire 1982–96 period

---

[22] Such movements range widely, having included middle-class debtors organizations, independent labor unions, neighborhood groups, student protests, associations of earthquake victims, and popular defense committees.

(McKinley and Alarcón 1995, 1575; David et al. 2000, 1682). Public social development spending, upon which the countryside was disproportionately dependent, declined in the 1980s at a rate of roughly 6 percent *per year*, until reversed with the initiation of Carlos Salinas' PRONASOL program (Friedmann et al. 1995, 344–6).

The evidence suggests that rural poverty has reached catastrophic levels, and even the "recovery" of the mid-1980s did little to reverse the trend. In 1989 rates of poverty and indigence in the countryside stood at 49 and 23 percent respectively. By 1994, after "the return to growth" of the Salinas *sexenio*, the rates had declined only to 47 and 20 percent, respectively. By 1996 the effects of the peso crisis had reversed what little improvement had taken place, bringing poverty to a majority of the countryside and indigence to a quarter – 53 and 25 percent, respectively (David et al. 2000, 1682). National rates of poverty, on the other hand, in 1989 were 23.6 percent, indicating that the poor were overwhelmingly concentrated in the countryside. Indeed, McKinley and Alarcón (1995, 1575–6) estimate that fully 70 percent of all the poor reside in the countryside and among the poor, the very poorest are even more disproportionately rural.

This begs an important question: if peasants are already in many cases on the margins of subsistence, and if the neoliberal reforms of the 1980s have had such materially devastating consequences for them, why have the public expressions of discontent in this sector been muted, fragmented, and largely politically inefficacious? This is particularly notable by contrast with the much more widespread and effective resistance manifested in urban areas. And because even under the decidedly more authoritarian political and less severe economic conditions that prevailed before the debt crisis, Mexican peasants *were* historically able to organize their grievances and force at least some national-level response. More stunning even than this is that this sector has instead remained the electoral bastion of the neoliberal party that provoked its very material decline.

Collective Action in the Mexican Countryside: Exit, Occupied Space, and Fragmentation

It is the rural demobilization provoked by neoliberalism that has made the simultaneous pursuit of economic and political reform in Mexico a possibility – despite many scholars' initial suspicion that they could only effectively be carried out in an authoritarian context (as indeed they were in Chile).[23] Surprisingly, the short-term (medium?) pain involved in economic opening has not posed the insurmountable political problems anticipated by many.[24] Nor has it resulted in economically suboptimal "partial reform equilibria" dominated by the rent-seeking beneficiaries of unevenness in the pace of transformation.[25] But most critically it has also been a principal foundation of the Mexican democratic transition. Without a large and predictable base of support in the countryside, PRI presidents would have been unable to continue dramatic economic reforms without recourse to increasingly authoritarian practices.

Why have peasants supported the PRI and its neoliberal reforms in such large numbers? Beyond the social atomization and heightened economic vulnerability brought about by liberalization, three further factors have hindered collective rural political activity. First, the viability of individualistic exit strategies made apolitical responses more likely and removed dissidents from the rural sector altogether. Second, the absence of strong *rural* partisan competition – based in the limited differences between the agrarian programs of the three main political parties[26] – has hindered the utilization of external resources

---

[23] For examples of this perspective, see Sheahan (1987) and Petras and Leiva (1994).

[24] Williamson (1994) and Bunce (1995) have emphasized the difficulties in pursuing painful reforms in politically open settings. Others have suggested that specifically labor-backed parties, able to use institutional resources to mitigate potential dissent might make painful reform possible in democratic contexts. The latter approach is promising, but in some senses incomplete. Control over labor has certainly prevented effective resistance to reform in the economic sphere, but it has not (at least in Mexico) provided the necessary *political* support for the reformist parties. This support has come from the countryside, and has in large measure not been retained because of existing corporatist institutional resources, but in large measure despite their very dramatic erosion.

[25] This is a pattern identified by Hellman (1998) in his analysis of the transition to market economies in the formerly communist world. Certainly rents were taken during the process of reform, but the rent seekers did not stop the process in an suboptimal "intermediate" state.

[26] This is obviously most true of the PRI and PAN. In many ways the PAN represents an alternative to the PRI that is even less attractive for peasants, insofar as it has called for the reduction of the remaining public subsidies that help to stabilize rural subsistence. No opposition party has made agrarian redevelopment, particularly that of peasant agriculture, an important piece of its national political agenda. While it is unsurprising that the PAN has a liberal economic orientation, even the

to underwrite rural mobilization. Finally, an "organizational field" already occupied by officialist and quasi-official organizations inhibited the creation of powerful and autonomous new groups.

Exit. Understanding the capacities of Mexican peasants to engage in political action begins with an evaluation of the plausible alternatives. Because economic policy changes have the character of public (or at least collective) goods, organizing large groups to pursue them ought be difficult (Olson 1965). Where material deprivation is severe enough, one might still expect collective action even though incentives to free ride exist because the costs of inaction could be catastrophic – the actors in question are indeed not far removed from the subsistence line.[27] But where the possibility of individual-level solutions exist, collective political organization is unlikely. And precisely that option is available to many Mexican peasants in the form of migration.

The political consequences of the migratory escape valve are actually quite paradoxical. On the one hand migration should be associated with lower levels of collective organization. Peasants will exit crushingly poor areas rather than act in concert to demand mitigation of their poverty. Only where migration is less realistic will a stronger premium be placed on political activity as a strategy to stabilize subsistence. On the other hand, because the existence of the migratory option reduce vulnerability and dependence on local elites (particularly if it brings remittance payments), it would simultaneously facilitate oppositional behavior that did not entail costly collective action – for example, voting for reformist political parties.

The evidence on these points is necessarily indirect and impressionistic. Nevertheless, the states of Mexico presently known for their comparatively high levels of peasant mobilization (and the only ones with measureable insurrectionary movements) are Chiapas, Guerrero, and Oaxaca. Of these, land invasions – a historic form of peasant collective

---

PRD's (http://www.prd.org.mx/programa/programa1.html, accessed February 26, 2001) platform outlining its proposals to reorient the Mexican political economy contains only a one-line reference to "agricultural development," and no mention of agrarian reform, relief from international competition, or prevention of monopsonistic practices by local middlemen.

[27] The relationship between threats to peasant subsistence and collective action are most closely associated with the work of Scott (1976, 1985).

TABLE 6.1 *Geographic Mobility and the Foundations of PRI Support (OLS Estimates with Huber/White Standard Errors)*

	1994 Presidential Elections	1994 Deputies' Elections[a]	1997 Deputies' Elections[a]
Constant	0.548**	0.558**	0.427**
	(0.027)	(0.027)	(0.023)
Proportion Migrant	−0.179*	−0.114	−0.194*
[0, 0.392]	(0.099)	(0.098)	(0.110)
Proportion Rural	0.128**	0.136**	0.103**
[0, 1]	(0.010)	(0.010)	(0.009)
Proportion Poor	−0.072**	−0.100**	−0.099**
[0, 0.98]	(0.022)	(0.022)	(0.019)
Mean Years of Schooling	−0.0083**	−0.0088**	0.0089**
[0.6, 11.1]	(0.0036)	(0.0035)	(0.0031)
N	2384	2351	2387

[a] Data are from the party votes for the proportional representation component of the deputies' election.
* Statistically significant at the $p < 0.10$ level.
** Statistically significant at the $p < 0.05$ level.
Sources: Independent variables are from INEGI (1990). Electoral results are from IFE (1994, 1997).

action – are prevalent mostly in Chiapas as a result of the failure of the land reform to have effectively reached this state (Harvey 1996, 155). But these are also states with moderate levels of out-migration. Guerrero and Oaxaca are average in terms of international emigration. Chiapas, on the other hand is 31 of 32 in rates of international exit.[28] It is the latter that is most informative: sustained mobilization occurs in a state in which the migratory option (for whatever reasons) is largely foreclosed.

More interesting, however, are the better data that are available connecting the exit option with electoral behavior. Table 6.1 presents the results of regression of municipal level migration rates (from 1990) on voting patterns for the 1994 and 1997 House of Deputies election, as well as the 1994 presidential election, controlling for poverty, rural residence, and education. These data suggest that there is a fairly consistent result connecting the relative availability of an individualized

---

[28] For these purposes the Federal District of Mexico City is counted as a state. Data are from INEGI (2000, Tables Migración 2 and Migración 9).

exit option (migration) from economic hardship with opposition to the long-governing PRI. That is, where dependence is reduced (either through the viability and thus threat of exit, or through the remittances produced by earlier migrants) the ability of the PRI to mobilize electoral supporters declines fairly dramatically. While the estimates of this decline do not attain statistical significance in all cases, the magnitudes of the coefficients are consistently high (accounting for a predicted decline in PRI support of between 5 to 8.7 percentage points in multiparty contests). At the same time the overall relationship between rural residence and PRI support remains quite strong.

Voiceless: Interest Fragmentation and Political Space. While I contend that the Mexican countryside, like the Chilean, is rife with barriers to collective action that are attributable to the implementation of neoliberal reforms, the mechanisms by which this comes to pass are somewhat different. This difference reflects the legacies of the social revolution, agrarian reform, and corporatism that were the hallmarks of Mexican "soft authoritarianism" since the 1920s. The core effects of the neoliberal transformation have been similar: communities are divided from each other as a function of differential endowments and/or agricultural subsector; they are divided from within by differentiation in the control over land, the informalization of labor processes, and heightened economic stratification. At the same time, the power of PRI-affiliated local elites – be they *caciques* embedded in the ejidal power structure, large landholders, or those with local monopolies over distribution and marketing channels – has been heightened dramatically.

   That being said, there are still substantial differences in the opportunity structure facing peasants in rural Mexico compared to Chile; the barriers are no less high, but they are built of different materials. Perhaps the most important feature of the Mexican social landscape that affects the collective action and the organization of rural interests has to do with the continued presence of the *ejido*. This organization stands as an institutional intermediary between individual peasants (in the reform sector) and extracommunity political actors that might be the focus of political pressure. While *ejidal* elites certainly no longer control access to the gamut of material resources essential to everyday peasant life chances that they used to,[29] they remain obvious targets of local action. In this way they help to defuse conflicts that might be generalizable, keeping them at a local (and generally undemocratic) level. They also help to divide peasant efforts, by obscuring whether national or local politics are the essential points of entry for the amelioration of grievances.

Probably more important to the ability of peasants to organize independently is the fact that the organizational field in which they must operate is – in marked contrast to Chile – already occupied by a plethora of organizations. This by no means is restricted to the remaining vestiges of the corporatist system embodied in formerly important, officially PRI-linked groups like the CNC for peasants, or the Confederación Nacional de Pequeños Propietarios (National Confederation of Small Propietors, or CNPP) for private-sector smallholders. To this must be added the gamut of organizations that were in the 1980s and 1990s initially (quasi-)independent, but that have been incorporated into official channels of representation and bargaining in ways that have dramatically reduced their ability to autonomously represent peasant interests (Bartra 1985).

The independent movements that do emerge, often find maintaining their indepence difficult. Such was the case of Antorcha Campesina (Peasant Torch), which had its origins in student radicalism and ended as a semiofficial paramilitary arm of the PRI (Snyder 2001b, 174). Similarly, the Unión de Organizaciones Regionales Campesinas Autónomas (Union of Autonomous Regional Peasant Organizations, or UNORCA), a principal independent peasant voice in the 1980s succumbed to corporatist inclusion. Most notably, its president, Hugo Andrés Araujo, joined the CNC leadership (Snyder 2001b, 148). In each case the material benefits of incorporation came at the cost of political autonomy.

Understanding the dynamics of collective action in an occupied organizational field is more complicated than the simple fragmentation and demobilization produced under neoliberal conditions in the Chilean context. In the first place, efforts to organize any particular latent group

---

[29] Combined with the official peasant organizations, this once included such critical issues as access to land, the availability of credit and inputs, and even assistance in acquiring housing.

among the peasantry (whether as a class, sectoral, regional, or other interest) faces the probability that already one or (frequently) more groups already claim to "represent" that sector; and in reality they do this to greater and lesser extents. Thus the latent groups already face the dilemma of having a portion of their potential constituency already bound up in existing (but politically not autonomous) organizational relationships, and thus is unlikely to be available for participation in a contending group.

When the state enters into this analysis, organization becomes even more problematic. The Mexican state quite often has *bargained* with rural actors, rather than exclusively resorting to repression, thereby providing an incentive for groups to engage in cooperative behavior. Frequently real material resources are at stake in these negotiations (but *not* major reorientations of policy). But the state *selects* the groups with which it will negotiate and which ones it will exclude – inducing compliant and nonconfrontational behavior. Moreover, organizational entrepreneurs seeking to maintain their autonomy face a severe problem: they marginalize themselves from small but immediate benefits (and sometimes not-so-small personal benefits for leaders) in the hopes of inducing long-term political changes. But they must also maintain the commitment of their membership in the face of a situation in which incremental gains are possible through participation in less autonomous groups that do receive public attention. Even an individual willing to pay the personal costs of participation would likely opt out of autonomous organizations where more moderate alternatives exist, and where persistent autonomous mobilization carries real material risks (of exclusion from land, material benefits, or even physical repression).

The consequence is that Mexican rural society is a hostile environment for the emergence of autonomous, politically active groups. Where organization does emerge, it tends to be local in orientation, given that strong incentives exist to fragment participation along regional, ethnic, subsectoral, and land-tenure lines. And within these fragments, powerful incentives also present for peasants to participate in partially or wholly subordinate institutional channels.[30] Thus

---

[30] Indeed, even where the governing party was forced to negotiate with relatively autonomous peasant groups, official organizations are always included in the discussion

rather than facing an all-or-nothing choice in engaging in political activity, Mexican peasants face incentives to keep their demands – should they manage to articulate them – local, sector-specific, and channeled through "recognized" organizations.[31]

Understanding the ability of peasants to engage in autonomous collective action is not strictly an internal question. It must be placed in the context of the likely opponents of such efforts at self-organization, in this case local elites (whether landlords or ejidal *caciques*). Liberalization, by dramatically reducing the role of the state in critical aspects of peasant life (the provision of credit, distribution channels, guaranteeing prices, distributing land, crop insurance, and inputs), has forced peasant reliance on local providers. But these providers are very often the historically dominant local elites – only they are now freed from competition through publicly provided marketing and distribution channels.[32] It is important to remember that I do not argue here that this has recreated a traditional form of patron-client relationship.[33] Instead it is a market-mediated dependence that discourages political activity or economic mobilization, but without implying the day-to-day level of oversight or interaction characteristic of a traditional manorial economy like the pre–land reform Chilean hacienda or the heavy-handed corporatism of Mexico's past.

My argument then is that peasants in contemporary Mexican rural society face a triple burden in aggregating their interests and introducing them into the national political debate: (1) they face standard collective action problems consequent upon the introduction of socially atomizing neoliberal reforms, (2) they must operate in a political field populated with less-than-autonomous groups that dominate the remaining linkages to the state, and (3) they must do so in the face

as a way to frame the boundaries of debate to less central points and to mitigate dissent as much as possible.

[31] "Recognition" extends well beyond the official corporatist organizations to include peasant groups with which the state has officially agreed to "discuss" matters of importance to the rural sector. But such inclusion has generally come at the cost of reduction of autonomy in the expression of peasant grievances (Bartra 1985).

[32] Indeed, these very channels were constructed, largely in the 1970s, as a result of widespread peasant agitation, in an effort to overcome exactly these sorts of exploitative monopsonies.

[33] Classical patron-client dependence is by its nature much more multifaceted and encompassing. Here the ties are dependent, but quite narrow.

of PRI-linked local elites whose power has in many ways increased dramatically as a consequence of economic liberalization.

My hypothesis thus suggests a rather paradoxical political outcome in the countryside: despite being (absolutely and relatively) materially disadvantaged by free market economic reforms, it is among peasants that neoliberal elites in the PRI have managed to sustain a viable mass base, one on whom increasingly their party's future depends. The reasons for the viability of this sandwich coalition of urban beneficiaries and rural losers from reform hinge on the inability of peasants to articulate concrete alternative perspectives, to aggregate them to the extent they are articulated, and the vulnerability of peasants to the political pressures of local elites. In the following sections I will explore the scope and weight of this peasant base.

Subnational Variations: State-Level Corporatism and Peasant Politics

There are important differences in the context and manner in which free market reforms were introduced in the Mexican and Chilean contexts. Most critically, reforms in Mexico were implemented by a governing party that was internally divided as to their wisdom in a political system that was organized along federal lines. By contrast, while reforms were certainly not implemented as a package in Chile, they were introduced without substantial regional variation or open intragovernmental dissent. The result was that while the Mexican national government was clearly committed to a broad free market developmental model by the late 1980s, the leaders of many of its federal subunits were not. Instead, they sometimes responded to the withdrawal of the national government from economic regulation and management with state-level corporatist efforts to fill the void.

The political implications of these different state-level development strategies – what Snyder (2001b) has called "reregulation" – sets up a further test of the marketization and atomization hypothesis that is central to this book. The expectations are simple: in states where populist governors respond to national-level liberalization by expanding the scope of state government intervention and corporatism, organization and mobilization should be substantially greater than in areas where governors' policies are in keeping with the national neoliberal trajectory.

A penetrating recent set of analyses by Snyder (1999, 2001b) have help to shed light on how geographic differences in implementation of policy reforms have affected agrarian political organization and mobilization. This work centers on four state-level responses to national-level liberalization of the coffee sector. Beginning in 1989, the Mexican government dismantled the Mexican National Coffee Institute (Instituto Mexicano del Café, INMECAFE), which until that point had dominated all aspects of the coffee trade save cultivation itself. The governors of two principal coffee-producing states – Oaxaca and Guerrero – bucked the national-level neoliberal trend and sought to recreate corporatism in the coffee sector through state-level organizations aimed at smallholders. Two others – Chiapas and Puebla – instead adopted elite-centered and much more deregulated coffee-sector policies that were much more consonant with the national neoliberal consensus (on this choice, see Snyder 2001b, 24–5).

The contrasts that resulted across these four states are telling. In Oaxaca, the incentives for peasants to participate politically and economically embedded in a persistently regulatory local environment produced "a veritable explosion of official rural organizations," while at the same time engendering dramatic expansion and unification among independent peasant groups (Snyder 2001, 67, 70). Not only did neo-corporatism help create organization, but it did so well it escaped political control! In Guerrero, efforts at neocorporatist reregulation in the coffee sector provoked a different kind of mobilization: resistance rather than participation, ending in the "politicization of the coffee sector, which resulted in an exclusionary policy framework that delivered few, if any benefits to producers" (Snyder 2001, 132). In Chiapas exclusionary efforts by the state governor's office were met with fierce peasant resistance, but it was resistance that was based in a far less liberalized context than most of the rest of agrarian Mexico. It was also resistance that for idiosyncratic reasons – the Zapatista rebellion – had the strong support of reformist federal officials (Snyder 2001, 135). In Puebla, the clearest case of federal- and state-level liberalization in the coffee sector, "independent organizations were unable to capitalize on the dismantling of INMECAFE" (Snyder 2001b, 170).

The point is that even in a sector unusual for its preexisting level of organization and dependence on indpendent farmers' liberalization induced atomization and decline. The exceptions – where the state government reregulated the coffee economy along neocorporatist lines or where strong indigenous identity, weak liberalization, and external support made collective action easier – are those that would be expected.

Alternative Explanations: State-Clientelism and Neopopulism or Free Market Dependence?

The difficulty with the atomization argument outlined in this book is that it is in Mexico in many ways observationally equivalent with its most plausible rival: the neopopulism hypothesis. This approach treats the support for the PRI in the countryside as a function of the effective channeling of social welfare resources in an effort to "compensate" for the costs of neoliberal reforms and "buy" support during the crucial time of transition. And it is certainly the case that very substantial sums were spent for such purposes during the heyday of reform, most notably with PRONASOL of President Salinas, but also including the much less ambitious PROGRESA program of President Zedillo (Kurtz 2002).

Thinking of peasant support as a consequence of either the last vestiges of corporatist control or the side payments made through new social welfare programs carries decidedly different implications from the hypothesis put forward in this book that roots peasant conservatism in the atomizing and dependency-inducing effects of agrarian neoliberalism. Both approaches predict the same overall outcome in the short run: substantial support for free market political forces among the peasant victims of neoliberalism. But they have decidedly different longer term implications. The neopopulist perspective views welfare schemes as side payments to get through a patchy transition moment, but the logic of continued liberalization should with time undermine the efficacy of this form of social control and electoral engineering. As liberalization removes the state from an active role in managing the economic affairs of the countryside and the end of privatization revenues and the commitment to fiscal responsibility scales back the use of public funds for patronage purposes, one would expect peasant support for the PRI to decline. On the other hand, if liberalization is a fundamental reason for the survival of the PRI, through a reconstituted form of social control over the rural sector, one would expect that further liberalization would only heighten not diminish the defects of agrarian democracy.

It is well known that the Mexican state, most particularly under Salinas, *sought* to use PRONASOL funds to help build political support (Bartra 1996). What is decidedly less clear, however, is whether it actually functioned in this fashion. Certainly some have argued that this is indeed the case, but empirical analyses have relied almost entirely on extremely aggregated data not well suited to directly evaluating the claims made. This is in part inevitable – the relevant data are largely unavailable. Those supporting the new clientelism thesis are, however, also bedeviled by other problems: they tend simultaneously to emphasize the importance of remaining corporatist channels even though these were purposely bypassed in the construction of new social spending institutions, and they bracket the question of why such compensatory programs failed utterly to generate political support in *urban* areas. This is particularly true given that spending in the most important program areas of PRONASOL disproportionately benefited *urban* areas (Lustig 1994, 91, 96).

There are other empirical reasons to doubt the compensation hypothesis, however intuitively attractive it is as an explanation for opposition politicians who have long attempted to compete with the PRI. Because the level of compensation offered through PRONASOL was vastly less than the decline in living standards induced during neoliberal restructuring, for peasants to continue to support the PRI (as they do) as a consequence of neopopulist distribution they must either (1) misunderstand their own interests, or (2) reasonably believe that critical (if marginal) benefits will be withdrawn if they fail to support PRI candidates.

The former mechanism is implausible, as Mexican peasants have long been capable of quite substantial collective action in defense of their interests, even in the face of a decidedly hostile state – evidence of this spans the country and much of the century, from the insurrections of the *Cristiada* after the revolution, to the mobilizations in the Laguna region during the land reform, to the wave of mobilization that provoked President Echeverría to reinitiate the land reform in the 1970s.[34]

---

[34] This is not, however, in contradiction with my argument that collective action is *presently* extremely difficult in the Mexican countryside. Indeed, the advent of formal

Nor are these peasants irrational traditionalists. They have responded quite adeptly and rationally to price signals as they have changed across time in Mexican agriculture, most recently by shifting their output into the protected corn and bean subsectors as tariff walls fell. A group that misunderstands their interests peasants are not.

The possibility that peasants support the PRI out of fear of the withdrawal of social welfare supports is more complicated to deal with. Certainly the PRI struggled mightily in the 1990s to undermine the notion that ballots were secret for poorer voters, even as they were in actuality becoming much more so. Nevertheless, the capacity to pierce ballot secrecy, while probably present to some extent in rural areas in 1988, was undermined by the time of the 1994 presidential elections, and almost all would agree that by 2000 was virtually impossible on any substantial scale (see Fox 1996 on the 1994 elections). The problem for the neopopulism argument is that throughout the 1990s Mexican balloting became far less fraud ridden – and hence something on which social benefits could not easily be conditioned. And by the 1990s there was little evidence that substantial portions of the social welfare budget, particularly once they were administered through the much more technocratic PROGRESA program of the Zedillo administration – were ever systematically withheld from those who failed to support the PRI.[35]

To evaluate empirically the compensation hypothesis, its causal mechanisms must be clearly specified. There are two plausible (and polar) alternatives here. Either PRONASOL and PROGRESA spending was targeted at areas of opposition strength in order to recapture votes that were lost in the disputed 1988 elections, or they were targeted to PRI-supporting communities with the goal of locking down a crucial support base. I examine both of these hypotheses with the available disaggregated data on PRONASOL spending in Table 6.2.[36]

---

democracy has not brought with it a greater ability of peasants to organize and promote their own interests. Rather, because it has been associated with neoliberalism it has provoked precisely the opposite, although without recourse to the level of heavy-handed repression characteristic of the past.

[35] PROGRESA at least theoretically envisions a strict targeting based on socioeconomic needs, and in this sense contrasts markedly with the preceding PRONASOL program (Poder Ejecutivo Federal 1998).

[36] Several caveats are important here. Most analyses of PRONASOL spending have relied on state-level aggregate figures, making it very difficult to evaluate claims about

TABLE 6.2 *The Dynamics of PRONASOL Spending[a]: Politics or Poverty?*
(OLS Regression Estimates with Huber/White Standard Errors)

	Model I	Model II	Model III	Model IV
Constant	−0.161	−0.331	−0.573**	−0.657**
	(0.118)	(0.237)	(0.230)	(0.289)
Poverty[b] (Percentage of	0.00318**	0.00431**	0.00363**	0.00367**
Employed Earning <	(0.00104)	(0.00116)	(0.00116)	(0.00124)
Minimum Wage)				
Education[b] (Mean Years		0.0203	0.0550**	0.0558**
of Schooling)		(0.0171)	(0.0179)	(0.0180)
Rural Composition[b]			0.331**	0.331**
(Proportion Rural)			(0.0620)	(0.0651)
PRI Vote Share (1994	0.649**	0.687**	0.465	0.547**
Presidential)	(0.253)	(0.276)	(0.285)	(0.237)
PAN Vote Share (1994				0.0600
Presidential)				(0.392)
PRD Vote Share (1994				0.116
Presidential)				(0.405)
N	1,110	1,110	1,110	1,110

[a] Data are measured as total per capita spending across the four main components of the 1988–94 Programa Nacional de Solidaridad program, measured at the municipal level. The components included are Niños de Solidaridad (children), Fondos Municipales (municipal development), Escuela Digna (schools), and Solidaridad para la Producción (production). Data were collected independently by the states, but reports were accessible only for a subset of the thirty-two states (and Federal District) of the Mexican Federation: Aguascalientes, Chiapas, Durango, Federal District, Guanajuato, Guerrero, Mexico, Morelos, Nayarit, Nuevo León, Puebla, Querétaro, Sinaloa, Tabasco, Tamulipas, Tlaxcala, Veracruz, Zacatecas. This represents more than half the states and slightly less than half the municipalities of the country.

[b] Data are taken from the indicators of well-being derived from the XI Censo de Población y Vivienda, 1990. See INEGI (1990). The poverty measure has a range of [0, 98.4] while education spans the interval [0.6, 11.1], and rural composition spans the interval [0, 1]. PRONASOL data from COPLADE (1994).

** $p < 0.05$

What predicts PRONASOL spending? What can we say about its political use? Officials of the PRI have long publicly contended that the program was technocratically targeted at poor communities and had no political pupose at all. By contrast, opponents had long argued that it

targeting. The data employed here are at the municipal level, but because reporting was done independently by states and data acquisition was difficult, they are incomplete. Roughly half the states and municipalities are accounted for in the dataset. While not an obviously biased subsample, this does restrict the degree to which one can rely on the conclusions of this analysis to make claims about Mexico as a whole.

was targeted at their strongholds (or alternatively, at PRI strongholds). At least in the municipalities for which data were available, there seems to be only at best a weak political logic to PRONASOL spending. First, levels of poverty are clearly associated with per capita spending efforts, as is the proportion of the population that is rural resident (which makes sense given the particularly great social and infrastructural needs of peasant communities). By contrast, there is almost no association between the per capita amount of PRONASOL spending over the 1988–94 period and the level of support for either major opposition party. The hypothesis that PRONASOL spending was targeted at opposition areas does not seem consistent with this result – areas receiving little aid were roughly as supportive of the opposition as those receiving quite a lot.

On the other hand, there is a statistically significant relationship between PRI support and PRONASOL spending. This is however not a terribly significant *substantive* effect. Using Model IV, the effect of a one standard deviation increase in PRI support is associated with an increase in PRONASOL funding of 82.05 pesos per capita. But given that the range of the dependent variable is from N$356 to N$5576, this is not terribly compelling. While the data inadequacies make a strong refutation impossible, they nevertheless are not consistent with standard accounts that emphasize the clientelistic results (importantly, not efforts) produced by this social spending. The principal problem is that the highly disaggregated results of the 1988 presidential election have never been made public. Indeed, officials at the Federal Electoral Institute deny that such records exist any longer. Thus, this analysis relies on the assumption that the 1994 election results are at least correlated with those of 1988. There is, however, quite valid and consistent support for the notion that rurality and poverty, if not partisan politics, account for much of the spending's targeting, and the estimated effects are substantively much greater.[37]

---

[37] The exception here is the level of education, which contradicts expectations. In two of the models the effect is positive – higher mean years of schooling in a municipality are associated with greater spending. But because PRONASOL spending was "demand driven" in large measure, through the construction of local solidarity committees, this suggests that more educated areas were more likely to be able to organize collectively to petition for support. While from a welfare perspective this result is both inefficient and inappropriate, it does not reflect specifically political bias.

TABLE 6.3 *Social Spending and the Foundations of PRI Support at the Municipal Level (OLS Regression Estimates using Huber/White Standard Errors[a])*

	1994 Presidential	1994 Deputies	1997 Deputies
Constant	0.557**	0.592**	0.443**
	(0.032)	(0.032)	(0.031)
Education	−0.0146**	−0.0179**	−0.0148**
	(0.0041)	(0.0040)	(0.0038)
Rural Composition	0.132**	0.134**	0.109**
	(0.018)	(0.027)	(0.0267)
Poverty (Proportion <	−0.0367	−0.0773**	0.078**
Minimum Wage)	(0.0268)	(0.0265)	(0.026)
PRONASOL	0.0362	0.0344	0.0520**
	(0.0266)	(0.0313)	(0.0115)
N	1,110	1,087	1,114

[a] Parallel analyses were undertaken using a weighted least squares approach to the correction of inherently heteroskedastic data (variables are population averages over differently sized units). Weighting cases by the natural logarithm of population produced results that did not differ substantively from those presented in this table.

** $p < 0.05$

Sources: Data are from IFE (1994, 1997) for electoral returns, the remainder are the same as in Table 6.2.

The data presented in the preceding paragraphs do not fully adjudicate between the compensation hypothesis and the notion that dependence rooted in rural liberalization is critical to the PRI's survival. The analyses in Table 6.3 are designed to evaluate these propositions against each other. Examining the municipal level results from the 1994 and 1997 elections, it appears that the critical predictors of support for the PRI are rural residence and low levels of education (indeed, these are highly collinear). Both of these account for substantial changes in the PRI vote share in a three-way election process. By contrast, the effect of PRONASOL spending is significant in only one instance, and there the effect is minimal at best (a one-standard-deviation change in PRONASOL spending accounts for a 0.8 percent increase in PRI vote share [1997 Deputies election]). Even with this result, it would be difficult to attribute all of the effect to clientelistic payoffs – they could in part reflect genuine electoral gratitude for the provision of much needed physical infrastructure. By contrast, similar one-standard-deviation changes in rural composition and education account for 2.8

TABLE 6.4 *Social Foundations of PRI Support at the Municipal Level (OLS Ecological Regression Estimates, Huber/White Standard Errors*[a]*)*

	1994 Presidential	1994 Deputies	1997 Deputies
Constant	0.546**	0.558**	0.427**
	(0.027)	(0.027)	(0.023)
Average Education	−0.0096**	−0.0097**	−0.010**
[0.6–11.1]	(0.0035)	(0.0035)	(0.0030)
Rural Population	0.130**	0.137**	0.104**
[0.0–1.0]	(0.010)	(0.009)	(0.009)
Poverty (proportion <	−0.071**	−0.0987**	0.100**
minimum wage) [0, 1]	(0.022)	(0.0221)	(0.019)
N	2,384	2,351	2,387

[a] Parallel analyses were undertaken using a weighted least squares approach to the correction of inherently heretoskedastic data (variables are population averages over differently sized units). Weighting cases by the natural logarithm of population produced results which did not differ substantively from those presented above.
** Statistically significant at the $p < 0.05$ level.
Sources: Electoral data are from IFE (1994, 1997), the rest from the same sources as in Table 6.2.

and 2.7 percent increases in PRI support, respectively (for the same 1997 Deputies election).

The possibility remains that these results are biased because they are based in a subset of the states of the Mexican republic. Parallel analyses that do not consider the effect of PRONASOL spending – in any event generally statistically insignificant, or of only moderate importance – carried out on data from all of Mexico support the same basic conclusions. It is obvious that the crucial bastions of electoral support for the PRI is centered in the unlikeliest of places – among the peasants and the less educated (see Table 6.4). These are certainly two groups that have massively and disproportionately suffered from the policies enacted at least since the start of the Salinas administration.

What is clear from Table 6.4 is that more rural municipalities are strongly supportive of the PRI, even controlling for education and poverty levels. Strikingly, education is also negatively associated with voting for the PRI. Because educational deficits are in important ways a rural phenomenon, these results suggest that the countryside is a critical bastion of the governing party, both because it contains a concentration of the least educated citizens and because of characteristics specific to rural residence. Surprisingly, the results linking income and voting outcomes (once education and rurality are controlled) are quite inconsistent. In 1994 poorer areas were less likely to support the PRI, while by 1997 the effect had reversed and higher rates of poverty became positively associated with support for the PRI. Most importantly, the effect estimates are broadly similar to those of the subsample of states in Table 6.3, suggesting that significant biases in data availability are not a problem, at least with respect to the variables of interest here.

Unfortunately, aggregate data such as these cannot easily be used to make the individual level inferences that are central to the argument being evaluated here – that rural voters are the crucial bastion of support for the PRI. Rather, they establish only that more rural areas are more supportive of the PRI (but one does not know with certainty who within those areas actually voted for the PRI). To overcome this problem and check for the possibility of aggregation biases, ecological inference techniques (King 1997) were employed to estimate the relative probabilities of an urban- or rural-resident voting for the PRI.

The data suggest that the differences between urban and rural areas are indeed pronounced (see Table 6.5). Indeed, estimates suggest that in a three-way race, the urban-rural gap in support for the PRI was roughly 15 percent in 1994, growing to almost 20 percent by 1997. Indeed, it is clear that without strong rural support the PRI would not have retained the presidency in 1994 and would have lost its majority in the congress well before 1997. In short, the ability to consolidate

TABLE 6.5 *Rural PRI Support in 1994–1997 Ecological Inferences with Municipal Level Data*[a]

	1994 Presidential	1994 Deputies	1997 Deputies
Probability of a Rural	0.608	0.616	0.522
Vote for the PRI	(0.011)	(0.011)	(0.011)
Probability of an Urban	0.443	0.447	0.328
Vote for the PRI	(0.003)	(0.003)	(0.003)
N	2,325	2,325	2,325

[a] Ecological inferences made using the technique of King (1997). The mean probability of a rural vote for the PRI was allowed to vary depending on the rural composition of a municipality. Urban probabilities were assumed to be constant across different urban/rural population compositions.

Sources: IFE (1994, 1997) for elections and INEGI (1995) for population.

neoliberal reforms beyond the Salinas *sexenio* depended on votes from the very peasants who were among its greatest victims.

The Zapatistas: An Exception that Proves the Rule?

No discussion of contemporary rural politics and its linkages to national-level democracy in Mexico would be complete without mentioning the ongoing struggle of the EZLN. At first blush, the explosion of rural rebellion in Chiapas on January 1, 1994 belies the thesis of this book: that agrarian liberalization provokes atomization, social quiescence, and political dependence. But for all the national and international media attention generated by this insurgency, what is most notable about the movement is not so much its successes, but rather its failures. It remains geographically extremely isolated, it has not sparked similar mobilization in other parts of the country, and it has not forced the Mexican state to address its demands. Despite the recent and much ballyhooed "Zapatour" culminating in an address to the Mexican Congress, the rebellion has produced only a set of constitutional modifications that in many senses mark regress and not progress in terms of indigenous rights.

But that still begs a very important question: why was mobilization possible in Chiapas while similar autonomous political expression has been decidedly difficult in the rest of the country?[38] The short answer is that Chiapas is not like the rest of Mexico in ways that are absolutely determinative from the perspective of rural autonomy and organization. First and foremost, the repressive and co-optative elements of the state have been least developed here, most clearly absent in precisely the regions of the Lacandon forest where the movement has its base. Second, economic liberalization has not come to Chiapas in the same way as it has in other parts of the country, both in terms of the removal of the state's role or the exposure to international forces. Finally, the social foundations for collective action in parts of Chiapas are much

---

[38] It is tempting to think of the Chiapas conflict as principally a guerrilla insurrection. This characterization accurately describes only a brief period in early 1994. Instead it must be thought of as part of larger and longer ongoing struggle over the access to land and the establishment of local political autonomy that has been present in Chiapas in different forms since at least the 1930s and most directly since the 1980s.

more present because of the activity of the local Catholic Church and the salience of indigenous identity.

It is important to begin by noting that *not all* of rural Chiapas is up in arms. Indeed, the principal locus of the rebellion is in one of the most geographically remote parts of the state: the Lacandon forest. This is a region that is of comparatively recent settlement, populated by surplus population expelled from highland Tzeltal and Chol Indian communities. In fact, many of the original settlers of this jungle region came not only because of land scarcity in the highlands but also because they resisted the domination of PRI-affiliated indigenous *caciques* or were expelled from their homes by the property encroachments of local landed elites (Harvey 1998, 61). This selection process alone makes them more likely to be involved in opposition activity. Being communities of recent construction in remote areas, the presence of the state in them was quite limited. While the PRI, the CNC, and the police were largely absent, the Catholic Church was by contrast quite active, having been involved in local development projects as well as supporting the formation of (often quite radical) indigenous organizations since the appointment of Archbishop Ruíz in 1960.

Nor did the opening of the Mexican agrarian economy transform Chiapas, particularly this part, in the same ways that it did the rest of the country. While, for example, the reforms to Article 27 of the constitution in 1992 spelled the definitive end to land redistribution in the rest of the country (which had in practice largely ceased well before), in Chiapas it by no means settled the land question. In the 1980s, with land reform stalled nationally, the Mexican state redistributed 80,000 hectares of land in Chiapas. But this hardly sated demand; at the time of the imposition of the constitutional reform, the backlog of agrarian reform petitions (*rezago agrario*) was enormous, this small state representing 27 percent of the national total. Nor did the distributions end: over the next two years the bulk of these pending claims were adjudicated resulting in an overall success rate for peasants of nearly 50 percent (Harvey 1996, 157–63).

This ongoing process of land distribution was not the goal of the Mexican state. Indeed, the governmental response (both federal and local) was frequently quite violent. But it did reflect the local realities of effective organization and land hunger. And, of course, where redistribution was forced it was used in classic corporatist fashion as a strategy of political control. In many instances, mobilizations that resulted in the successful expropriation of latifundia or the colonization of new areas were not rewarded. Instead, lands seized by one group would be distributed to peasants affiliated with the PRI-controlled CNC. This served to discourage membership in autonomous groups, divide indigenous groups and communities, and increase the leverage of the state over the peasantry. By contrast, *liberalizing* activity by the state was stunted in Chiapas. For example, nowhere was the PROCEDE land-titling program as ineffective. The important fact here is that unlike the rest of the country the Mexican state *did not* withdraw from the management of the countryside in parts of Chiapas. This made the state a target of collective action, and increased the probability of a successful outcome to efforts at collective action (in a context where peasants had very little to lose).

Peasant mobilization in Chiapas is also different because it is not in important ways *peasant* mobilization; rather, indigenous identity is a (if not *the*) central organizing principle. This is important insofar as constructing a firm foundation for collective action is both difficult and essential. The reference to indigenous identity and the discrimination and repression common to Indian groups help to overcome the conflicts of interest and social fragmentation that impede mobilization in class terms as peasants in other parts of Mexico. To this must be added a population structure containing a number of already politicized individuals (the migrants to the Lacandon region) and an especially young age structure. When important (and politically and culturally *legitimate*) organizational resources provided by the Catholic Church were added to the mix, collective action and autonomous politics in the face of rural neoliberalism became possible. But it is a form of collective action that is exceedingly limited in scope and successful only because of the *absence* of sustained economic liberalization in lowland Chiapas. In this sense it comports directly with the thesis of this book. By contrast, were the conflict to generalize across the peasantry, or even in a substantial way outside Chiapas, the liberalization thesis of this book would be under severe threat. This has, however, decidedly not been the case.

As we have seen, the dynamics of agricultural liberalization in Mexico did not unfold in precisely the same fashion as in Chile. Nevertheless, the broad result was the same: the political construction of an electoral base for neoliberal political forces among the very peasants who were primary victims of economic openness. What the Mexican case shows is that free market policies can induce atomized politics even where they are implemented gradually in a comparatively politically open environment. The specific problems that bedevil peasant organization and autonomy may vary somewhat from the Chilean experience – including the presence of a plethora of controlled, officialist organizations – but these problems of collective action nevertheless shape rural politics decisively. Neither traditional corporatism nor contemporary welfarism can by themselves account for the rural (but not urban) support that the PRI continues to have – that is in important measure a function of agrarian liberalism.

PART III

CONCLUSIONS AND IMPLICATIONS

7

Political Competitiveness, Organized Interests, and the Democratic Market

The surprisingly easy consolidation of free market democracy in important parts of Latin America has confounded critics of neoliberal reforms. Indeed, the political explosions anticipated by many in the wake of economic austerity, privatization, trade opening, and attendant deindustrialization and mass unemployment have either simply not lived up to expectations (e.g., Chile, Mexico, Brazil) or have taken place in those political economies that were *least* liberalized (e.g., Venezuela, Ecuador). Nevertheless, it is also true that economic liberalization has generally not improved living standards, reduced inequality, expanded the middle classes, or in many cases even produced a consistent return to growth that many of its proponents had contended was its chief virtue. Often, the opposite was the case. Thus, the comparative facility with which markets and democracy have been reconciled in Latin America remains as perplexing as ever on a continent with a long and troubled historical relationship with both.

One potential answer, favored by more radical critics, is that free market democracy is simply a façade masking a transformation of authoritarianism and continued class dominance. This is contradicted, however, by a reality of free and fair elections that resulted in both Mexico and Chile in opposition victories in presidential contests, producing governments of the reformist center-right and socialist center-left, respectively. Moreover in each case politicians committed to free market policies have been able to command, if not majorities, veto-level minorities in free electoral contests. Whatever one may think of the wisdom of neoliberal policies, their political proponents are not without quite substantial electoral support.

On the other hand, does the fact that political parties who are strongly committed to free markets and have dominated the presidency in Mexico and sustained at least a legislative veto position in Chile in open electoral contests – despite the association of such policies with authoritarian rule, material deprivation, and political exclusion – imply that there are no tensions between neoliberalism and democracy? The answer is "no": there are in fact tensions between free markets and democratic politics, but they are not rooted in economic outcomes such as growth, welfare, or inequality. The answer I give is in this book has been that these tensions are fundamentally social, not socioeconomic. It is not that neoliberalism produces poverty and inequality that is destabilizing for democracy (though produce them it does), but rather that it undermines the social foundations of political participation, characteristically in rural areas. The result is a sectorally divided democracy where the ability of one particular segment of society – peasants – to self-organize and participate in politics is exceedingly limited. Thus the tension between free markets and democracy hinges not on inequality and the contentious politics the former are often thought to produce, but on the new collective action problems that marketization creates, and the sectoral participatory deficit that results.

This participatory aridity is not, however, simply a function of poverty or inequality. Disadvantaged urban groups *have* managed to organize and place their issues on the national political agenda. It is only in the countryside that collective action problems become so severe as to violate basic democratic requirements of independent interest aggregation and expression. But this same (rural) sectoral exclusion produced by neoliberalism is the key to the comparatively easy national-level marriage of free markets to democratic politics. On its foundation, neoliberal parties can contstruct a sandwich coalition of urban winners and rural losers backing free market reforms. These forces, however, need not be hegemonic. To successfully stabilize democracy, they need only be sufficiently powerful to ward off threats to the survival of the broad outlines of the market reforms themselves; in so doing this unequal alliance gives elites capable of reversing democratization a stake in the survival of the democratic regime.

The sectoral unevenness of the political effects of economic opening also explains why the implementation of reforms – materially painful to the vast majority of the population in almost all cases – has not generally necessitated recourse to authoritarian practices or produced successful populist counterattacks. It is the urban-rural elite/peasant coalition that is a political solution to the paradox of economic reform (Gibson 1997). And it is a solution that can stabilize democratic politics without being vulnerable to the emergence of bottom-of-the-well "partial reform equilibria" (Hellman 1998).

The problem, of course, is that the solution is only partly democratic. Because the neoliberal political coalition is founded on rural social atomization, disorganization, and dependence, it stands in the way of democracy's broadening or deepening. And it is here where the real paradox of free market democracy lies: if the commitment of powerful elites to the democratic regime is contingent on their control of peasant votes – providing a veto over potentially threatening policies – how can the countryside be democratized without threatening regime survival?

INTEREST GROUPS, NEOLIBERALISM, AND THE
CONSOLIDATION OF DEMOCRACY

In a prescient review of the literature on democratic transition, now nearly a decade past, Hagopian called for a renewed emphasis on societal transformations in understanding the development of postdemocratization politics. She argued that without such a focus, scholars would develop a narrow conceptualization of democratic consolidation as little more than an effort to "correct the institutional deficiencies that led to the breakdown of democracy..." (1993, 466). Unfortunately, this advice was little heeded. Scholarship on the politics of consolidation has made many advances, but almost all of them are confined to the institutional front.[1] With notable exceptions, very few have emphasized the societal transformations and reorganization of

---

[1] Thus there have been sustained debates on the merits of presidential versus parliamentary systems, the design of electoral institutions, or changes in the structure and organization of political parties and party systems (Linz and Valenzuela 1994; Lijphart and Waisman 1996; Siavelis 2000).

state–society relations under preceding authoritarian rulers (but see Garretón 1983; Hagopian 1996; Roberts 1998; Houtzager 2001; and Shadlen 2002). The approach of this book has been to endeavor to "bring society back in" to the study of democratic consolidation, but in a way that is complementary to the progress made over the past decade of institutionalist scholarship. The goal is to help fill the lacunae first identified by Hagopian, by emphasizing the way in which market-led societal transformations impinge on Dahl's two fundamental pillars of polyarchic politics – citizen participation and elite contestation for office (1971, 5–7).

Here is where the potential tensions between markets and democracy are located: if citizens – even only a sector of them – cannot form and aggregate interests independently, how can they participate in democratic politics? If they cannot form and sustain interest groups, how can they hold their representatives accountable, either at elections or between them? Indeed, it is the between-election accountability of elites that is the most difficult to reconcile with a commitment to free market economics. Thus, the approach to understanding democratic consolidation and deepening I employ focuses not on how institutions or bargains can mitigate conflict or "stabilize" democracy, but on how social transformations can affect government accountability and political participation.

The crucial intermediary here is the oft-maligned interest group. My argument has been that without a dense network of competing groups, representing a plethora of social interests, democratic politics is coordinated more along the lines of a technocratic organizational hierarchy than a competitive "marketplace of ideas," even if its leaders are periodically elected. The metaphor is instructive, and suggests that if we are interested in the deepening of free market democracy we should place emphasis on the sorts of public policies that will *increase* the competitiveness of political (electoral) markets. By this I mean, of course, the spectrum of societal interests that can participate in politics, not the "closeness" of particular electoral contests.

Interest Groups and Democracy

Why are interest groups so important? It has long been recognized that social organization, beginning with political parties but including an enormous variety of interest groups, is a fundamental part of any democratic system. In particular such groups – alongside political parties – are generally considered essential to giving meaning to the electoral contests that are the mechanism for democratic accountability. Even an exceedingly spare understanding of democracy such as that of Schumpeter (1976 [1942], 270–1), who is usually seen as requiring only the existence of competitive elections, points to the mobilization and competition of groups as fundamental to free politics. Successive scholars, often writing from a perspective concerned with distinguishing democratic regimes from state socialist ones, took a stronger position. Lipset et al. (1956, 15–16) account for democracy's very emergence in terms of the ongoing conflict between a host of "special" interests, be they class, religious, economic, or sectional. Dahl has hailed the existence of "a significant number of social groups and organizations that are relatively autonomous with respect to one another and to the government itself" as the essence of pluralist democracy (1989, 219). And of course similar understandings have been taken up into the literature on democratization and democratic consolidation (O'Donnell et al. 1986). And of course defects of associational life have recently been identified as serious problems in even the most consolidated of democracies (Cohen and Rogers 1992; Schmitter 1992a; Putnam 1993, 2000).

How are interest groups such a critical, if oft-maligned, component of democratic politics? It is here where recent formal theory has made an important contribution, by highlighting the specific roles that such groups must play not only in giving elections meaning, but in maintaining the accountability of elites in interelectoral periods. Viewed from the perspective of elected representatives, interest groups provide valuable and scarce information. Not all of this is technical; just as crucially, threats to inform group members and mobilize opposition if undesirable positions are taken is important political information (Austen Smith 1998, 277–8). They also play an essential role in providing information to citizens so that informed voting (and thus accountability) can take place (McKelvey and Ordeshook 1986). Indeed, by conceptualizing the relationship between voters and legislators as a principal-agent problem, formal theorists have shown that interest groups are critical to maintaining democratic representation except in the unlikely case that voters are completely informed and can punish legislators immediately (Potters and Sloof 1996, 426–7). Thus, the activity that is from one perspective perceived as a constant clamor of "special interests" for "rents" can from another be seen as the only mechanism capable of holding politicians to account, particularly in periods between electoral contests.

The point is that interest group politics serves a vital democratic function – accountability – in both providing information to voters and in monitoring and political leaders. The emphasis in most of this literature, however, has been on an undifferentiated treatment of political groups, with an underlying expectation that in practice they are well distributed in relation to a wide spectrum of latent interests. This assumption is, however, problematic on two grounds. First, however, not all interests are equivalent. It is well known that there is a distinction between the interests of (big) business and all others: in market economies capitalists can make their interests felt in the political system *even without collective action or coordination* (Lindblom 1977; Przeworski and Wallerstein 1988). One need not concur with a strong version of Ferguson's (1995) "investment theory" of political parties – that parties and candidates respond to economically powerful donors not voters – to believe that these interests tend to be privileged in the democratic politics of market economies.

Second, more than the asymmetry of interest group influence, is the question of what happens to democratic accountability when interest group activity is essentially impossible to organize for an important segment of the populace? Here the problem is *not* of an asymmetry of influence founded in differential resources, but rather a situation in which one major group is effectively barred from playing the democratic game altogether. It has, of course, been the point of this book to problematize the issue of rural social organization, showing that collective action problems under neoliberalism have become so severe as to undermine peasant political participation. The difference is between a game with mismatched opponents and one in which only one team can play. The former is a contest, the latter a forfeit.

As one might expect, the effect of problems of social organization on rural democracy is profound. In the first place, without collective action the aggregation of peasant interests is difficult, and their political expression nearly impossible. Second, without strong rural organizations it is impossible for peasants to effectively monitor the activities of their representatives and consequently difficult to hold them to account at election time. Indeed, if any group were in need of the sort of information that interest groups provide it is the peasantry. Not only are they the social stratum with least access to individual information sources (print media, radio, and even television), but they are also the group with the fewest political skills (literacy, experience, education) necessary for the evaluation of government policy outputs or proposals. These problems are naturally made worse where rural inequality and poverty heighten such skill deficits.

We are in such contexts left with a hierarchy of problems for the consolidation of free market democracy. First, the interests of powerful economic actors have a privileged position – particularly insofar as economic liberalization facilitates capital mobility. Second, marketization of social life has in general reduced the associational foundation of political participation bringing with it a decline in the ability of voters to monitor politicians. Finally, collective action problems and atomization have had asymmetric effects in class terms – rendering the peasantry, nearly always the poorest and most marginal stratum, in some contexts essentially unable to participate.

The result is a form of free market democracy in which leaders are selected in periodic free and fair elections, but are not meaningfully accountable to *all* the voters. Without groups to organize and mobilize them it is hard to imagine how a sector as fragmented and marginalized as the peasantry could coordinate in opposition to politicians even where their actions have manifestly produced material harm. In such contexts not only are there no rural groups that could credibly threaten the reelection of elites, but it is not clear how even at a minimal level peasants as individuals could obtain the political information necessary to effectively engage in punishment at the polls. And as we shall see in the following text, both the opportunities and information necessary for "retrospective" punishment of political figures in Chile and Mexico are strongly constrained by institutional rules and social realities.

MARKETS, DEMOCRACY, AND DEMOCRATIC MARKETS

The organizational defect in the countryside has been linked in the preceding chapters to the social effects of free market economic policies. This is a relationship that should not be surprising, and it points to the problematic point of intersection between free market and democratic goals. It has been customary to see the tensions between these twin goals as rooted in socioeconomic inequality – the argument is generally made that market-based policies generate such skewed distributions of wealth and income as to alternatively (1) produce insoluble and polarizing political conflicts, or contrariwise (2) so weaken the working and popular classes as agents as to render them incapable of resisting growing poverty and the "discipline" of capitalist markets.

Ignoring for a moment the contradictory implications drawn from the same economic phenomenon in such arguments, it is my contention that while neoliberalism may well tend to generate inequality and poverty, this is *not* in itself a problem for democracy. Instead it is the tenuous relationship between free market policies and interest groups politics – that is, a social not socioeconomic conflict – that is at the core of contradiction that can emerge in free market democracy. To be sure, there is nothing about a commitment to liberal economic policies that militates against the establishment of an elected political regime. Indeed, to the extent to which periodic political competition serves to reduce corruption, increase the supply of crucial public goods, or promote efficient administration there is much to recommend democracy from a free market perspective. The principal problem comes in the periods *between* elections, where organized interests are the most crucial mediators of accountability.

The paradox for anything more than an exceedingly minimalist notion of democracy is that from a free market perspective interest groups are typically considered economically, and therefore socially, pernicious. They are rent seekers who aim to impose deadweight costs on the economy in the furtherance of their own private interests (Krueger 1974). The principal challenge for leaders or institutions is to *prevent* precisely such groups from exercising influence over the state. Indeed, to some (Olson 1982), the very success and failure of market economies hinges on the relative weight of these "predatory" interests.[2] What is interesting in this standard neoliberal formulation is not only that the political activity of interest groups is seen as inefficient and welfare reducing, but that even competition among interest groups is seen as

---

[2] The only caveat here is when these interests become so large as to be encompassing, and thus are capable of taking the long-run national interest into account. More will be said on this.

harmful – it only triggers a spiral of short-term rent redistribution by politicians unable to resist these political pressures. In fact, such scholars frequently counsel insulation of decision making, often through constitutional provisions that prevent elites from responding to political pressures, the reduction of channels of state–society interaction, political fragmentation that increases the number of veto players and hence prevents policy enactment, and an administrative decentralization that reduces the possibility of redistribution.

All of these moves, however, are an effort to induce the coordination of the political sphere along the lines of an organizational hierarchy. This is oddly paradoxical. Efficiency in markets is seen as a product of the competition of a wide variety of firms, none of which has the potential to be dominant. But in the political sphere many have argued that competition among groups should be as limited as possible (Krueger 1974; Bhagwati 1982; Olson et al. 2000).[3] Certainly presidents or prime ministers should be accountable at the quadrennial or sexennial electoral "shareholders meeting," but outside this moment, politics should be muted. Even the second best option – encompassing organization through societal corporatism – is still a form of political oligopoly, deemed efficient for precisely such a reason (Olson 1982).

But this is more than a stylistic problem – if interest group politics does indeed promote illiberal (e.g., rent-seeking) political outcomes, then free markets and free interest group politics are not so readily compatible. And indeed, unless interests are weak, democracy and liberalism may run into serious conflicts. Thus the political telos for an economic liberal is minimalist government, technocratic decision making, bureaucratic insulation from "politics," and the use of market mechanisms to implement policy wherever feasible. The problem is twofold: (1) this vision is democratic only in a limited sense, and (2) it emphasizes outcomes rather than procedures. But this is in some ways not democracy, the essence of which is *uncertainty* about outcomes with clarity about the procedures through which outcomes are realized (Przeworski et al. 2001, 16). Thus it is where interests – particularly those of subordinate groups – are weak that free market democracy most easily flourishes.

---

[3] Indeed, Olson et al. (2000) go so far as to make government insulation from politics an explicit part of their definition of good government.

How then are we to know whether free market democracy has been consolidated? The answer is not to be found in the absence of polarizing conflict, nor the successful transmission of authority from elected leaders of one political party to another, nor in the emergence of a normative consensus. While these may all be important, the critical test is whether free market democracy can survive the real resurrection of civil society (particularly rural society), an outcome that has been much assumed but little examined since the wave of democratization began in the 1980s. Just as the test of statist democracy in Chile's history (1932–73) came when it was forced to confront the election of a Marxist president, the contemporary question is whether powerful elites will tolerate the *real* policy uncertainty implicit in a system characterized by a vibrant and broadly participative civil society.

INTEREST GROUPS, INSTITUTIONS, AND DEMOCRATIC ACCOUNTABILITY IN CHILE AND MEXICO

In this book I have emphasized the atomizing and demobilizing effects of neoliberal economic policies on the peasantry. This does not imply, however, that liberalization has not had political effects in other sectors, or that changes in the institutional organization of politics have been unimportant. First, even in urban areas problems of collective action have mounted, though they have not posed the same overall threat to popular participation as they have in the countryside. The on-the-ground social organization of politics in Chile and Mexico has indeed been restructured, and in class asymmetric ways, but urban political competition remains comparatively vibrant. Second, the negative implications of liberalization for participation, however, have been magnified rather than mitigated by the particular institutional rules that govern political competition in each system.

In Chile it is well documented that in the wake of the military government's neoliberal transformation, the terrain of interest group politics has thinned nationwide. While during the struggle for democratization in the late 1980s there was some hope that emergent organizations of, for example, squatters, the informal sector, neighborhoods, or women (but notably not peasants) might constitute a new civil society and a foundation for the new democratic regime (Oxhorn 1995). Unfortunately, the vast majority of such groups did not survive the democratic transition or continue in a very reduced fashion (Barrera 1998, 146–7). Meanwhile, the traditional constituencies that made Chilean democracy before 1973 so vigorous – from the *gremios* (small business and professional associations) to labor and peasant unions – have all experienced marked declines in scope and activity. And it is important to note that this is true even of the *allies* of the military government and the right in the gremio movement.

One of the crucial institutional changes that interacts with a transformed social world can be found in redefinition of the role and structure of the legislative arena. Historically in Chile it was the national legislature that organized and mediated the conflicts among these groups and between them and the state, while mayors accomplished the task at the local level (A. Valenzuela 1977). Indeed, given the deeply polarized and extreme social and ideological cleavages in precoup Chilean society, the effectiveness with which the legislature functioned as a site of bargaining and compromise is evidenced by the comparative durability of democratic politics in the face of seemingly intractable political and economic conflicts. Indeed, it may not be that the structure of the Chilean political system that impelled polarization and democracy's collapse (A. Valenzuela 1978; Collier and Collier 1991), but rather that the institutional features of the political system helped to postpone collapse even three years into a minority Marxist government's experiment with socialist transition. And despite the conflicts that rocked the country in 1971–2, there are some who have suggested that the political system still had room for elite bargaining that might have prevented catastrophe (Oppenheim 1999, 95).

The institutional structure that governs Chilean legislative politics under the 1980 constitution (and accessory organic constitutional laws implemented by the military) is quite different from that of the 1925 constitution. Crucially, the legislature's authority has been scaled back very dramatically to the benefit of the executive. For a variety of crucial bills initiation must come from the executive, and these cannot be amended to include spending on items not contemplated in the original bill. More importantly, the congress is prohibited even from amending fiscal legislation to either increase outlays or to cut taxes beyond the levels indicated in executive proposals (*Constitución Política* of 1980, art. 64; *Ley Orgánica Constitucional del Congreso Nacional*, art. 24). Without substantial control over fiscal policy it is thus difficult for the national legislature to function as a site of compromise and group accommodation (Siavelis 2000, 160–3). A recreation of the old regime, tellingly labeled by Chileans the *Estado de Compromiso* ("Compromise State") is thus precluded, forcing interest groups to press their demands in less institutionalized ways.

Even if legislators were inclined to attempt such a mediating function, the mechanisms rendering them accountable to (and thus representative of) contending social constituencies have been dramatically diminished. Historically, linkages among legislators, parties, and interests were extremely tight. Not only are these linkages now far weaker as a result of the generalized decline of social organization, but in many cases legal prohibitions inhibit their very formation (*Código de Trabajo* 1992).

This problem of accountability is magnified by the use of the two-member district "binomial" electoral system for legislative seats. In a political system where electoral competition is largely confined to two blocs (that negotiate internally the list of two candidates for each district), in the overwhelming majority of districts each bloc is assured one of the available two seats. In each district one seat goes to the first-place list, the other to the second. Only where the second-place finisher's vote total is doubled by the winner are both seats awarded to the latter. In a two-way race this means that roughly 34 percent vote share is sufficient to ensure one candidate is elected. Given this, the vote swing necessary to unseat a representative is generally enormous (as any result between 34 and 66 percent of the vote produces the same outcome). It is only in the few districts where one bloc is on the cusp of doubling the electoral strength of the other that real electoral sanction can occur.[4] In the others, even improbably large swings in vote shares (in what is a notoriously stable electorate) would be insufficient to impose costs on incumbent politicians.[5] This system contrasted markedly with the open-list proportional representation used before the coup of September 1973, which heightened the direct accountability of representatives to voters.

---

[4] The electoral districts were defined by the outgoing military government in 1988 on the basis of plebiscite results that identified its support base geographically. Naturally, very few areas where the center-left Concertación was likely to "double" were created.

[5] They can protect themselves from internal (intralist) competition through the party-controlled negotiations by which the lists are constructed. These negotiations have in practice tended to protect incumbents of all cooperating parties.

Nor is the executive branch particularly accountable or capable of serving as a site of social bargaining. Because the president is limited to a single consecutive six-year term, desire for reelection cannot function to enforce accountability to voters directly or indirectly through interest groups. And even were the presidency to be a site for compromise and interest group inclusion and articulation, it could hardly meaningfully include representation from the necessary breadth of social forces: it is by construction a unitary and partisan office. Consequently, interests allied with opposition political forces would be excluded from real access. Indeed, bargaining, compromise, and accountability would be particularly difficult where the president is elected from either the socialist left (as is currently the case) or the neoliberal right ends of the political spectrum.

The inability of normal representational channels to function effectively is manifest in the tendency of those interest groups that do manage to organize to press their demands less through legislative lobbying and more through open public confrontation. In posttransition Chile, successive Concertación governments have faced widespread protests from students, doctors, bus drivers, teachers, and even the labor movement. What is striking about this is the existence of protest, including multicampus student strikes and mass resignations of doctors, and the fact that most of these groups are political *allies* of the government. The most telling example is that of the labor movement – a cornerstone of both the Socialist and Christian Democratic parties that have governed since 1990 – that has consistently engaged in sustained protest over the adjustments in the minimum wage (Siavelis 2000). Indeed, this was the result of the government's effective abandonment of political negotiations of this issue with its labor allies in the early 1990s.

While neoliberalism has largely silenced peasant groups, it has also weakened other actors – as manifested by the inability of the labor movement to compel action even from its political allies. Coupled with institutional peculiarities of Chilean democracy – a weak legislature and an insulated executive – this has served to heighten the challenge to democratic accountability induced by the associational deficit produced by neoliberalism.

Reduced democratic accountability and weak interest articulation in the wake of neoliberalism are also problems in Mexico. The associational decay under neoliberalism here is not as severe as that experienced by Chile – both because the free market transition in Mexico is less complete, and because the legacies of corporatist state–society linkages have for so long fostered (albeit often undemocratic) organization. But the ability of interest groups to aggregate citizen preferences and hold elites to account is nevertheless quite limited. Where groups in Chile have a difficult time forming in the first place, in Mexico if constructing interest groups is somewhat less problematic, asserting their influence is more problematic: at every turn interests must contend with preexisting, co-opted quasi-official organizations that claim an identical representational function and are typically privileged by state actors.

But neoliberalism has still brought substantial organizational decay as it with time undermines corporatist legacies and creates barriers to autonomous collective action. If one surveys for a moment the set of interests most strongly and effectively organized in Mexico, just as in Chile, they are far from representative. The much-ballyhooed debtors' movement, *El Barzón*, represents those fortunate enough to have had access to formal credit markets – generally from the middle sectors and above. The *Consejo Coordinador Empresarial* (Business Coordinating Council, or CEE) represents the captains of industry, and has only seen its influence increase with liberalization, capital mobility, trade opening, and the transfer of power to the neoliberal PAN. Students, most notably in the recent strike action at the national autonomous university (UNAM), while hardly wealthy, are disproportionately from comparatively privileged strata.

On the other hand, the vast majority of the population in the working, informal, and peasant classes are largely without effective representation. We have seen the tremendous effects of liberalization on peasants. For urban labor, democratization has also brought with it an unexpected *decline* in organizational and mobilization effectiveness – even given the loosening of the authoritarian controls to which it had been subject since the revolution. It must be recalled that under the highly restrictive labor regime imposed by the long-governing PRI, labor retained some mobilizational capacity (Fig. 7.1). But as liberalization *and* political opening took place from the mid-1980s onward, a surprising effect can be seen: labor activity suddenly and completely evaporated. That is, just as repressive controls were inevitably weakening with democratization, and the catastrophic economic situation created powerful new grievances, the ability of labor

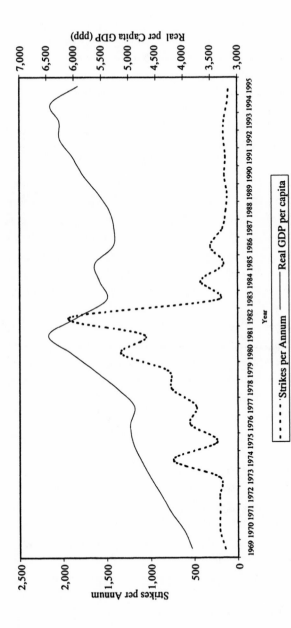

FIGURE 7.1 Labor Mobilization and Economic Liberalization in Mexico (strikes per annum; real GDP per capita). *Sources*: For strikes, ILO (2001); for GDP/capita, World Bank (2001).

to mount effective efforts to recoup some of these economic losses was eviscerated.

But workers and peasants were not the only sectors whose ability to act politically was shattered by liberalization. Even some business interests, most notably small to medium firms, have seen the combination of democratization-cum-liberalization actually *undermine* rather than increase their ability to articulate demands and place pressure on elected representatives (see Shadlen 2002 for an insightful discussion). Similarly, the efflorescence of self-help organization that arose in the wake of the calamity of the 1985 earthquake in Mexico City proved unsustainable.

So if the organizational playing field is slanted toward the more privileged sectors in Mexico (as it is in Chile) by neoliberalism, institutional features of the Mexican political system further act to undercut the accountability of elected political elites that is essential to democracy. The problem of responsiveness is structured by the continued presence of co-opted or officialist organizations that are the legacies of corporatism – some linked to the PRI (workers, peasants, and the "popular sector"), others to the government (industrial chambers of commerce that long had compulsory membership). The existence of such pliable groups gives politicians a ready ability to claim both to be "representing" societal pressures, at least those "emanating" from these groups, and it simultaneously undercuts the legitimacy of more autonomous organizations. Not only does the presence of officialist groups muddy the informational waters for citizens, it also allows politicians to *appear* responsive, albeit only to organizations that they in large measure control.

Unlike Chile, however, the Mexican political system is not structured around an inherently strong presidency – though this was historically the case as a consequence of uninterrupted control of both Chamber of Deputies and Senate by the PRI for virtually all of the postrevolutionary period. But with democratization, and the absence of governing majorities for the current president, a meaningful separation of powers has emerged. Given the fairly broad formal authority assigned to the legislature under the Mexican constitution, there is a hopeful possibility for public negotiation and compromise in the legislative arena that would encourage greater civic engagement, political participation, and interest group oversight of public policy.

That said, however, there are still serious barriers to political accountability on the part of elected representatives. First and foremost, it is a hallmark of the Mexican system that no office permits re-election – a prohibition that applies to deputies, senators, state governors and legislators, and the president. As a consequence, once elected, a legislator is in no direct way responsible to voters, because a future re-election is precluded. Indeed, a typical political career in Mexico involves a tremendous amount of office switching, as politicians move between and among the Chamber of Deputies, a party office, the Senate, the bureaucracy, state legislatures, and/or governorships. Thus for politicians, in securing an upward career trajectory the approval of party elites is far more determinative than that of voters. As a consequence one might expect elected representatives to be very sensitive to the preferences of party leaders; but what mechanism exists to make them sensitive to societal demands?

The upshot is that neoliberalism interacts with the structure of political institutions in Chile and Mexico to produce a form of free market democracy that is in important ways anæmic. But the weakness of free market democracy is not the same as democracy in the earlier statist era: it is not vulnerable to polarization, balkanization, and collapse (or, by contrast, corporatist authoritarianism). Rather than the sorts of calamitous failures of democracy that were repeated across South America in the 1960s and 1970s, free market democracy can persist in sectorally uneven equilibria. This is also a condition that is conducive to the implementation and consolidation of neoliberal reforms – even where these produce far more losers than winners. The threat to consolidation here, however, is that free market democracy can shade over into political exclusion; it is not an exclusion enforced by the barrel of a soldier's rifle, but by the quotidian reality of atomization, disorganization, dependence, and collective action failure.

DEMOCRATIC POLITICS AS A MARKET

If one accepts as fundamental the participation of a plethora of freely formed interest groups as a foundational element of any democratic political system, then the collective action problems sometimes attendant upon neoliberalism can be threats to democracy. More precisely, they might properly be thought of as failures of the democratic market.

If the presence of vibrant, competing interests, none capable of imposing hegemony, is the hallmark of a competitive market, then at least
some sectors of the free market democratic systems examined here suffer from serious problems of oligopoly and monopoly. The question,
however, is what lesson we take from this?

Viewed from the optic of a market analogy, the tendency toward
uncompetitive outcomes in the countryside in particular should not be
surprising. It is well known that vigorous economic competition is far
from automatic, but rather must regularly be nurtured, regulated, and
protected by the state. Applying this lesson to the democratic sphere
is perhaps the broadest implication of this book. What neoliberalism
has provoked, at least in the countryside, is a problem of entry costs
into political markets. These costs are the barriers to collective action
outlined in the preceding chapters. With entry costs high, however,
political competitiveness is reduced, as is the accountability of politicians to voters. The logic is the same as in an economic monopoly –
responsiveness to customer desires in such contexts is similarly weak.

The problem that has shaped this book is not new – indeed, it was
Polanyi (1944) who first recognized that unregulated markets have the
potential to be corrosive of human society and social organizations.
It is precisely this corrosion that has weakened rural social life and
democratic competition in Chile and Mexico. The question is how can
this problem be ameliorated? The somewhat paradoxical answer may
be that under free market conditions, the state may have to take on
some responsibility for reducing the entry costs facing nascent political
groups where political markets fail. That is, the state may have to
actively intervene to promote competition in democratic markets, just
as it does so to restore the competitiveness of economic markets.

The difficulty, of course, is that such intervention may simply create a new democratic defect – a more vibrant associational world, but
one that is tied directly to, and politically dependent upon, the state.
In essence, this could be akin to the undemocratic forms of corporatism that have at different points plagued Mexico, Brazil, Peru, and
Argentina. What would be essential then is that the state help in foster-
ing social organization as a form of public good – resources received by
one group could not reduce those available to others, nor could there
be any excludability on partisan grounds. Only in this way would the

perils of domination by the state, or capture by extant interests, be avoided.

It is beyond the scope of this book to identify the mechanisms by which this could be accomplished (Schmitter 1992a, 1992b). But examples of efforts taken along these lines abound. Public financing mechanisms can be created to provide material resources for new groups to enter political competition. Social organization can be directly fostered through community development grant programs (ranging from the Community Development Block Grant program in the United States in the 1960s, to the social development components of some Latin American social welfare programs). The state need not rely on direct action, it can also promote the work of churches and non-governmental organizations (NGOs) that have community development goals, and that were, at least in Chile, historically crucial to the political incorporation of the peasantry in the 1960s.

Free markets create problems for social organization. Until these problems are overcome, democratic politics tends toward anæmic competition and limited accountability. To be sure, in such systems there is generally competition among parties with distinct programmatic appeals. But unless groups can hold elites accountable, one runs the risks that these will be distinctions without differences. The sectoral analysis provided here suggests how this can emerge. It is not coincidental that the major differences among contending political parties in free market Chile and Mexico have to do fundamentally with issues of importance to the urban sector. Without an engaged and organized peasantry – *pace* Chiapas – rural issues will recede into irrelevance, competing policies will not emerge from above, and political demands will not be articulated from below. Until the problem of rural collective action is solved, however, free market democracy will not live up to its promise. It will instead produce and reproduce locally exclusionary and oligarchic forms of economic and political governance. But paradoxically this is the foundation on which national-level and consolidated free market democracy is constructed.

References

Abbott, Eduardo G. 1976. "Strategies of Opposition to Peasant Unionization: Some Considerations on the Limits of Law as a Tool of Social Change." Master's thesis, University of Wisconsin, Madison.

Achen, Christopher and W. Phillips Shively. 1995. *Cross-Level Inference* (Chicago: University of Chicago Press).

Acuña, Lila, José Bengoa, Rolf Foerster, Verónica Oxman, Pedro Segure, and Gozalo Tapia. 1983. *Informe acerca de la organización sindical campesina en Chile* (Santiago, Chile: GIA).

Affonso, Almino. 1988. *Trayectoria del movimiento campesino chileno* (Santiago, Chile: GIA).

Affonso, Almino, Sergio Gómez, Emilio Klein, and Pablo Ramírez. 1970. *Movimiento campesino chileno* (Santiago, Chile: ICIRA).

Appendini, Kirsten. 1998. "Changing Agrarian Institutions: Interpreting the Contradictions" in Wayne Cornelius and David Myhre, eds., *The Transformation of Rural Mexico: Reforming the Ejido Sector* (San Diego: Center for U. S.–Mexican Studies).

Armijo, Marianela and Cecilia Montero. 1991. "La agricultura chilena a comienos de los años 90: Fortalezas y debilidades." Apuntes CIEPLAN no. 101 (June).

Austen-Smith, David. 1998. "Allocating Access for Information and Contributions." *Journal of Law, Economics, and Organization* vol. 14: 2.

Auyero, Javier. 1999. " 'From the Client's point(s) of View': How Poor People Perceive and Evaluate Political Clientelism." *Theory and Society* vol. 29.

Axelrod, Robert. 1984. *The Evolution of Cooperation* (New York: Basic Books).

Aylwin, Andrés. 1967. *Carta informe sobre experiencias sindicales campesinas* (Santiago, Chile: Cámera de Diputados).

Banco Central de Chile. 1991. *Indicadores económicos y sociales regionales 1980– 1989* (Santiago, Chile: Banco Central de Chile).

———. 1989. *Indicadores económicos y sociales 1960–1988* (Santiago, Chile: Banco Central de Chile).

Banfield, Edward. 1958. *The Moral Basis of a Backward Society* (New York: The Free Press).

Barham, Bradford, Mary Clark, Elizabeth Katz, and Rachel Schurman. 1992. "Nontraditional Agricultural Exports in Latin America." *Latin American Research Review* vol. 27: 2.

Barnes, Andrew. 2001. "Property, Power, and the Presidency: Property-Rights Reform and Russian Executive-Legislative Relations, 1990–1998." *Communist and Post-Communist Studies* (March).

Barrera, Manuel. 1998. "Macroeconomic Adjustment in Chile and the Politics of the Popular Sectors" in Philip Oxhorn and Graciela Ducatenzeiler, eds., *What Kind of Democracy? What Kind of Market?: Latin America in the Age of Neoliberal Reform* (University Park: The Pennsylvania State University Press).

Barría, Liliana, Luz Cereceda, Hugo Ortega, and Hamilton Aliaga. 1988. *El campesinado chileno: sus organizaciones productivas* (Santiago, Chile: Insituto Chileno de Educación Cooperativa, Insituto de Sociología de la Universidad Católica de Chile, and Desarrollo Campesino).

Bartra, Armando. 1996. "A Persistent Rural Leviathan" in Laura Randall, ed., *Reforming Mexico's Agrarian Reform* (Armonk, NY: M. E. Sharpe).

———. 1985. *Los herederos de Zapata: Movimientos campesinos posrevolucionarios en México, 1920–1980* (Mexico City: Ediciones Era).

Bates, Robert. 1981. *Markets and States in Tropical Africa: The Political Basis of Agricultural Policies* (Berkeley: University of California Press).

Bates, Robert and William Rogerson. 1980. "Agriculture in Development: A Coalitional Analysis." *Public Choice* vol. 35.

Bauer, Arnold. 1975. *Chilean Rural Society: From the Spanish Conquest to 1930* (Cambridge: Cambridge University Press).

Bellin, Eve. 2000. "Contingent Democrats: Industrialists, Labor, and Democratization in Late-Developing Countries." *World Politics* vol. 52: 2 (January).

Bengoa, José. 1990. *Haciendas y campesinos: Historia social de la agricultura chilena* Tomo II (Santiago, Chile: Ediciones SUR).

———. 1988. *El poder y la subordinación: Historia social de la agricultura Chilena* Tomo I (Santiago, Chile: Ediciones SUR).

———. 1983a. *Historia del movimiento campesino* (Santiago, Chile: Grupo de Investigaciones Agrarias).

———. 1983b. *Trayectoria del campesinado chileno: Elementos para su interpretación.* Documento de Trabajo No. 8 (Santiago, Chile: Grupo de Investigaciones Agrarias).

Bhagwati, Jagdish. 1982. "Directly Unproductive, Profit-Seeking Activities." *Journal of Political Economy* vol. 90: 5.

Bienen, Henry and Jeffrey Herbst. "The Relationship between Political and Economic Reform in Africa." *Comparative Politics* vol. 29: 1 (October).

Bonilla, Javier and Gérard Viatte. 1994/5. "Radical Reform in Mexican Agriculture." *The OECD Observer* no. 191 (December/January).

Bresser Pereira, Luiz Carlos, José María Maravall, and Adam Przeworski. 1994. "Economic Reforms in New Democracies: A Social-Democratic Approach" in William Smith, Carlos Acuña, and Eduardo Gamarra, eds., *Latin American Political Economy in the Age of Neoliberal Reform* (New Brunswick, NJ: Transaction Publishers).

Büchi, Hernán. 1993. *La transformación económica de chile: Del estatismo a la libertad económica* (Barcelona: Group Editorial Norma).

Bunce, Valerie. 2000. "Comparative Democratization: Big and Bounded Generalizations." *Comparative Political Studies* vol. 33: 6–7 (August/September 2000).

———. 1995. "Sequencing of Political and Economic Reforms" in John Hardt and Richard Kaufman, eds., *East-Central European Economies in Transition* (Armonk, NY: M. E. Sharpe for the Joint Economic Committee of the Congress of the United States).

Calhoun, Craig. 1983. "The Radicalism of Tradition: Community Strength or Venerable Disguise and Borrowed Language." *American Journal of Sociology* vol. 88: 5 (March).

Carreño, Dora and G. Fu. 1986. "1985: Coyuntura agraria: Más dólares que alimentos." *Documento de Trabajo No. 25* (Santiago, Chile: GIA).

Carrière, Jean. 1981. *Landowners and Politics in Chile: A Study of the 'Sociedad Nacional de Agricultura,' 1932–1970* (Amsterdam: Center for Latin American Research and Documentation [CEDLA]).

Carter, Michael and Bradford Barham. 1996. "Level Playing Fields and *Laissez Faire*: Postliberal Development Strategy in Inegalitarian Agrarian Economies." *World Development* vol. 24: 7.

Carter, Michael R. and Dina Mesbah. 1992. "¿Es posible reducir la probreza rural con políticas que afectan el mercado de la tierra?" *Colección Estudies CIEPLAN* vol. 34 (June).

Carter, Michael, Bradford Barham, and Dina Mesbah. 1996. "Agricultural Export Booms and the Rural Poor in Chile, Guatemala, and Paraguay." *Latin American Research Review* vol. 31: 1.

Caviedes, César. 1991. *Elections in Chile: The Road Toward Redemocratization* (Boulder, CO: Lynne Rienner).

———. 1979. *The Politics of Chile: A Sociogeographical Assessment* (Boulder, CO: Westview Press).

Centro de Estudios Públicos (CEP). 1992. *El ladrillo: Bases de la política económica del gobierno militar chileno* (Santiago, Chile: CEP).

Centro de Información de Recursos Naturales (CIREN). 1987. *Catastro frutícola nacional: Regiones V a VII* (Santiago, Chile: CIREN/CORFO).

Cereceda, Luz Eugenia and Fernando Dahse. 1980. *Dos décadas de cambios en el agro chileno* (Santiago, Chile: Instituto de Sociología de la Pontificia Universidad Católica de Chile).

Chaudhry, Kiren. 1993. "The Myths of the Market and the Common History of the Late Developers." *Politics & Society* vol. 21: 3.

Cohen, Joshua and Joel Rogers. 1992. "Secondary Associations and Democratic Governance." *Politics & Society* vol. 20: 4 (December).

Collier, Ruth Berins and David Collier. 1991. *Shaping the Political Arena: Critical Junctures, the Labor Movement, and Regime Dynamics in Latin America* (Princeton, NJ: Princeton University Press).

Collins, Joseph and John Lear. 1995. *Chile's Free Market Miracle: A Second Look* (Oakland, CA: Food First).

Comité de Planificación para el Desarrollo (COPLADE). 1994. *Memoria sexenial de solidaridad, 1989–94.* Various volumes, published independently in eighteen states.

Collier, David, ed. 1979. *The New Authoritarianism in Latin America* (Princeton, NJ: Princeton University Press).

Collier, David and Steven Levitsky. 1997. "Democracy with Adjectives: Conceptual Innovation in Comparative Research." *World Politics* vol. 49: 3 (April).

Collier, Ruth Berins and David Collier. 1991. *Shaping the Political Arena: Critical Junctures, the Labor Movement, and Regime Dynamics in Latin America* (Princeton, NJ: Princeton University Press).

Comite Interamericano de Desarrollo Agraricola (CIDA). 1966. *Chile: Tenencia de la Tierra y Desarrollo Socio-económico del Sector Agrícola* (Santiago, Chile: CIDA/ECLA/FAO).

Cornelius, Wayne and David Myhre, eds. 1998. *The Transformation of Rural Mexico: Reforming the Ejido Sector* (La Jolla, CA: Center for U.S.–Mexican Studies).

Cortázar René and Jorge Marshall. 1980. "Índice de precios al consumidor en Chile, 1970–1978." *Colección Estudios CIEPLAN* (Santiago, Chile: CIEPLAN).

Corvalán, Antonio. 1976. "El empleo en el sector agrícola: Realidad y perspectivas." *Documento No. 52* (Santiago, Chile: CEPLAN).

Crisp, Brian. 1998. "Lessons from Economic Reform in the Venezuelan Democracy." *Latin American Research Review* vol. 33: 1.

Crispi, Jaime. 1980. *El agro chileno después de 1973: expansión capitalista y campesinización pauperizante.* Unpublished manuscript (Santiago, Chile: GIA).

————. 1982. "El agro chileno después de 1973: Expansión capitalista y campesinización pauperizante." *Revista Mexicana de Sociología* vol. 44: 2 (April–June).

Cruz, María Elena. 1991. Transcribed speech in Armijo, Marianela and Cecilia Montero, eds. "La agricultura chilena a comienos de los años 90: Fortalezas y debilidades." *Apuntes CIEPLAN* no. 101 (June).

de la Cuadra A., Fernando. 1991. *Estado y Movimiento Campesino: Trayectoria Histórica de su Relación.* Serie Materiales de Capacitación No. 4.

Curso de Capacitación a Profesionales y Técnicos de Organizaciones No Gubernamentales de Apoyo al Sector Rural. Unpublished manuscript (Santiago, Chile: Grupo de Investigaciones Agrarias).

Dahl, Robert. 1989. *Democracy and Its Critics* (New Haven, CT: Yale University Press).

———. 1971. *Polyarchy* (New Haven, CT: Yale University Press).

Dahse, Fernando. 1979. *Mapa de la extrema riqueza* (Santiago, Chile: Editorial Aconcagua).

David, M. Beatriz, Martine Dirven, and Frank Vogelgesang. 2000. "The Impact of the New Economic Model on Latin America's Agriculture." *World Development* vol. 28: 9 (September).

Departamento de Economía Agraria (DEA-UC). 1980. *Panorama económico de la agricultura* (Santiago, Chile: Departamento de Economía Agraria, Pontificia Universidad Católica de Chile).

Dewalt, Billie R., Martha W. Rees, and Arthur D. Murphy. 1994. "The End of the Agrarian Reform in Mexico: Past Lessons, Future Prospects." *Transformation of Rural Mexico* paper no. 3 (San Diego: Center for U.S.–Mexican Studies).

Diamond, Larry. 1992. "Economic Development and Democracy Reconsidered." *American Behavioral Scientist* vol. 35: 4/5 (March/June).

Dirección del Trabajo. 1991. *Informe estadístico: negociación colectiva 1990* (Santiago, Chile: Dirección del Trabajo).

———. 1990. *Informe estadístico: negociación colectiva 1979–89* (Santiago, Chile: Dirección del Trabajo).

Domínguez, Jorge and Abraham Lowenthal. 1996. *Constructing Democratic Governance: Latin America and the Caribbean in the 1990s* (Baltimore: The Johns Hopkins University Press).

Dornbusch, Rudiger and Sebastián Edwards. 1991. *The Macroeconomics of Populism in Latin America* (Chicago: University of Chicago Press).

Echenique, Jorge and Nelson Rolando. 1991. *Tierras de Parceleros. ¿Dónde están?* (Santiago, Chile: AGRARIA).

———. 1989. *La pequeña agricultura: una reserva de potencialidades y una deuda social* (Santiago, Chile: AGRARIA).

Edwards, Sebastian and Alejandra Cox Edwards. 1987 [1991]. *Monetarism and Liberalization: The Chilean Experiment* (Chicago: University of Chicago Press).

Ellis, Frank. 1988. *Peasant Economics: Farm Households and Agrarian Development* (Cambridge: Cambridge University Press).

Etchemendy, Sebastián. 2001. "Constructing Reform Coalitions: The Politics of Compensations in the Argentine Path to Economic Liberalization." *Latin American Politics and Society* vol. 43: 3 (Fall).

Evans, Peter. 1996. "Government Action, Social Capital and Development: Reviewing the Evidence on Synergy." *World Development* vol. 24: 6.

Fainsod, Merle. 1957. *How Russia is Ruled* (Cambridge, MA: Harvard University Press).

Ferguson, Thomas. 1995. *Golden Rule: The Investment Theory of Party Competition and the Logic of Money-Driven Political Systems* (Chicago: University of Chicago Press).

Flores-Quiroga, Aldo. 1998. "The Domestic Politics of Mexico's Tariff Structure." Unpublished manuscript, Claremont Graduate University.

Food and Agricultural Organization (FAO). 2000. FAOSTAT agriculture data. Available at http://apps.fao.org/page/collections.

Fox, Jonathan. 1996a. "What Makes Civil Society Thicken? The Political Construction of Social Capital in Rural Mexico." *World Development* vol. 24: 6.

———. 1996b. "National Electoral Choices in Rural Mexico" in Laura Randall, ed., *Reforming Mexico's Agrarian Reform* (Armonk, NY: M. E. Sharpe).

———. 1994. "The Difficult Transition from Clientelism to Citizenship: Lessons from Mexico." *World Politics* vol. 46: 2 (January).

———. 1993. *The Politics of Food in Mexico: State Power and Social Mobilization* (Ithaca, NY: Cornell University Press).

Foxley, Alejandro. 1983. *Latin American Experiments in Neo-Conservative Economics.* (Berkeley: University of California Press).

———. 1979. *Redistributive Effects of Government Programmes: The Chilean Case* (Oxford: Pergamon Press).

Ffrench-Davis, Ricardo. 1980. "Liberalización de importaciones." *Colección Estudios CIEPLAN* 4 (Santiago, Chile: CIEPLAN).

Frieden, Jeffry. 1991. *Debt, Development, and Democracy: Modern Political Economy and Latin America, 1965–1985* (Princeton, NJ: Princeton University Press).

———. 1988. "Classes, Sectors, and the Foreign Debt." *Comparative Politics* vol. 21: 1 (October).

Friedman, Milton. 1962. *Capitalism and Freedom* (Chicago: University of Chicago Press).

Friedmann, Santiago, Nora Lustig, and Arianna Legovini. 1995. "Mexico: Social Spending and Food Subsidies during Adjustment in the 1980s" in Nora Lustig, ed., *Coping with Austerity: Poverty and Inequality in Latin America* (Washington, DC: The Brookings Institution).

Friedrich, Carl J. and Zbigniew K. Brzezinski. 1956. *Totalitarian Dictatorship and Autocracy.* (Cambridge, MA: Harvard University Press).

Fukuyama, Francis. 1989. "The End of History?" *The National Interest* vol. 16 (Summer).

Gacitúa, Estanislao. 1985. *Toward an Explanatory Model of Mapuche Mobilizations under the Chilean Military Regime.* Master's thesis, Kansas State University, Manhattan.

Garretón, Manuel Antonio. 1986. "The Political Evolution of the Chilean Military Regime and Problems in the Transition to Democracy" in Guillermo

O'Donnell, Philippe Schmitter, and Laurence Whitehead, eds., *Transitions from Authoritarian Rule: Latin America* (Baltimore: The Johns Hopkins University Press).

———. 1983. *El proceso político chileno* (Santiago, Chile: FLACSO).

Gibson, Edward. 1997. "The Populist Road to Market Reform: Policy and Electoral Coalitions in Mexico and Argentina." *World Politics* vol. 49 (April).

Gómez, Sergio. 1987. "Organizaciones empresariales rurales: los casos de Brazil y de Chile." *Revista Paraguaya de Sociología* vol. 24: 70 (December).

———. 1986. "Evolución orgánica e ideológica de las organizaciones empresariales rurales." Documento de Trabajo No. 323 (Santiago, Chile: FLACSO).

Gómez, Sergio and Jorge Echenique. 1988. *La agricultura chilena: las dos caras de la modernización* (Santiago, Chile: Facultad Latinoamericana de Ciencias Sociales and Organismo de Desarrollo Campesino y Alimentario [AGRARIA]).

Goodman, Louis, Steven Sanderson, Kenneth Shwedel, and Paul Haber. 1985. "Mexican Agriculture: Rural Crisis and Policy Response." Working Paper No. 168 (Washington, DC: The Wilson Center/Latin American Program).

Gore, Charles. "The Rise and Fall of the Washington Consensus as a Paradigm for Developing Countries." *World Development* vol. 28: 5.

Grupo de Investigaciones Agrarias (GIA). 1991. *Síntesis estadística* vol. I–XIII (Santiago, Chile: GIA).

Gunther, Richard, P. Nikiforos Diamandouros, and Hans-Jürgen Puhle. 1995. *The Politics of Democratic Consolidation: Southern Europe in Comparative Perspective* (Baltimore, MD: The Johns Hopkins University Press).

Gwynne, Robert and Jorge Ortiz. 1997. "Export Growth and Development in Poor Rural Regions: A Meso-Scale Analysis of the Upper Limari." *Bulletin of Latin American Research* vol. 16: 1.

Hagopian, Frances. 1996. *Traditional Politics and Regime Change in Brazil* (Cambridge: Cambridge University Press).

———. 1993. "After Regime Change: Authoritarian Legacies, Political Representation, and the Democratic Future of Latin America." *World Politics* vol. 45: 3 (April).

Harding, Timothy and James Petras. 1988. "Introduction: Democratization and the Class Struggle." *Latin American Perspectives* vol. 58: 15.

Harvey, Neil. 1998. *The Chiapas Rebellion: The Struggle for Land and Democracy* (Durham, NC: Duke University Press).

———. 1996. "Impact of Reforms to Article 27 on Chiapas: Peasant Resistance in the Neoliberal Public Sphere" in Laura Randall, ed., *Reforming Mexico's Agrarian Reform* (Armonk, NY: M. E. Sharpe).

von Hayek, Friedrich A. 1944. *The Road to Serfdom*. (Chicago: University of Chicago Press).

Heller, Patrick. 2000. "Degrees of Democracy: Some Comparative Lessons from India." *World Politics* vol. 52 (July).

Hellman, Joel. 1998. "Winners Take All: The Politics of Partial Reform in Postcommunist Transitions." *World Politics* vol. 50: 2 (February).

Heredia, Blanca. 1994. "Making Economic Reform Politically Viable: The Mexican Experience" in William Smith, Carlos Acuña, and Eduardo Gamarra, eds., *Democracy, Markets, and Structural Reform in Latin America: Argentina, Bolivia, Brazil, Chile, and Mexico* (New Brunswick, NJ: Transaction Publishers for the North-South Center).

Hirschman, Albert. 1968. "The Political Economy of Import-Substituting Industrialization in Latin America." *Quarterly Journal of Economics* vol. 82: 1 (February).

———. 1958. *The Strategy of Economic Development* (New Haven, CT: Yale University Press).

Horcasitas, Juan and Jeffrey Weldon. 1994. "Electoral Determinants and Consequences of National Solidarity" in Wayne Cornelius, Ann Craig, and Jonathan Fox, eds., *Transforming State-Society Relations in Mexico: The National Solidarity Strategy* (San Diego, CA: Center for U.S.–Mexican Studies).

Houtzager, Peter. 2001. "Collective Action and Political Authority: Rural Workers, Church, and State in Brazil." *Theory and Society* vol. 30: 1 (February).

———. 1998. "State and Unions in the Transformation of the Brazilian Countryside, 1964–1979." *Latin American Research Review* vol. 33: 2.

Houtzager, Peter and Marcus Kurtz. 2000. "The Institutional Roots of Popular Mobilization: State Transformation and Rural Politics in Brazil and Chile, 1960–1995." *Comparative Studies in Society and History* vol. 42: 2 (April).

Huntington, Samuel. 1989. "The Modest Meaning of Democracy" in Robert Pastor, ed., *Democracy in the Americas: Stopping the Pendulum* (New York: Holmes and Meier).

———. 1984. "Will More Countries Become Democratic?" *Political Science Quarterly* vol. 99: 2 (Summer).

———. 1969. *Political Order in Changing Societies* (New Haven, CT: Yale University Press).

Instituto de Capacitación e Investigación en Reforma Agraria. 1979. *Análisis de la situación de los Asignatarios de Tierras a junio de 1978* (Santiago, Chile: Ministerio de Agricultura).

———. 1977. *Análisis de la Situación de los Asignatarios de Tierras a Diciembre de 1976* (Santiago, Chile: Ministerio de Agricultura).

———. 1972. "Diagnóstico de la reforma agraria chilena, Noviembre 1970–Junio 1972." Unpublished manuscript (Santiago, Chile: ICIRA).

Instituto Federal Electoral. 1997. Electoral results. www.ife.org.mx.

———. 1994. Electoral Results. www.ife.org.mx.

Instituto Nacional de Estadística. 1993. *Censo de Poblacion y Vivienda. Resultados Generales, Chile 1992* (Santiago, Chile: INE).

———. 1992a. *Compendio Estadístico* (Santiago, Chile: Instituto Nacional de Estadística).

———. 1992b. *Empleo: Encuesta Nacional 1986–1991. Total País* (Santiago, Chile: Instituto Nacional de Estadística [INE]).

———. 1981. *V Censo Nacional Agropecuario, Año Agrícola 1975–6* (Santiago, Chile: INE).

Instituto Nacional de Estadística, Geographía e Informática. 2000. Tables Migración 2 and Migración 9. www.inegi.gob.mx.

———. 1995. Conteo de Población 1995. CD-ROM (Mexico City: INEGI).

———. 1990. XI Censo de Población y Vivienda. CD-ROM.

International Labor Organization (ILO). 2000. LABORSTA database available at http://laborsta.ilo.org/.

de Janvry, Alain. 1981. *The Agrarian Question and Reformism in Latin America* (Baltimore, MD: The Johns Hopkins University Press).

Jarvis, Lovell. 1992. "The Unravelling of the Agrarian Reform" in Cristóbal Kay, ed., *Development and Social Change in the Chilean Countryside: From the Pre-Land Reform Period to the Democratic Transition* (Amsterdam: CEDLA).

———. 1985. *Chilean Agriculture under Military Rule: From Reform to Reaction, 1973–1980* (Berkeley: Institute of International Studies).

Jonas, Suzanne. 1989. "Elections and Transitions: The Guatemalan and Nicaraguan Cases" in James Booth and Mitchell Seligson, eds., *Elections and Democratization in Central America* (Chapel Hill: The University of North Carolina Press).

Junta Militar de Gobierno. 1973a. *Bando No. 5* (Santiago, Chile: Gobierno de Chile).

———. 1973b. *Declaración de principios del Gobierno de Chile* (Santiago, Chile: República de Chile).

Kahler, Miles. 1990. "Orthodoxy and its Alternatives: Explaining Approaches to Stabilization and Adjustment" in Joan Nelson, ed., *Economic Crisis and Policy Choice: The Politics of Adjustment in the Third World* (Princeton, NJ: Princeton University Press).

Karl, Terry Lynn. 1990. "Dilemmas of Democratization in Latin America." *Comparative Politics* vol. 23: 1 (October).

Kaufman, Robert. 1989. "Economic Orthodoxy and Political Change in Mexico: The Stabilization and Adjustment Policies of the de la Madrid Administration" in Barbara Stallings and Robert Kaufman, eds., *Debt and Democracy in Latin America* (Boulder, CO: Westview Press).

———. 1972. *The Politics of Land Reform in Chile, 1950–1970* (Cambridge, MA: Harvard University Press).

Kaufman, Robert and Barbara Stallings. 1991. "The Political Economy of Latin American Populism" in Rudiger Dornbusch and Sebastian Edwards, eds., *The Macroeconomics of Populism in Latin America* (Chicago: University of Chicago Press).

Kay, Cristóbal. 1981. "Political Economy, Class Alliances, and Agrarian Change in Chile." *Journal of Peasant Studies* 8: 4 (July).

―――. 1971. "Comparative Development of the European Manorial System and the Latin American Hacienda System: An Approach to a Theory of Agrarian Change for Chile." Ph.D. diss., University of Sussex.

Kessler, Timothy. 1998. "Political Capital: Mexican Financial Policy under Salinas." *World Politics* vol. 51: 1.

King, Gary. 1997. *A Solution to the Ecological Inference Problem* (Pinceton, NJ: Princeton University Press).

Krueger, Anne. 1974. "The Political Economy of the Rent-Seeking Society." *American Economic Review* vol. 64: 3 (June).

Kurtz, Marcus. 2002. "Understanding the Third World Welfare State after Neoliberalism: The Politics of Social Provision in Chile and Mexico." *Comparative Politics* vol. 34: 3 (April) 293–313.

―――. 2001. "State Developmentalism without a Developmental State: The Public Foundations of the 'Free Market Miracle' in Chile." *Latin American Politics and Society* 43: 2 (Summer).

―――. 1999a. "Chile's Neo-Liberal Revolution: Incremental Decisions and Structural Transformation, 1973–89." *Journal of Latin American Studies* vol. 31: 2 (May).

―――. 1999b. "Free Markets and Democratic Consolidation in Chile: The National Politics of Rural Transformation." *Politics & Society* vol. 27: 2 (June).

Kurtz, Marcus and Andrew Barnes. 2002. "The Political Foundations of Post-Communist Regimes: Marketization, Agrarian Legacies, or International Influences." *Comparative Political Studies* vol. 35: 5 (June).

Lawson, Stephanie. 1993. "Conceptual Issues in the Comparative Study of Regime Change and Democratization." *Comparative Politics* vol. 25 (January).

León, Arturo. 1994. "Urban Poverty in Chile: Its Extent and Diversity." *Democracy and Social Policy Series*. Working Paper No. 8 (Notre Dame, IN: The Kellogg Institute).

Lijphart, Arend and Carlos Waisman. 1996. "The Design of Markets and Democracies: Generalizing Across Regions" in Arend Lijphart and Carlos Waisman, eds., *Institutional Design in New Democracies: East Europe and Latin America* (Boulder, CO: Westview Press).

Lindblom, Charles. 1977. *Politics and Markets: The World's Political Economic Systems* (New York: Basic Books).

Linz, Juan. 1990. "The Perils of Presidentialism." *Journal of Democracy* vol. 1.

―――. 1978. *The Breakdown of Democratic Regimes: Crisis, Breakdown, and Reequilibration* (Baltimore, MD: The Johns Hopkins University Press).

Linz, Juan and Alfred Stepan. 1996. *Problems of Democratic Transition and Consolidation: Southern Europe, South America, and Post-Communist Europe* (Baltimore, MD: The Johns Hopkins University Press).

Linz, Juan and Alfred Stepan, eds. 1978. *The Breakdown of Democratic Regimes* (Baltimore, MD: The Johns Hopkins University Press).

Linz, Juan and Arturo Valenzuela. 1994. *The Failure of Presidential Democracy: Comparative Perspectives* (Baltimore, MD: The Johns Hopkins University Press).

Lipset, Seymour. 1993. "The Social Requisites of Democracy Revisited." *American Sociological Review* vol. 59: 1 (February).

Lipset, Seymour, Martin Trow, and James Coleman. 1956. *Union Democracy: The Inside Politics of the International Typographical Union* (New York: The Free Press).

Lipton, David and Jeffrey Sachs. 1990. "Creating a Market Economy in Eastern Europe: The Case of Poland." *Brookings Papers on Economic Activity* no. 1.

Llambí, Luís. 1991. "Latin American Peasantries and Regimes of Accumulation." *European Review of Latin American and Caribbean Studies* 51 (December).

Londregon, John. 2000. *Legislative Institutions and Ideology in Chile* (Cambridge: Cambridge University Press).

Loveman, Brian. 1976. *Struggle in the Countryside: Politics and Rural Labor in Chile, 1919–1973* (Bloomington: Indiana University Press).

Luebbert, Gregory. 1991. *Liberalism, Fascism, or Social Democracy: Social Classes and the Political Origins of Regimes in Interwar Europe* (New York: Oxford University Press).

Lustig, Nora. 1994. "Solidarity as a Strategy of Poverty Alleviation" in Wayne A. Cornelius, Ann L. Craig, and Jonathan Fox, eds., *Transforming State-Society Relations: The National Solidarity Strategy* (San Diego, CA: Center for U.S.–Mexico Studies).

———. 1991. "La política de reparto agrario en México (1917–1990) y las reformas al artículo 27 constitucional" in Alejandra Massolo et al., eds., *Procesos rurales y urbanos en el México actual* (Mexico City: UAM-Iztapalapa).

Mackinlay, Horatio. 1991. "La política de reparto agrario en México (1917–1990) y las reformas al artículo 27 constitucional" in Magda Fritscher Mundt and Cristina Steffer, eds., La Agricultura Mexicana en la Novena Década: Un Destino Incierto (Mexico City: Universidad Autónoma Metropolitana-Iztapalapa).

Maffei, Eugenio and Emilio Marchetti. 1972. "Estructur agraria y consejos comunales campesinos: Situación actual, análisis y estrategía" in *Cuadernos de la Realidad Nacional* (Santiago, Chile: Universidad Católica de Chile/Centro de Estudios de la Realidad Nacional [CEREN]).

Magagna, Victor. 1991. *Communities of Grain: Rural Rebellion in Comparative Perspective* (Ithaca, NY: Cornell University Press).

Mainwaring, Scott. 1992. "Transitions to Democracy and Democratic Consolidation: Theoretical and Conceptual Issues" in Scott Mainwaring, Guillermo O'Donnell, and J. Samuel Valenzuela, eds., *Issues in Democratic*

Consolidation; The New South American Democracies in Comparative Perspective (Notre Dame, IN: The University of Notre Dame Press).

Mainwaring, Scott and Timothy Scully, eds. 1995. *Building Democratic Institutions: Party Systems in Latin America* (Oxford: Oxford University Press).

Mallon, Florencia. 1983. *The Defense of Community in Peru's Central Highlands: Peasant Struggle and Capitalist Transition, 1860–1940* (Princeton, NJ: Princeton University Press).

Mamalakis, Markos. 1965. "Public Policy and Sectoral Development: A Case Study of Chile 1940–1958" in Markos Mamalakis and Clark Reynolds, eds., *Essays on the Chilean Economy* (Homewood, IL: Richard D. Irwin, Inc.).

Marín, Juan Carlos. 1972. *Las tomas* (Santiago, Chile: ICIRA).

Martínez, Javier and Margarita Palacios. 1990. "Tendencias políticas y cambios electorales en las comunas de Chile, 1949–1973." Documento de Trabajo No. 113 (Santiago, Chile: Centro de Estudios Sociales y Educación SUR).

McAdam, Doug. 1983. *Political Process and the Development of Black Insurgency, 1930–1970* (Chicago: University of Chicago Press).

McBride, George. 1936 [1970]. *Chile: su tierra y su gente* (Santiago, Chile: Editorial ICIRA).

McCarthy, John D. and Mayer Zald. 1977. "Resource Mobilization and Social Movements: A Partial Theory." *American Journal of Sociology* vol. 82: 6 (May).

McKelvey, Richard and Peter Ordeshook. 1986. "Information, Electoral Equilibria, and the Democratic Ideal." *Journal of Politics* vol. 48: 4 (November).

McKinley, Terry and Diana Alarcón. 1995. "The Prevalence of Rural Poverty in Mexico." *World Development* vol. 23: 9.

McNall, Scott. 1988. *The Road to Rebellion: Class Formation and Kansas Populism, 1865–1900* (Chicago: University of Chicago Press).

El Mercurio. September 18, 2001. "Despacho de la reforma laboral." No pagination. Available at http://www.emol.com/Diario_ElMercurio/modulos/Buscar/_portada/detalle_diario.asp?idnoticia=0118092001001a0030062.

――――. Santiago, Chile. September 28, 1973. "Anuncia Ministro de Agricultura: Asignación Progresiva de Títulos de Propiedad" p. 20.

――――. September 26, 1973. "Bandos de la Junta de Gobierno Militar: Los Siguientes Son los Bandos Emitidos hasta la Fecha por la Junta de Gobierno Militar." pp. 22–3.

Ministerio de Agricultura. 1987. "Sabemos hacia donde vamos" (Santiago, Chile: Ministerio de Agricultura).

Ministerio del Interior. 1998. Unpublished data from Subsecretaría de Desarrollo Regional y Administrativo (SUBDERE), for 1996. Available on request. Current information available through the Sistema Nacional de Indicadores Municipales (SINIM) at http://www.sinim.cl/.

――――. 1997. Distribución de votación partidaria por comuna. http://www.elecciones97.cl/RESULTADOS/P_v9_TT_97D.htm. Accessed December 1997.

———. 1996. *Reporte Estadístico Comunal.* Online data from Chilean Ministry of the Interior. http://www.interior.cl/cgi-reporte/. Accessed October 1996.

Ministerio de Trabajo y Previsión Social. 1992. Unpublished data on agricultural union membership (Santiago, Chile: Ministerio de Trabajo).

Montes, J. Esteban, Scot Mainwaring, and Eugenio Ortega. 2000. "Rethinking the Chilean Party System." *Journal of Latin American Studies* vol. 32: 3 (October).

Moore, Barrington. 1966. *Social Origins of Dictatorship and Democracy: Lord and Peasant in the Making of the Modern World* (Boston: Beacon Press).

Munck, Gerardo. 1994a. "Democratic Transitions in Comparative Perspective." *Comparative Politics* vol. 26: 3 (April).

———. 1994b. "Democratic Stability and Its Limits: An Analysis of Chile's 1993 Elections." *Journal of Interamerican Studies and World Affairs* vol. 36: 2 (Summer).

Munck, Gerardo and Jay Verkuilen. 2000. "Measuring Democracy: Evaluating Alternative Indexes." Paper presented at the 2000 Annual Meeting of the American Political Science Association. Washington, DC, August 31–September 3.

Mundt, Magda Fritscher and Cristina Steffen. 1991. "La agricultura mexicana en la novena década: un destino incierto" in Alejandra Massolo, et al., eds., *Procesos rurales y urbanos en el México actual* (Mexico City: UAM-Iztapalapa).

Murray, Warwick. 1997. "Competitive Global Fruit Export Markets: Marketing Intermediaries and Impacts on Small-Scale Growers in Chile." *Bulletin of Latin American Research* vol. 16: 1.

Myhre, David. 1998. "The Achilles' Heel of the Reforms: The Rural Finance System" in Wayne Cornelius and David Myhre, eds., *The Transformation of Rural Mexico: Reforming the Ejido Sector* (San Diego, CA: Center for U.S.–Mexican Studies).

———. 1994. "The Politics of Globalization in Rural Mexico: Campesino Initiatives to Restructure the Agricultural Credit System" in Philip McMichael, ed., *The Global Restructuring of Agro-food Systems* (Ithaca, NY: Cornell University Press).

Nelson, Joan. 1992. "Poverty, Equity, and the Politics of Adjustment" in Stephan Haggard and Robert Kaufman, eds., *The Politics of Economic Adjustment: International Constraints, Distributive Conflicts, and the State* (Princeton, NJ: Princeton University Press).

———, ed. 1989. *Fragile Coalitions: The Politics of Economic Adjustment* (New Brunswick, NJ: Transaction Books).

North, Douglass. 1990. *Institutions, Institutional Change, and Economic Performance* (Cambridge: Cambridge University Press).

O'Brien, Philip and Jackie Roddick. 1983. *Chile, The Pinochet Decade: The Rise and Fall of the Chicago Boys* (London: Latin America Bureau).

O'Donnell, Guillermo. 1978. "State and Alliances in Argentina, 1956–1976." *Journal of Development Studies* vol. 15: 1 (October).

――――. 1973 [1979]. *Modernization and Bureaucratic Authoritarianism: Studies in South American Politics* (Berkeley: Institute of International Studies).

O'Donnell, Guillermo and Philippe Schmitter. 1986. *Transitions from Authoritarian Rule: Tentative Conclusions about Uncertain Democracies* (Baltimore, MD: The Johns Hopkins University Press).

O'Donnell, Guillermo, Philippe Schmitter, and Laurence Whitehead, eds., 1986. *Transitions from Authoritarian Rule: Lain America* (Baltimore, MD: The Johns Hopkins University Press).

Oficina Coordinadora de Asistencia Campesina (OCAC). 1980. *Análisis coyuntural de la realidad campesina, 2. El movimiento sindical agrario* (Santiago, Chile: OCAC).

Oficina de Estudios y Políticas Agrarias (ODEPA). 1992. *Sintesis agro-regional* (Santiago, Chile: Ministerio de Agricultura).

Oficina de Planificación Nacional (ODEPLAN). 1987. *Sabemos hacia donde vamos: Algunos logros del gobierno del presidente Augusto Pinochet Ugarte* (Santiago, Chile: ODEPLAN).

――――. 1979. *Chilean Economic and Social Development 1973–1979* (Santiago, Chile: Imprenta Calderón y Cía).

――――. 1977. *Informe Económico Anual 1977* (Santiago, Chile: ODEPLAN).

――――. 1974a. *Primer plan nacional indicativo de desarrollo 1975–1980* (Santiago, Chile: ODEPLAN).

――――. 1974b. *Informe Económico Año 1974* (Santiago, Chile: ODEPLAN).

Olavarría, Carlota. 1978. *La asignación de tierras en Chile (1973–1976), sus efectos en el empleo agrícola* (Santiago, Chile: PREALC).

Olson, Mancur. 1982. *The Rise and Decline of Nations: Economic Growth, Stagflation, and Social Rigidities* (New Haven, CT: Yale University Press).

――――. 1965. *The Logic of Collective Action* (Cambridge, MA: Harvard University Press).

Olson, Mancur, Naveen Sarna, and Anand Swamy. 2000. "Governance and Growth: A Simple Hypothesis Explaining Cross-Country Differences in Productivity Growth" *Public Choice* vol. 102: 3/4 (March).

Oppenheim, Lois. 1999. *Politics in Chile: Democracy, Authoritarianism, and the Search for Development* (Boulder, CO: Westview Press).

Ortega, Emiliano. 1987. *Transformaciones agrarias y campesinado: De la participación a la exclusión* (Santiago, Chile: CIEPLAN).

Otero, Luis. 1990. *Pueblos y aldeas rurales en el marco de las principales regiones agroproductivas del país* (Santiago, Chile: Pontificia Universidad Católica de Chile).

Oxhorn, Philip. 1995. *Organizing Civil Society: The Popular Sectors and the Struggle for Democracy in Chile* (University Park: The Pennsylvania State University Press).

———. 1994. "Understanding Political Change after Authoritarian Rule: The Popular Sector and Chile's New Democratic Regime." *Journal of Latin American Studies* vol. 26.

Paige, Jeffery. 1997. *Coffee and Power: Revolution and the Rise of Democracy in Central America* (Cambridge, MA: Harvard University Press).

———. 1975. *Agrarian Revolution: Social Movements and Export Agriculture in the Underdeveloped World* (New York: The Free Press).

Paré, Luisa. 1990. "The Challenges of Rural Democratization in Mexico." *Journal of Development Studies* vol. 26: 4 (July).

Pastor, Manuel and Carol Wise. 1998. "Mexican Style Neoliberalism: State Policy and Distributional Stress" in Carol Wise, ed., *The Post-NAFTA Political Economy: Mexico and the Western Hemisphere* (University Park: The Pennsylvania State University Press).

Perry, Elizabeth. 1980. *Rebels and Revolutionaries in North China, 1845–1945* (Stanford, CA: Stanford University Press).

Petras, James and Fernando Ignacio Leiva. 1994. *Democracy and Poverty in Chile: The Limits to Electoral Politics* (Boulder, CO: Westview Press).

Petras, James and Maurice Zeitlin. 1967. "Miners and Agrarian Radicalism." *American Sociological Review* vol. 32: 4 (August).

Piñera, José. 1991. *El cascabel al gato: La batalla por la reforma provisional* (Santiago, Chile: Zig-Zag).

———. 1990. *La revolución laboral en Chile* (Santiago, Chile: Zig-Zag).

Poder Ejecutive Federal. 1998. *Progresa: Programa de educación, salud y alimentación* (Mexico City: República de México).

Polanyi, Karl. 1944. *The Great Transformation* (Boston: Beacon Press).

Popkin, Samuel. 1979. *The Rational Peasant: The Political Economy of Rural Society in Vietnam* (Berkeley: University of California Press).

Potters, Jan and Randolph Sloof. 1996. "Interest Groups: A Survey of Empirical Models That Try to Assess Their Influence." *European Journal of Political Economy* vol. 12: 3.

Prebisch, Raúl. 1959. "Commercial Policy in the Underdeveloped Countries." *American Economic Review* vol. 49 (May).

Provoste, Patricia and Wilson Cantoni. 1971. *Descripción numérica de la organización sindical chilena, 1968–1969* (Santiago, Chile: FEES).

Puryear, Jeffrey M. 1994. *Thinking Politics: Intellectuals and Democracy in Chile, 1973–1988* (Baltimore, MD: The Johns Hopkins University Press).

Putnam, Robert. 2000. *Bowling Alone: The Collapse and Revival of American Community* (New York: Simon and Schuster).

———. 1993. *Making Democracy Work: Civic Traditions in Modern Italy* (Princeton, NJ: Princeton University Press).

Przeworski, Adam. 1986. "Some Problems in the Study of Transitions to Democracy," in Guillermo O'Donnell, Philipe Schmitter, and Laurence Whitehead, eds., *Transitions from Authoritarian Rule: Latin America* (Baltimore, MD: The Johns Hopkins University Press).

Przeworski, Adam and Fernanado Limongi. 1997. "Modernization: Theory and Facts." *World Politics* vol. 49: 2.

Przeworski, Adam and Michael Wallerstein. 1988. "The Structural Dependence of the State on Capital." *American Political Science Review* vol. 82: 1 (March).

Przeworski, Adam. 1995. *Sustainable Democracy* (Cambridge: Cambridge University Press).

Przeworksi, Adam, Michael Alvarez, José Antonio Cheibub, and Fernando Limongi. 2001. *Democracy and Development: Political Institutions and Well-Being in the World, 1950–1990* (Cambridge: Cambridge University Press).

Rabkin, Rhoda. 1996. "Redemocratization, Electoral Engineering, and Party Strategies in Chile, 1989–1995." *Comparative Political Studies* vol. 29: 3 (June).

Raczynski, Dagmar. 1993. "Social Policies in Chile: Origin, Transformations and Perspectives." *Democracy and Social Policy Series* Working Paper No. 4 (Notre Dame, IN: Kellogg Institute).

———. 1981. "Naturaleza rural-urbana y patrones geográficos de la migración interna." *Colección Estudios CIEPLAN* vol. 5.

Raczynski, Dagmar and Pilar Romaguera. 1995. "Chile: Poverty, Adjustment, and Social Policy in the 1980s" in Nora Lustig, ed., *Coping with Austerity: Poverty and Inequality in Latin America* (Washington, DC: The Brookings Institution).

Remmer, Karen. 1990. "Democracy and Economic Crisis: The Latin American Experience." *World Politics* vol. 42: 3 (April).

de los Reyes, Paulina. 1990. "The Rural Poor: Survival Strategies and Living Conditions among the Rural Population in the Seventh Region" in David Hojman, ed., *Neoliberal Agriculture in Rural Chile* (New York: St. Martin's Press).

Rivera, Rigoberto. 1988. *Los campesinos chilenos*. Serie Grupos de Investigaciones Agrarias No. 3 (Santiago, Chile: GIA).

Rivera, Rigoberto and María Elena Cruz. 1984. *Pobladores rurales: Cambios en el poblamiento y el empleo rural en Chile* (Santiago, Chile: GIA).

Roberts, Kenneth. 1998. *Deepening Democracy: The Modern Left and Social Movements in Chile and Peru* (Stanford, CA: Stanford University Press).

———. 1996. "Neoliberalism and the Transformation of Populism in Latin America: The Peruvian Case." *World Politics* vol. 48: 1.

———. 1995. "From the Barricades to the Ballot Box: Redemocratization and Political Realignment in the Chilean Left." *Politics & Society* vol. 23: 4 (December).

Rodríguez, Daniel and Sylvia Venegas. 1991. *Los trabajadores de la fruta en cifras* (Santiago, Chile: GEA).

———. 1989. *De Praderas a parronales: Un estudio sobre estructura agraria y Mercado laboral en el valle de Aconcagua* (Santiago: Grupo de Estudios Agro-Regionales [GEA]/Academia de Humanismo Cristiano).

_____. 1988. *Las regiones frutícolas de Chile: Caracterización productiva y del mercado laboral.* Proyecto Mercado Laboral Frutícola (Santiago, Chile: Grupo de Estudios Agro-Regionales [GEA], Universidad Academia de Humanismo Cristiano).

Rodrik, Dani. 1996. "Understanding Economic Policy Reform." *Journal of Economic Literature* vol. XXXIV (March 1996).

_____. 1993. "The Positive Economics of Policy Reform." *American Economic Review* vol. 83: 2. Papers and Proceedings of the Hundred and Fifth Annual Meeting of the American Economics Association (May).

Ros, Jaime. 1994. "On the Political Economy of Market and State Reform in Mexico" in William Smith, Carlos Acuña, and Eduardo Gamarra, eds., *Democracy, Markets, and Structural Reform in Latin America: Argentina, Bolivia, Brazil, Chile, and Mexico* (New Brunswick, NJ: Transaction Publishers for the North–South Center).

Rubio, Blanca. 1997. "La política agropecuaria neoliberal y la crisis alimentaria (1988–1996)" in José Luis Calva, ed., *El campo mexicano: Ajuste neoliberal y alternativas* (Mexicali, Mexico: Centro de Investigaciones Económicas, Sociales y Tecnológicas de la Agroindustria y la Agricultura Mundial [CIESTAAM]/Unión Nacional de Trabajadores Agrícolas [UNTA]).

Rueschemeyer, Dietrich, Evelyne Huber Stephens, and John Stephens. 1992. *Capitalist Development and Democracy* (Chicago: University of Chicago Press).

Rustow, Dankwart. 1970. "Transitions to Democracy." *Comparative Politics* vol. 2 (April).

Sáez, Arturo. 1986. *Uvas y manzanas, democracia y autoritarismo: El empresario frutícola chileno (1973–1985).* Documento de Trabajo No. 30 (Santiago, Chile: Grupo de Investigaciones Agrarias [GIA]).

Sáez, Raúl. 1993. "Las privatizaciones de empresas en chile" in Oscar Muñoz, ed., *Después de las privatizaciones: hacia el estado regulador* (Santiago, Chile: CIEPLAN).

Salinas, Raúl. 1985. *Trayectoria de la organización sindical campesina.* Documento de Trabajo No. 1 (Santiago, Chile: AGRA Ltda.).

Samuels, David and Richard Snyder. 2001. "The Value of a Vote: Malapportionment in Comparative Perspective." *British Journal of Political Science* vol. 31: 4 (October).

Sanderson, Steven. 1985. "The 'New' Internationalization of Agriculture in the Americas" in Steven Sanderson, ed. *The Americas in the New International Division of Labor* (New York: Homes and Meier).

Schady, Norbert. 2000. "The Political Economy of Expenditures by the Peruvian Social Fund (FONCODES), 1991–95." *American Political Science Review* vol. 94: 2 (June).

Schamis, Hector. 1999. "Distributional Coalitions and the Politics of Economic Reform in Latin America." *World Politics* vol. 51: 2.

Schejtman M., Alexander. 1971. *El inquilino de Chile central* (Santiago, Chile: Instituto de Capacitación e Investigación en Reforma Agraria).

Schmitter, Phillippe. 1995. "Democracy's Future: More Liberal, Preliberal, or Postliberal?" *Journal of Democracy* vol. 5: 1 (January).

――――. 1992a. "The Irony of Modern Democracy and Efforts to Improve Its Practice." *Politics & Society* vol. 20: 4 (December).

――――. 1992b. "The Consolidation of Democracy and the Representation of Social Groups." *American Behavioral Scientist* vol. 35: 4–5 (March/June).

――――. 1974. "Still the Century of Corporatism?" *Review of Politics* vol. 36.

Schumpeter, Joseph. 1976 [1942]. *Capitalism, Socialism and Democracy* (New York: Harper Torchbooks).

Scott, James. 1992. *Domination and the Arts of Resistance* (New Haven, CT: Yale University Press).

――――. 1985. *Weapons of the Weak* (New Haven, CT: Yale University Press).

――――. 1976. *The Moral Economy of the Peasant* (New Haven, CT: Yale University Press).

――――. 1972. "Patron-Client Politics and Political Change in Southeast Asia." *American Political Science Review* vol. 66: 1 (March).

Scully, Timothy. 1992. *Rethinking the Center: Party Politics in Nineteenth and Twentieth Century Chile* (Stanford, CA: Stanford University Press).

Scully, Timothy and J. Samuel Valenzuela. 1993. "From Democracy to Democracy: Continuities and Changes of Electoral Choices and the Party System in Chile." *Working Paper* No. 199 (Notre Dame, IN: Kellogg Institute).

Shadlen, Ken. 2002. "Orphaned by Democracy: Small Industry in Contemporary Mexico." *Comparative Politics* vol. 35: 1 (October).

Sheahan, John. 1987. *Patterns of Development in Latin America: Poverty, Repression, and Economic Strategy* (Princeton, NJ: Princeton University Press).

Siavelis, Peter. 2000. *The President and Congress in Postauthoritarian Chile: Institutional Constraints to Democratic Consolidation* (University Park: Pennsylvania State University Press).

Siavelis, Peter. 1997. "Continuity and Change in the Chilean Party System: On the Transformational Effects of Electoral Reform." *Comparative Political Studies* vol. 30: 6 (December).

Siavelis, Peter and Arturo Valenzuela. 1996. "Electoral Engineering and Democratic Stability: The Legacy of Authoritarian Rule in Chile" in Arend Lijphart and Carlos Waisman, eds., *Institutional Design in New Democracies: East Europe and Latin America* (Boulder, CO: Westview Press).

Silva, Eduardo. 1996. *The State and Capital in Chile: Business Elites, Technocrats, and Market Economics* (Boulder, CO: Westview Press).

Silva, Patricio. 1993. "Landowners and the State: Beyond Agrarian Reform and Counter-Reform" in David Hojman, ed., *Change in the Chilean Countryside: From Pinochet to Aylwin and Beyond* (London: The MacMillan Press, Ltd.).

_____. 1992a. "The State, Politics, and Peasant Unions" in Cristóbal Kay and Patricio Silva, eds., *Development and Social Change in the Chilean Countryside: From the Pre-Land Reform Period to the Democratic Transition* (Amsterdam: CEDLA).

_____. 1992b. "Landowners and the State: From Confrontation to Cooperation?" in Cristóbal Kay and Patricio Silva, eds., *Development and Social Change in the Chilean Countryside: From the Pre-Land Reform Period to the Democratic Transition* (Amsterdam: CEDLA).

_____. 1992c. "Technocrats and Politics in Chile: From the Chicago Boys to the CIEPLAN Monks." *Journal of Latin American Studies* vol. 23.

_____. 1987. *Estado, neo-liberalismo y política agraria en Chile, 1973–1981* (Amsterdam: CEDLA).

Snyder, Richard. 2001a. "Scaling Down: The Subnational Comparative Method." *Studies in Comparative International Development* vol. 36: 1 (Spring).

_____. 2001b. *Politics after Neoliberalism: Reregulation in Mexico* (Cambridge: Cambridge University Press).

_____. 1999. "After Neoliberalism: The Politics of Reregulation in Mexico." *World Politics* vol. 51: 2 (January) 173–204.

Snyder, Richard and James Mahoney. 1999. "The Missing Variable: Institutions and the Study of Regime Change." *Comparative Politics* vol. 32: 1 (October).

Stephen, Lynn. 1998. "The Cultural and Political Dynamics of Agrarian Reform in Oaxaca and Chiapas" in Richard Snyder and Gabriel Torres, eds., *The Future Role of the Ejido in Rural Mexico* (San Diego, CA: Center for U.S.–Mexico Studies).

Tapia, Gonzalo. 1982. *Aspectos constitutivos de la organización campesina en Chile, 1920–1964* (Santiago, Chile: GIA).

Tarrow, Sidney. 1998. *Power in Movement: Social Movements and Contentious Politics* 2nd ed. (Cambridge: Cambridge University Press).

La Tercera (Santiago, Chile) December 11, 2002. "Acuerdo unánime para eliminar a senadores designados el 2006." www.tercera.cl/diario/2002/12/11/03.POL.UNAMINIDAD.html.

_____. June 16, 1997. "Renovación sigue buscando los votos." www.tercera.cl/diario/1997/06/15/53.html.

Thompson, Edward P. 1971. "The Moral Economy of the English Crowd in the Eighteenth Century." *Past and Present* vol. 50.

Thompson, Gary D. and Paul N. Wilson. 1994. "Ejido Reforms in Mexico: Conceptual Issues and Potential Outcomes." *Land Economics* vol. 70: 4 (November).

Tilly, Chales. 1978. *From Mobilization to Revolution* (New York: Random House).

Tironi, Eugenio and Felipe Agüero. 1999. ¿Sobrevivirá el Nuevo paisaje político Chileno? *Estúdios Públicos* no. 74 (Autumn).

de Tocqueville, Alexis. 1969. *Democracy in America* vol. II (New York: Harper and Row).

Tornell, Aaron. 1995. "Are Economic Crises Necessary for Trade Liberalization and Fiscal Reform: The Mexican Experience" in Rudiger Dornbusch and Sebastian Edwards, eds., *Reform, Recovery, and Growth* (Chicago: University of Chicago Press for the NBER).

United Nations Food and Agriculture Organization (UN FAO). 1985. *Production Yearbook* (Rome: UN FAO).

————. 1975. *Production Yearbook* (Rome: UN FAO).

Valenzuela, Arturo. 1978. *The Breakdown of Democratic Regimes: Chile* (Baltimore, MD: The Johns Hopkins University Press).

————. 1977. *Political Brokers in Chile: Local Government in a Centralized Polity* (Durham, NC: Duke University Press).

Valenzuela, Elvira. 1979. "La política agraria de la junta militar chilena (1973–1978)." *Tareas* 45 (July–September).

Venegas, Sylvia. 1993. "Programas de apoyo a temporeros y temporeras en Chile" in Sergio Gómez and Emilio Klein, eds., *Los pobres del campo: El trabajador eventual* (Santiago, Chile: FLACSO/PREALC/OIT).

————. 1987. *Family Production in Rural Chile: A Socio-Demographic Study of Agrarian Changes in the Aconcagua Valley, 1930–1986.* Ph.D. diss., University of Texas, Austin.

Vergara, Pilar. 1994. "Market Economy, Social Welfare, and Democratic Consolidation in Chile" in William Smith, Carlos Acuña, and Eduardo Gamarra, eds., *Democracy, Markets, and Structural Reform in Latin America: Argentina, Bolivia, Brazil, Chile, and Mexico* (New Brunswick, NJ: Transaction Publishers).

————. 1984. "Auge y caída del neo-liberalismo en Chile: Un estudio sobre la evolución ideológica del régimen militar." Documento de Trabajo No. 216 (Santiago, Chile: FLACSO).

Wade, Robert. 1992. "East Asia's Economic Success: Conflicting Perspectives, Partial Insights, Shaky Evidence." *World Politics* vol. 44: 2 (January).

Ward, Peter. 1993. "Social Welfare Policy and Political Opening in Mexico." *Journal of Latin American Studies* vol. 25: 3.

Waterbury, John. 1999. "The Long Gestation and Brief Triumph of Import-Substituting Industrialization." *World Development* vol. 27: 2.

Weyland, Kurt. 1998. "Swallowing the Bitter Pill: Sources of Popular Support for Neoliberal Reform in Latin America." *Comparative Political Studies* vol. 31: 5 (October).

————. 1996. *Democracy without Equity: Failures of Reform in Brazil* (Pittsburgh, PA: The University of Pittsburgh Press).

Williamson, John. 1994. "In Search of a Manual for Technopols" in John Williamson, ed., *The Political Economy of Policy Reform*. Washington, DC: Institute for International Economics.

Wolf, Eric. 1969. *Peasant Wars of the Twentieth Century* (New York: Harper and Row).

World Bank. 2001. *World Development Indicators.* CD-ROM (Washington, DC: World Bank).

———. 1995. *Chile: Estrategia para elevar la competitividad agrícola y aliviar la pobreza rural* (Washington, DC: IBRD).

———. 1980. *Chile: An Economy in Transition.* World Bank Country Study (Washington, DC: Latin American and Caribbean Regional Office).

Wright, Thomas C. 1982. *Landowners and Reform in Chile: The Sociedad Nacional de Agricultura, 1919–1940* (Urbana: The University of Illinois Press).

Yashar, Deborah J. 1999. "Democracy, Indigenous Movements, and the Postliberal Challenge in Latin America." *World Politics* vol. 52: 1 (October).

Zeitlin, Maurice and Richard Ratcliff. 1988. *Landlords and Capitalists: The Dominant Class of Chile* (Princeton, NJ: Princeton University Press).

Index

Printed in the United States
86300LV00004B/322-351/A

9 780521 534741

1732   38